PARAGRAPH PRACTICE

PARAGRAPH
PRACTICE

KATHLEEN E. SULLIVAN
MERRITT COLLEGE

WRITING

THE

PARAGRAPH

AND THE

SHORT

COMPOSITION

SEVENTH EDITION

Longman

New York   San Francisco   Boston
London   Toronto   Sydney   Tokyo   Singapore   Madrid
Mexico City   Munich   Paris   Cape Town   Hong Kong   Montreal

Editor: Barbara A. Heinssen
Production Supervisor: Jane O'Neill
Production Manager: Nicholas Sklitsis
Text and Cover Designer: Hothouse Designs

This book was set in Janson and Helvetica by Digitype and was printed and bound
by R. R. Donnelley and Sons. The cover was printed by New England Book Components.

Macmillan Publishing Company
866 Third Avenue, New York, New York 10022

Macmillan Publishing Company is part of
the Maxwell Communication Group of Companies.

Maxwell Macmillan Canada, Inc.
1200 Eglinton Avenue East
Suite 200
Don Mills, Ontario M3C 3N1

Library of Congress Cataloging-in-Publication Data

Sullivan, Kathleen E.
    Paragraph practice : writing the paragraph and the short
composition / Kathleen E. Sullivan. — 7th ed.
        p. cm.
    ISBN 0-02-418351-2
    1. English language — Rhetoric. 2. English language — Paragraphs.
I. Title.
PE 1408.S779 1994
808'.042 — dc20   93-14700
                    CIP

Printing: 7 8 9 10   Year: 5 4 3

In Memory of
Aurora Quiros ("Tita") Haggard

PREFACE

The seventh edition of *Paragraph Practice: Writing the Paragraph and the Short Composition* has been revised to improve both Part One on the paragraph and Part Two on the short composition. The revisions in Part One make the text clearer, and new short-answer exercises help bridge the gap between text and longer, more challenging writing exercises. Part Two also features revisions in the text and includes new exercises on the thesis statement as well as a new section on titling the composition. Moreover, a new Chapter 15, "Writing More Sophisticated Sentences," has been added to this edition. It covers strong and weak sentence positions, active and passive voice, conciseness and wordiness, variety, and parallelism. To sum up, the objective of this edition is to broaden the reach of *Paragraph Practice*, to make early chapters more accessible and later chapters more challenging and comprehensive.

The sixth edition of *Paragraph Practice* introduced the opening chapter, "Getting Started." This chapter prompts students to experience the writing process before they later begin to analyze it. The chapter opens with a recognition of the blank paralysis beginners often feel when asked to take up the unfamiliar activity of writing, proceeds to validate their ordinary daily experiences as valuable source material and themselves as authentic and dynamic voices, and then moves on to methods they may use to trigger their best written responses. The major portion of the chapter consists of prewriting exercises, using Gabriele Rico's technique of clustering, each followed by simple paragraph exercises. The chapter concludes with a list of additional topics for clustering and paragraphing and with some easy relaxation exercises to help allay tension before writing.

With the expansion of Part One in the fifth edition, which introduced the chapter "Coherence and Continuity," and the enlargement of Part Two in the fourth edition, which added new chapters in organizing, developing, introducing, and concluding the short composition, *Paragraph Practice* virtually combines two little books into one. The first half of the book concentrates on the topic sentence and the paragraph, and the second half focuses on the thesis statement and the short composition. This edition also contains Appendix B, "Correction Symbols," which was expanded in the third edition into a minihandbook of grammar and usage.

Like its predecessors, the seventh edition is a workbook designed not so much to *talk about* the paragraph as to provide models and exercises in *writing* the paragraph. It is intended to give the same experience with the topic sentence, the thesis statement, and the short composition. The main theme of this workbook, as Professor Strunk might have put it, is *practice, practice, practice!*

Why practice the paragraph? The paragraph is ideally suited to meet the needs of college students who, for one reason or another, need extra practice in writing. The paragraph is comparatively short and contains many of the basic elements to be considered in studying any form of writing. Because of its brevity, the paragraph permits frequent writing practice without overburdening either the student or the instructor. In addition, the brevity of the paragraph makes it ideal as a medium for controlled composition in which specific mechanics or techniques of writing can be studied.

Organization is the primary concern of this workbook. Organization does not come naturally to most students in college composition courses. Because it is unfamiliar and strikes many students as unnecessary pain, they often resist it. As a result, instructors frequently neglect it. Nonetheless, organization is vital to good composition. It is the aim of this workbook to make it as painless to learn and as enjoyable to teach as possible. Consequently, the book begins with relatively simple problems and proceeds, by degrees, to problems of greater complexity.

The order of the text and exercises in Part One that precede the actual practice of the paragraph may be modified. For example, the section in Chapter 4 called "Find the Right Word" may be deferred as a refinement that digresses from more essential requirements of the topic sentence. It can easily be taken up later when, for instance, problems of variety and imagination are introduced in Chapter 8.

Paragraph Practice may be used in combination with other books or by itself as a reader and as a workbook in composition. The subject matter of the model sentences, paragraphs, and compositions can serve as topics for class discussions and for written exercises based on the discussions that will be of genuine interest to both instructor and students.

Several people have been very helpful in the development of this edition of *Paragraph Practice*. I would especially like to thank Anne Anderson, Sandra Fini, Marjorie Smith, and Marion Trentman for their valuable contributions. Special thanks are due to the reviewers of the seventh edition: Viralene J. Coleman, University of Arkansas at Pine Bluff; Kristin O. Lauer, Fordham University; Susan D. Walbert, Westmark Community College; Dr. Warren Westcott, Francis Marion College; and Teena Zindel-McWilliams, Richland Community College.

Above all, I want to thank my friend and colleague, Richard Vietti, to whom I have turned for assistance with most editions of *Paragraph Practice*. He has been steadfast in his support for many years, and I am deeply grateful for all the help he has given me with the book, the table pounding he has shared with me, and the quality control he has tried so hard to ensure.

K. E. S.

CONTENTS

PART ONE   PRACTICING THE PARAGRAPH

PART TWO   WRITING THE SHORT COMPOSITION

9 THE SHORT COMPOSITION   129

10 THE THESIS STATEMENT   134

APPENDIXES

PARAGRAPH PRACTICE

CHAPTER 1

STARTED

DO YOU RECOGNIZE THIS EXPERIENCE?

As a student you are probably familiar with the following experience: You are sitting in a classroom, paper in front of you, pencils sharp, pens poised for action. Your assignment is to write a 500-word composition within the hour. You understand the directions and are ready to begin. But the clock on the wall begins to jerk away the minutes as you stare at the blank page, defying you to write on it. What can you write about? What is there to say? You feel as blank as the page itself and sit there, paralyzed, waiting for inspiration. No ideas come. You begin to twist and turn in your hard chair, desperately looking around the room for some kind of miracle. Why can't you get started?

YOU HAVE PLENTY TO WRITE ABOUT

Deep down you know you have a lot to say. Just think about your last telephone call. Can you hear how you jabbered away to one of your best friends? You had plenty of ideas then. Think about the last time you griped to someone about your life. You were loaded with complaints, weren't you? Or consider all the effort you have made to find a decent job and the humiliation and frustration you have experienced. You have had no trouble sharing your feelings with people close to you, some of them in the same boat. How about the directions you recently gave a younger sister or brother who was trying to learn to do something you already knew all about? That effort took clear explanation as well as patience, didn't it? Think of all the skill you have developed in discussing controversial issues with your parents and others older if not wiser than

1

you. You have proved to be quite a survivor, haven't you? Remember the intricate beginnings when you met that very important person in your life. Conversation may not have been easy at first, but you ultimately learned to speak volumes to each other. Take stock of the fact that you are an authority about your life and your experiences, and that you have a lot to say and plenty to write about.

BE YOURSELF

You have within you a gold mine of source material to draw on for writing. Moreover, you are unique. No one else has lived your life. No one else knows quite what you know or sees through your particular eyes. Therefore, what you have to say is special and should be alive and interesting. If you can reveal what you know, value, think about, worry about, fear, or look forward to, you are bound to find an attentive audience. But you must write from yourself and with your own authentic voice. Do not be a phony. Do not try to sound like someone else, some stranger, and do not distance yourself from what you write, trying vaguely to deliver what you imagine is expected from those writing (or not writing) with you in the classroom. Do not depersonalize yourself or become bland, colorless, and dull. Be yourself when you pick up that pen to write. Be genuine. Be willing to risk showing your reader who you are.

Revealing who you are, of course, also includes letting your imperfections as a writer show. For example, you may not always be as clear or as well organized as you would like to be. Your vocabulary may not be as exact and as fully developed as you might wish. You may be shaky about mechanics such as spelling, grammar, and punctuation. However, you cannot afford to worry about these problems when you are first getting started. If you do, you may risk blocking yourself, being unable to write at all, becoming self-conscious, intimidated, confused, stiff, and wooden instead of your spontaneous, dynamic self! Since no one expects you to be perfect in the beginning, anyway, you may as well relax and be yourself, all the best and worst of you. Perfection can come later. First you must worry about getting your thoughts on paper, no matter how they may come out, before they slip away!

THINK ABOUT *WHAT* MORE THAN *HOW*

In the beginning, think about *what* you want to say more than *how* you want to say it. In most writing situations, you will be able to write more than one version or "draft" of what you want to say. In the first or "rough draft" of your composition, you should dwell on *content* — that is, on subject matter, the thoughts or ideas you want to express — more than on *form* or the various means by which you express those ideas. Your rough draft may be quite sketchy, in fact, and consist of little more than notes to yourself in a kind of shorthand that only you can read and understand.

Form is not important at this point. What is important is to pin down those thoughts that come to you just as they appear, direct and honest, maybe even crude or half-conceived, semithoughts, ghosts of thoughts, but possibly very vital fragments that you can later develop more clearly. If time permits, and your energy and motivation are strong enough, you may write several drafts, gradually developing and refining your composition. In your final drafts, your attention can rightly turn to form, structure, and mechanics, but not in the beginning, when you need to focus on content.

CONTENT MAY NEED TO BE TRIGGERED

Content will not always leap to your call. Although you have within you an abundant source of subject matter to draw on for writing, what you need at any given moment may not always be immediately accessible. You may not always know what you know or be able to bring it to mind with ease so that you can write about it. Suppose you can't think of anything? What can be done to trigger your thoughts or to tap into them?

THE OUTSIDE WORLD CAN BE HELPFUL

The thoughts or ideas that exist somewhere in the hidden reaches of your mind may be teased into your consciousness with the help of the outside world or may depend on your own ability to trigger them. Forces in the outer world can be very helpful. For instance, writing assignments are frequently preceded by classroom discussion that can stimulate your thoughts. Your instructor may put penetrating questions to the class that make you think, that remind you of something in your past experiences, that encourage you to put together new combinations or fresh applications of ideas. Besides your classroom activities, your personal world is probably full of people who can assist you. It may prove enjoyable as well as enormously helpful for you to go to family members or other people who know you well and ask them, "Can you remind me of what I know about this subject? Have I had experience with this topic? Help me remember." The result can be not only entertaining but can bring you still closer together.

To illustrate, suppose you are asked to write a composition in which you have to discuss your earliest experience with right and wrong behavior, particularly in relation to violation of law. You think back through your career as a less-than-perfect child, and you realize you are hazy on the subject, but fortunately a parent is available. You sit down together and begin to reflect on your childhood, one of you remembering one thing, the other another. The discussion calls to mind a poignant memory of your stealing a small item from a neighborhood store, and you remember how bothered you were as weeks went by and your guilt about the theft mounted until you finally revealed your secret to your parent. Sharing this memory, you both smile as you recall the lesson you learned that day when the two of you returned to that small store, your parent watching as you made your apology and paid the proprietor.

Bringing what you know to consciousness is not always so much a matter of *remembering* as it is of *realizing* something about which you may be only vaguely aware or that you may not have thought about at all. For instance, imagine a classroom discussion of a complex word such as *ambivalence*, which means feeling conflicting emotions about a person or thing, such as love and hate, at the same time. Suppose you are asked to write about the word and you wonder what to say. You have lunch with a friend after class, and you begin to toss the word around, trying it out. At some point your friend says, "Isn't that how you used to feel about your Ex? Didn't you sometimes love and hate him at the same time?" Of course, you "know that" or sometimes almost let yourself feel that, but it may take your friend to bring your dim awareness to full recognition. When you realize you have had real experience with the word — that is, with the feelings the word represents — you have much to write about. Thus can the outside world help you to tap into your inner resources.

YOU MAY NEED TO HELP YOURSELF

Although your writing can benefit from the outside world in this and other ways, some of your most vivid writing may depend on your ability to tap into your memory or to trigger your realization on your own. To do this requires a special state of mind and may also be facilitated by some special prewriting exercises.

CONSIDER A SPECIAL STATE OF MIND

All writing classes might well begin with relaxation exercises, for one of the greatest blocks to good writing is tension — feeling uptight, threatened, insecure, defensive. Notice how you hold your pen or pencil as you write in class. Do you squeeze it so tightly that it feels like a weapon stabbing the page and your dented hand in armed combat? While a rush of adrenaline or excitement may help you to write well, feeling tense and defensive will likely make it difficult for you to write. Hopefully, you will have a chance, before you write, to stretch, breathe deeply, and loosen up, just as you would before engaging in an athletic event requiring intense concentration and skill. (For some simple exercises designed to help you relax before writing, see the end of this chapter.) Further, early in your class, you may also have an opportunity to get acquainted with your classmates, at least those sitting in your vicinity, to discover that they are human, too, and quite possibly as unsure of themselves as you may be. Sharing your mutual anxiety can do much toward making it tolerable or even diminishing it to the point that it ceases to matter. These activities should help you feel more relaxed, confident, and ready to write.

Feeling stimulated but not tense and defensive, you are ready to experience the special state of mind called for in the beginning or rough draft stage of writing. (Remember, at this point you are concentrating on *content*, on *what* you want to express, *not* on *form* or *how* to express it, which comes later.)

First you need to look outward to your instructor or elsewhere for direction, for as clear a sense of the writing assignment as you can obtain. After that, however, you must become somewhat detached from the outer world and look inward. At this stage you need to tap into your inner resources, to become creative and original. This is when you want most to be your unique self, to dwell on subject matter, attitudes, or feelings only you know about. This is also the moment when you need most to trust yourself, indeed, to allow yourself to *be*, to see who you are, to learn how you think and feel. This can be a striking moment of self-discovery, certainly a prime benefit of writing. A scary but exciting time, this is when you need to take a risk, to be open and therefore vulnerable, if only to yourself. No one should intrude on this moment, nor should you look to others for help, for this is your time to be with yourself. Look inward to your own experience, to your own reality. Listen to yourself. Get in touch with your own inner voice. Discover, explore, and develop your unique core.

TRY SOME SPECIAL PREWRITING EXERCISES AND PRACTICE PARAGRAPHS

If you are still hesitant about plunging into the writing of your first rough draft, you may find the special prewriting exercises that follow helpful. They should get you started, ease you into the writing process, facilitate the flow of ideas, possibly even make you eager to begin writing. As noted earlier, you have within you a wealth of subject matter to draw on for writing. However, what you need at any given moment may not be immediately accessible. The outside world or you, yourself, may help to trigger your thoughts. The exercises that follow are designed to assist you to do that, to stimulate you to action, perhaps to little bursts of activity, and ultimately to the writing of your rough draft.

To begin with, your instructor may put a word on the blackboard, enclosing it in a circle or rectangle to set it off, and then ask you and your classmates to tell what you think of or associate with that word. Take, for example, the word *chance*. Imagine yourself in class now. What comes to mind when you think of that word? What else? Does something contrary also come to mind? Try to be free and spontaneous rather than studied or analytical. To tap your inner resources, you may need to surprise yourself, to catch yourself off guard. Therefore, do not be too careful. Do not think it through. Instead, say whatever pops into your mind about the word. Can you imagine what others in your class might say also? Picture your instructor writing each contribution from the class (a single word or group of words) on the board, encircling it, and making these "word bubbles" or "balloons," connected by little lines or "strings," float out and about the core word, *chance*. After a short period of class participation, with many members of the class contributing a bubble, the blackboard should be filled. A simplified version of it might look something like Figure 1–1.

The process represented in Figure 1–1 is called *clustering*, which is a special way of brainstorming designed to develop ideas, images, and feelings around a core or stimulus word (in this case, the word *chance*) that can motivate or help lead to writing.* After you sample the process two or three times as part of a group in class, you may be on your own (though you may want to share the results in class) to try the exercises that follow. Keep in mind that the words you see around the core word, *chance*, do not result from careful and deliberate planning but rather from spontaneous, free association, that is, from whatever you happen to think of when you see the word. Further, you do not need to arrange the word bubbles in any special way around the core word, though a pattern may emerge, but let them connect and float about as they may.

As represented in Figure 1–1 the right-hand side of the core or stimulus word is busier (contains more word bubbles) than any other space around it, suggesting greater interest or responsiveness in that direction. You may also see a kind of pattern

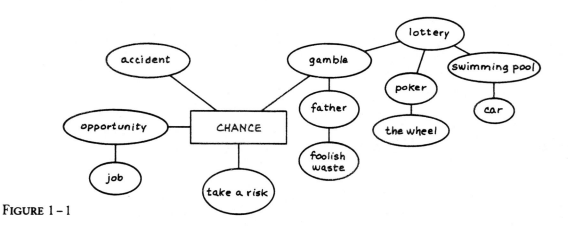

FIGURE 1–1

---

*Based on the process originated by Gabriele Rico, California State University, San Jose.

or form of thinking developing there. When such a pattern becomes clear in your own clustering, when it begins to call to you, the clustering process may give rise to the desire to write, to test the developing pattern. When you are clustering on your own, you may feel at such a point, "Aha! Maybe this is something I can write about!" When this feeling strikes you, it is time to stop clustering and to begin writing. Examine the following paragraph based on the clustering developed in Figure 1 – 1.

"A fool and his money are soon parted," I can imagine my father saying as I buy my state lottery ticket. "So I pay for a little fantasy life," I argue back, in my mind, as I consider how best to spend my millions, always including a swimming pool and a new car in my plans. Taking a chance on the lottery or a game of poker or, my favorite long shot at a Nevada gambling house, the big wheel, is certainly a debatable use of money. The rare times I gamble, I seem to have to clear the way for it with this little imaginary argument with my father. I think of him, too, when I throw away the ticket that had once shown such promise, or when I lose at poker, or when the big wheel flicks slowly toward my number but then dies next to it. "It's only a game, Dad," I mutter to myself, and then maybe I'll get in my old car and drive to the Y for a swim.

You need to follow your own star, so to speak, when clustering. That is, there is no one right way to cluster, no formula, no correct method. What you need most is to be tuned to your own impulses, to let happen what will, to permit yourself to go off in any direction that suits you. Thus everyone will cluster a word somewhat differently, often enormously differently, and the writing that comes from clustering will vary with each person. The preceding examples give only one way to cluster and write about the word *chance*. Keep in mind that there are numerous different ways, including others suggested but unexplored in Figure 1 – 1 as well as your own individual approach.

EXERCISE 1A
▬

Directions

Cluster the words ice cream, or choose another snack food such as pizza, popcorn, French fries, peanuts, or potato chips.

To encourage your spontaneous rather than planned and considered responses, limit yourself in time to approximately 3 minutes. An example for comparison follows; however, remember the example reflects the reactions of someone else whereas your own reactions are called for here.

Example

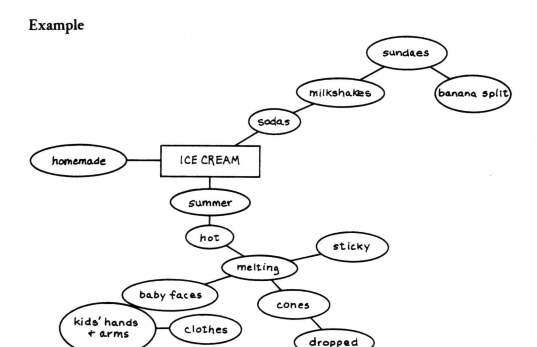

EXERCISE 1B

Directions

Write a paragraph — a group of sentences about one central topic — based on one point or aspect you developed in Exercise 1A.

In your clustering of the words <u>ice cream</u> (or some other word you chose), you very likely developed the core word in more than one worthwhile and interesting direction, but now you need to select just <u>one</u> direction on which to base a paragraph. Think about what you want to say — the <u>content</u> — as you write your paragraph. Do not worry about the form of the paragraph (you will study form in depth later in the book); concentrate on one topic and develop it until it feels finished. Follow through on one of the ideas that came to you or that you found most interesting as you clustered. Compare the following example to the cluster example in Exercise 1A. Can you see how the paragraph grew from the cluster?

Example

Ice cream makes me think of summer. It is hot, and everyone tries to keep cool by eating ice cream. I can imagine happy baby faces messy with ice cream, globs of it stuck to their noses and chins, layers of it smeared around their mouths and cheeks. I can see little kids with ice cream cones melting in their hands, running down their arms, and dripping on their clothes. Suddenly there is a tragedy. A cone slips from a small hand and lands, plop, on a hot sidewalk. Then what agony and flood of tears! An impatient parent scolds the child and they rush home. The fallen cone soon becomes a sticky feast for flies, then a faint stain in the concrete.

EXERCISE 2A

Directions

Cluster the word <u>throw</u>, or choose another action word such as <u>run</u>, <u>kick</u>, <u>jump</u>, <u>smash</u>, or <u>hold</u>.

To foster your spontaneous or free association rather than planned and studied responses, limit yourself in time to approximately <u>3 minutes</u>. Use the following example for reference or comparison, but keep in mind that your own reactions are what is called for here.

Example

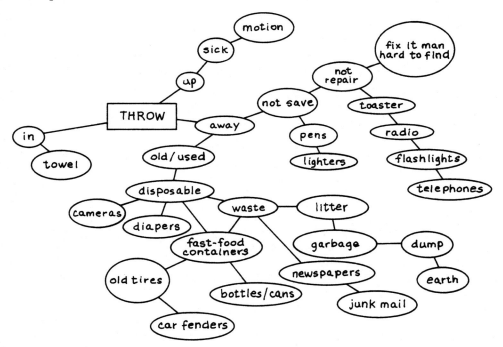

EXERCISE 2B

Directions

Write a paragraph — a group of sentences about one central topic — based on one point or aspect you developed in Exercise 2A.

Follow through on one of the ideas that came to you or that you found most interesting as you clustered in Exercise 2A. It may be helpful to compare the following example to the cluster example in Exercise 2A.

Example

This is a throwaway culture, maybe a throwaway world. People don't save things anymore, such as pens and lighters and clocks; they toss them out. They don't repair things anymore, like radios and toasters, unless by chance they find that rare member of a dying breed, a fix-it man, located in some offbeat place, dimly lighted and covered with dust. Most people just throw things away, whatever they may be: flashlights, car fenders, junk mail, fast-food containers, cameras, bottles, cans, diapers, newspapers, old tires, and telephones. Most things can be replaced; practically everything is disposable. As a result, the world is covered with litter. The great cities of the world, its rivers, lakes, and mountains, its seas and deserts, have become eyesores, slopped with garbage. That old movie line uttered by Bette Davis now applies to most parts of the earth, "What a dump!"

EXERCISE 3A

Directions

Cluster the word <u>hill</u>, or choose a word for another natural place such as <u>beach</u>, <u>meadow</u>, <u>creek</u>, <u>mountain</u> or <u>lake</u>.

To prompt a spontaneous rather than a planned reaction, limit yourself in time to approximately <u>3 minutes</u>. Use the following example for reference or comparison, but remember that your own responses, not those of someone else, are called for here.

Example

EXERCISE 3B

Directions

Write a paragraph—a group of sentences about one central topic—based on one point or aspect you developed in Exercise 3A.

Follow through on one of the ideas that came to you or that you found most interesting as you clustered in Exercise 3A. It may be helpful to compare the following example to the cluster example in Exercise 3A.

Example

The word <u>hill</u> strikes at my core. I am a hill person. The house where I live now is on a hill. The ranch where I grew up was on a hill in back of this one. I've always lived in hilly country. I feel strange and restless on flat land, as if I'm not tall enough, as if there's no way to get perspective on reality, no high place from which to look down and see and understand. As a youngster I used to get on my horse and ride to the highest hill I could find whenever I was troubled or had a problem to work out. There, on a golden, grassy, windswept peak, I could literally rise above it all. The valley below me retreated in a distant haze. Even the nearest barns and houses looked tiny and insignificant. Now when I walk to the top of this hill, I can look out on a beautiful bay with its great bridges, surrounding cities, and a mountain that looks like a sleeping lady. The view is lovely and complex, but the way to the peak is paved, and houses follow me as I go.

EXERCISE 4A

Directions

Cluster the word <u>afraid</u>, or choose another word that suggests strong feeling such as <u>angry</u>, <u>lonely</u>, <u>joyful</u>, <u>grateful</u>, or <u>embarrassed</u>.

To promote spontaneity rather than a studied, planned response, limit yourself in time to approximately <u>3 minutes</u>. Use the following example for reference or comparison, but bear in mind that your own reaction, not that of someone else, is called for here.

Example

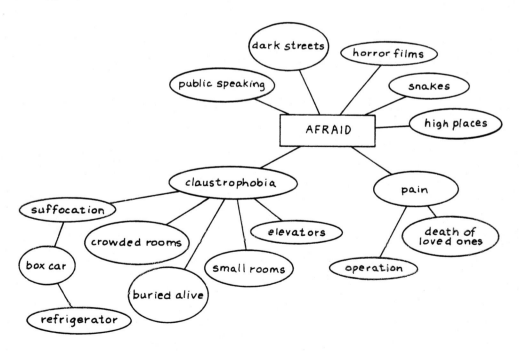

EXERCISE 4B

Directions

Write a paragraph — a group of sentences about one central topic — based on one point or aspect you developed in Exercise 4A.

Follow through on one of the ideas that came to you or that you found most interesting as you clustered in Exercise 4A. It may be helpful to compare the following example to the cluster example in Exercise 4A.

Example

Claustrophobia gives me nightmarish thoughts. . . . I am alone in an elevator, stuck between floors. The power in the building has gone off; it is dark, and no one can hear my call for help. . . . I am in a large room filled with people wedged together, moaning and screaming; I am at the center of the mass, held in place by sweating arms and elbows, so that I cannot reach a door. I can barely breathe. . . . I am locked in a boxcar on a railroad siding; the blazing sun has pushed the temperature to 120 degrees inside the car where I am writhing on the floor, throwing up and tearing at my clothes. . . . I am a curious child who has wandered alone into a junkyard, and I have found an open refrigerator. I will play house, I think, as I step inside and close the door, not realizing, until too late, that I cannot get out. . . . I am lying in a narrow box, my head and feet pressing against each end. I can hear dirt being dumped on the box, but there is no way of telling anyone that I am still alive. . . . Claustrophobia — the word alone makes me afraid.

EXERCISE 5A

Directions

Cluster the word <u>singer</u>, or choose another word for a performer such as <u>pianist</u>, <u>actor</u>, <u>dancer</u>, <u>magician</u>, or <u>acrobat</u>.

To encourage spontaneity rather than a carefully planned response, limit yourself in time to approximately <u>3 minutes</u>. Use the following example for reference or comparison, but keep in mind that your own reaction, not that of someone else, is called for here.

Example

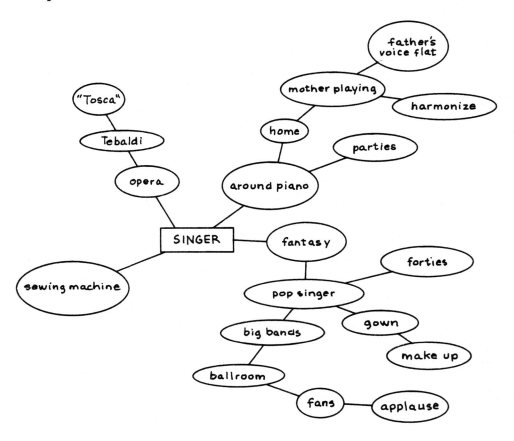

EXERCISE 5B

Directions

Write a paragraph—a group of sentences about one central topic—based on one point or aspect you developed in Exercise 5A.

Follow through on one of the ideas that came to you or that you found most interesting as you clustered in Exercise 5A. It may be helpful to compare the following example to the cluster example in Exercise 5A.

Example

The word <u>singer</u> calls to mind one of my favorite fantasies in which I am a professional popular singer. I can put my fantasy in a time warp and zing back into the late forties with the big bands and marvelous singers such as Helen Forrest, Anita O'Day, and Margaret Whiting. I imagine myself, a new star, standing in a shimmering gown in front of one of the big orchestras in a large and elegant ballroom filled with couples dancing. The band quiets down, and I step up to the microphone, a soft spot catching the sequins of my silver dress, my Lauren Bacallish face and figure, my glowing eyes with just the right color and amount of blue eye shadow, my lips glistening with a perfect reddish-purplish lipstick, my hair, lovely and long, slipping down my back, just so. I begin to sing in tones so sultry and intriguing that the people on the crowded floor turn my way, stop dancing, and move toward the bandstand, where they stand and gently sway to the music, captivated by my charm and talent. For a time it is as if we are all caught in a kind of magic spell that holds us enchanted until my song ends. Then I modestly acknowledge the applause and step back to my chair in front of the band, where I sit, looking cool and perfect, until my next number.

CONSIDER THESE AFTERTHOUGHTS ON CLUSTERING AND PARAGRAPHING

A. You have probably noticed, especially after gaining experience with the process, that when you cluster, you sometimes find yourself developing word bubbles (your ideas and impressions) first in one direction, then another, and then another with almost equal fullness. You may end up with a luxurious problem: having too much to write about! Since a paragraph can contain only one main topic lest it explode with overload, you have to make a decision. Which direction developed in clustering will you take in paragraphing? If you do not know right away because of gut feeling or intensity of interest, then you might decide another way. Try writing your paragraph on first one topic, then another, and then another to see which one writes best. A good paragraph sometimes has a way of almost writing itself, so when you feel that kind of ease as well as interest, your choice is clear. Such was the case in the last cluster and paragraph examples in the exercise on the word <u>singer</u>. The temptation to write a paragraph about <u>singer</u> in terms of being at home and singing around a piano was great, but the fantasy direction had a stronger pull. When that direction was tried out, the paragraph practically wrote itself.

B. One of the benefits that clustering brings to paragraphing is detail, without which writing is inclined to be not only vague but also limp and lifeless. Quite a bit of space is given elsewhere in this book to the subject of detailing, but it is helpful to think about it now and appreciate clustering as a valuable source of detail. When you tap your inner resources by means of clustering, what comes to you tends to be something like snapshots your mind has taken in the past but forgotten about. The stimulus or core word triggers your memory, and those old pictures come back to you, often in sharp detail. Thus you think about the word *hill*, for example, not in general terms or in some vague way but in relation to specific hills you have known, hills you have glimpsed or "snapped" in the past. You may see again such fine details as the grass on those hills, the color of the soil, the movement of the ground with a gopher underneath, the soil being pushed up, the bobbing nose, or whatever it was you saw originally. It is important to appreciate these details because they can make your writing rich, alive, and interesting. Be sure to make use of them, to note them in your word bubbles when clustering, and to use them in paragraphing.

C. At this early stage in your writing, you should concentrate on content, on what you want to say, more than on form or how to say it. However, you may realize by now that clustering gives you a sense of direction and some sense of form in paragraphing. The word bubbles you create around the core or stimulus word do not float about in total chaos. An idea (or perhaps two or three) tends to take shape somewhere in your clustering, a pattern of thought begins to grow. Examine again the cluster example of the word *afraid* on page 12. Clustering began with a miscellaneous assortment of things feared, which are given above and to the right of the core word. Then one of the worst fears, claustrophobia, came to mind. This word suggested a central topic, a whole category of fears, including various conditions or circumstances of claustrophobia. Thus clustering led not only to the content of the paragraph but also to its form. Similarly, with the cluster example of the word *throw* on page 9, once the word *away* came to mind, a topic was recognized, a series of related ideas and examples tumbled onto the page in a cluster, and a paragraph quickly followed. It is not surprising that the cluster prepares the way so well for the paragraph. After all, clustering means a gathering or grouping together of similar things. A paragraph, which is a group of sentences expressing one central idea, is little more than an expanded and modified cluster.

D. Do not stop clustering when you complete this chapter. If the process is working for you here, why not use it in later chapters that give you further exercises in paragraphing? Clustering should prove especially helpful to you in Chapter 6, "Problems of Form and Organization: Part A"; Chapter 7, Problems of Form and Organization: Part B"; and Chapter 8, "Problems of Variety and Imagination." You may find the process useful, as well, when you begin to practice the short composition in Chapter 15. In fact, you may get in the habit of clustering and want to use it before you write much of anything. One well-known innovator in the teaching of writing thinks so highly of the clustering process that she uses it even outside the field, for problem solving in general.

TRY CLUSTERING; THEN PRACTICE PARAGRAPHING SOME ADDITIONAL TOPICS

Remember what clustering is as you use the words in the following list. You should *not* try to define the words according to a dictionary or to collect ideas from other sources. *Your own free, spontaneous reaction* to the words is all that is called for here. How do you feel about the word? What impressions does it call to mind? What associations with the word do you have? What do you think of when you see it? To encourage your spontaneity rather than a planned and studied response, limit yourself to approximately *3 minutes* with each clustering exercise. Refer to the cluster and paragraph examples given earlier in this chapter if necessary.

A. Use the word *rain*, or choose another word for a weather element such as *snow, sunshine, fog, wind,* or *clouds.*

B. Use the word *twenty-one*, or choose another age such as *thirty, ten, eighteen, forty,* or *seventy.*

C. Use the word *green*, or choose another color such as *blue, red, pink, tan,* or *gold.*

D. Use the word *aggressive*, or choose another descriptive word such as *assertive, elegant, wimpy, shy,* or *dignified.*

E. Use the word *car*, or choose another land vehicle such as *truck, bus, bicycle, motorcycle,* or *sled.*

F. Use the word *handsome*, or choose another descriptive term such as *beautiful, sexy, romantic, earthy,* or *sensitive.*

G. Use the word *Help!*, or choose another exclamation such as *Stop!, Fire!, Look out!, Mayday!,* or *Thief!*

H. Use the word *rose*, or choose another flower such as *carnation, plumeria, orchid, magnolia,* or *tulip.*

I. Use the word *sailboat*, or choose another means of sea or air transport such as *canoe, surfboard, hang glider, airplane,* or *space shuttle.*

J. Use the word *carpenter*, or choose another occupation such as *farmer, dentist, chef, mechanic,* or *teacher.*

TRY THESE SIMPLE EXERCISES TO HELP YOU RELAX BEFORE WRITING

A. Sitting or standing as erect and tall as you can, stretch both arms straight up above your head as far as they will reach. Can you reach higher still, trying to touch the ceiling with your finger tips? Relax a moment, then try again, stretching as far as you can. Higher, please. Now relax.

B. Sitting or standing as erect and tall as you can, hold your arms out to each side, level with your shoulders. Minimizing any other movement of your body, first stretch your right arm out, reaching, reaching, as far as it will go. Next, do the same with your left arm, stretching, stretching, as far as you possibly can. Drop both arms and relax.

C. Sitting or standing, your arms relaxed at your side, draw your shoulders up as high as you can and then slowly roll them back and around several times.

D. Sitting or standing up straight, slowly bring your head down until your chin touches your chest. Then roll your head slowly toward your right shoulder, next to the back, then toward the left shoulder, finally back until it touches your chest again. Reverse the direction, making a slow move first toward the left shoulder, next to the back, then to the right shoulder, returning to the front. Straighten and relax.

E. Sitting or standing, dangle your arms and gently shake your wrists, as if you were trying to dry your hands.

F. Sitting or standing, let your body slump forward, bending your back, dangling your arms, letting your head slowly fall forward, your chin resting on your chest. If standing, bend your knees slightly. Hang that way for a few seconds. Then straighten up again.

G. Take a deep breath and slowly sigh. Take another deep breath and let it out slowly, humming softly from a middle to a lower note, sounding something like a faint foghorn. Inhale and exhale several times deeply and slowly. Can you breathe more slowly still? Keep breathing.

━

SUMMARY

You do not need to feel blank and paralyzed when you are asked to write a composition. You are an authority about your life, your experiences, and that means you have plenty to write about. Appreciate who you are and be yourself when you write, concentrating on content more than form in the beginning, becoming concerned with structure and mechanics later, after you have written your first rough drafts. You have within you an abundant source of subject matter to draw on for writing; however, this content may need to be triggered by forces in the outside world or by your own efforts. Special prewriting exercises using a process called *clustering* should help you get started. Follow these exercises with practice paragraphs. Before you begin, prepare yourself to write with relaxation exercises.

━

CHAPTER 2

WHAT IS A PARAGRAPH?

A *paragraph* is composed of a group of sentences expressing one central idea. A paragraph is complete in itself and is also a subdivision or part of something larger, such as a composition or a chapter in a book.

WHAT DOES A PARAGRAPH LOOK LIKE ON THE PAGE?

A paragraph begins with an empty space called an *indentation*. The indentation of a paragraph indicates where the paragraph begins. A composition, which contains several paragraphs, has several indentations, making it easy for the reader to see where each new paragraph or idea in the composition begins. One paragraph, however, contains only one indentation because there is only one beginning point. Figure 2 – 1 shows how a paragraph should look. Indent — once only! Figure 2 – 2 shows a paragraph indented too many times.

19

Xxxxxxxxxxxxxxxxxxxxxxxxxxxxxxxxxxxxxxxxxxxxxxxxxxxxxxxxxxxxx
xxxxxxxxxxxxxxxxxxxxxxxxxxxxxxxxxxxxxx. Xxxxxxxxxxxxxxxxxxxxxxxxxxxx
xxxxxxxxxxxxxxxxxxxxxxxxxxxxxxxxxxxxxxxxxxxxxxxxxxxxxxxxx. Xxxxxxxxx
xxxxxxxxxxxxxxxxxxxxxxxxxxxxxxxxxxxxxxxxxx. Xxxxxxxxxxxxxxxxxxxxxxxxx
xxxxxxxxxxxxxxxxxxxxxxxx. Xxxxxxxxxxxxxxxxxxxxxxxxxxxxxxxxxxxxxxxxxxx
xxxxxxxxxxxxxxxxxxxxxxxxxxxxxxxxxxxxxxxxxxxxxxxxxxxxxxxxxxxxxxxxxxxxx
xxxxxxxxxxxxxxxxxxxxxxxxxxxxxxxxxxxxxxxxxxxx. Xxxxxxxxxxxxxxxxxxxxxxxx

FIGURE 2 – 1   xxxxxxxxxxxxxxxxxxxxxxxxxxxxxxxxxxxxxxxxxxxxxxxxxxxxxxxxxxxxx.

Xxxxxxxxxxxxxxxxxxxxxxxxxxxxxxxxxxxxxxxxxxxxxxxxxxxxxxxxxxxxxxxxxxxx
xxxxxxxxxxxxxxxxxxxxxxxxxxxxxxxxxxxxxxx.

Xxxxxxxxxxxxxxxxxxxxxxxxxxxxxxxxxxxxxxxxxxxxxxxxxxxxxxxxxxxxxxxxxxxxx
xxxxxxxxxxxxxxxxxxxxxxxxxxxxxxxxxxxxxxxxxxxxxxxxxxxxx.

Xxxxxxxxxxxxxxxxxxxxxxxxxxxxxxxxxxxxxxxxxxxxxxxxxxxxxxxxxxxxxxxxxx
xxxxxxxxxxxxxxxxxxxxxxxxxxxxxxxxxxxxxxxx. Xxxxxxxxxxxxxxxxxxxxxxxxxxxx
xxxxxxxxxxxxxxxxxxxxxxxxxxxxxxxxxxxxxxxxxxxxxxxxxxxxxxxxx.

Xxxxxxxxxxxxxxxxxxxxxxxxxxxxxxxxxxxxxxxxxxxxxxxxxxxxxxxxxxxxxxxxxx

FIGURE 2 – 2   xxxxxxxxxxxxxxxxxxxxxxxxxxxxxxxxxxxxxxxxxxxxxxxxxxxxxxxx.

What Is the Difference Between a Paragraph and a Composition?

A paragraph is a part of a composition. Just as a group of related sentences composes a paragraph, so a group of related paragraphs makes up a composition. A group of compositions, in turn, can be the chapters that constitute a book. A book, then, is the largest unit; it covers more ground and is more complex than any one of its chapters. A chapter or composition is broader and says more than any one of its paragraphs. A paragraph is generally shorter, less complex, and expresses a great deal less than a composition. Figure 2–3 shows how a paragraph and composition are related.

Notice that the subdivisions of the book, which are indicated by increasingly smaller circles, each within the other, have been extended to the smallest unit of all, the word. Thus the paragraph, as well as the book and composition, can be subdivided.

In your college courses you will need to develop skill in writing compositions; therefore, it is useful to keep in mind the relationship between a paragraph and a composition.

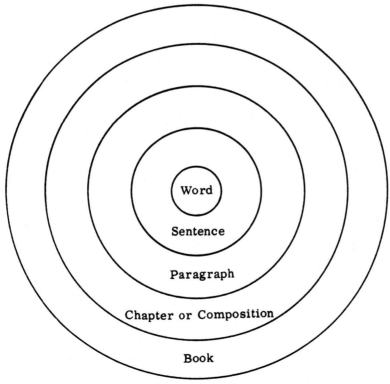

FIGURE 2–3

HOW LONG IS A PARAGRAPH?

If the idea of the paragraph is simple, the paragraph will usually be rather short. If the idea is complicated, the paragraph will probably be somewhat long. You should keep in mind this principle: *The paragraph should be neither so short that the subject of the paragraph is underdeveloped and insufficiently explained, nor so long that it tends to break down into too many subtopics that would be better organized into separate paragraphs.*

Paragraph length varies according to place and purpose as well as idea. In a newspaper, for example, where the column of newsprint is narrow, one-sentence paragraphs are common. Because comparatively few words can be contained in each line of newsprint, several lines are often necessary to print one sentence. To provide breaks or resting spots that make reading easier, newspapers indent or paragraph frequently. Purpose also determines the length of a paragraph. Newspapers, novels, textbooks, and college compositions each have particular purposes, and they use paragraphs accordingly.

Your paragraphs for the exercises in this book should be approximately *8 to 12 sentences long*, depending on sentence length and complexity. In some cases, your paragraphs should be longer.

HOW IS A PARAGRAPH ORGANIZED OR DEVELOPED?

All paragraphs have one basic aim: to communicate a single idea clearly and effectively. All paragraphs, however, are not organized in the same way. *How* they communicate depends on *what* they wish to express. You will face various types of "what" and "how" decisions in the exercises that follow.

Although all paragraphs are not exactly alike, they all nevertheless have some things in common. Consider some of the factors that should be present in any paragraph.

A. THE PARAGRAPH SHOULD CONTAIN ONLY ONE CENTRAL IDEA

A paragraph with more than one central idea is usually overworked and tends to break down under the strain. *Limit* the paragraph. Limiting the paragraph is something like taking a snapshot with a small camera. You should not try to get everyone in your hometown into your picture. Even your own family is too large or too interesting for your paragraph-sized camera. You had better settle on one member of your family, and keep in mind that you cannot tell everything about even one person in a single paragraph of 8 to 12 sentences. Make your picture a small portrait. See Figure 2–4.

FIGURE 2-4

Hometown   Family   Small Portrait

Like a small portrait, the paragraph should be limited to one part of a subject, although the subject is probably much larger than the single aspect discussed in the paragraph. To illustrate this idea, suppose you are asked to write something about your house in a paragraph. You cannot tell all about your house. The subject is too big. Even your living room may be too large a subject to discuss in a single paragraph. You need to select a part of the room, such as your fireplace or your favorite chair. Examine the following paragraph.

Example

My favorite chair is ugly, but I love it. It is a recliner. Because it is shapeless, heavy, and covered with horrible material, it is an eyesore in my living room. However, it is so comfortable that I would not trade it for the finest piece of furniture I might ever hope to own. There is nothing quite so delightful after a hard day at work as sinking my weary body into that chair. With my back eased into it and my feet eased up from it, I am in heaven. I notice other people like that chair, too. Whenever I have company, the first chair everybody heads for is my ugly, lovely recliner.

Limiting the paragraph is not an exact matter, but a useful rule of thumb may help you determine its approximate limitation: *The more deeply you go into a subject, the more the paragraph must be narrowed down or limited.*

A comparison of a paragraph to a camera is useful again. This time think of the process of enlargement. Suppose you take a picture of a standing figure. Then you decide that the expression in the face is good and you want to see it in more detail. You decide to have that portion of the picture enlarged. Then you decide there is something in the eyes that is fascinating (perhaps you see a mysterious figure reflected there) and you want to enlarge that portion of the face. The closer you get to the subject, the more you see in it. Similarly, the closer you get to the subject in the paragraph, the more you see to discuss, and consequently the more the subject must be narrowed if you want to discuss in one paragraph all that you see.

Figure 2 – 5 may clarify the rule of limitation.

As Figure 2 – 5 indicates, the paragraph must narrow down or limit its subject to the degree that it concentrates on it or any part of it. Figure 2 – 5A shows the whole subject, but at some distance. Such a paragraph, although it may give an overall view, cannot go into much detail. Figure 2 – 5B represents a paragraph that, by limiting itself, can develop its subject more fully. Figure 2 – 5C shows further limitation that makes further or closer examination of its subject possible.

Although some of the paragraphs you write may be like Figure 2 – 5A, your main aim is to develop skill in writing paragraphs like Figure 2 – 5B, or, in some cases, like Figure 2 – 5C.

Focus the paragraph. First, decide what the center of interest in your paragraph is and then make sure it is central and unmistakably clear. The following paragraph is focused.

Example

My father's face is rough. His complexion is leathery and wrinkled. There are large pores in the skin that covers his nose and cheeks. His nose, broken twice in his life, makes him look like a boxer who has lost too many fights. His mouth, unless he smiles, looks hard and threatening. His chin is massive and angular. Shaved or not, my father's face is rugged.

FIGURE 2 – 5

A   B   C

The following paragraph is out of focus.

Example

I want to talk about my father. He is strict with his children, especially me. He won't let me out of the house unless I've done all my homework. He is a tall and rather skinny man. Some people say he is good-looking. He has a nice streak of gray in his hair. He laughs a lot and enjoys life. My father is interesting.

The second paragraph fails to focus on a particular aspect or make a main point about its subject.

Focusing the paragraph is also like taking a good picture. Like the picture, the paragraph must have a center of interest that is obvious and unmistakable. Bad paragraphs are sometimes like the pictures in Figure 2–6, fuzzy or off-center.

B. THE PARAGRAPH SHOULD HAVE UNITY

Unity means the paragraph should be of one piece, a distinct unit that has one fundamental purpose. Remember that even though the paragraph is a subdivision or part of a larger unit, it should be complete in itself.

The previous example of a focused paragraph serves also as an example of a unified paragraph. Notice that although the paragraph discusses only one part of a much larger subject, the part discussed is complete in itself and does not need the

FIGURE 2–6

larger unit to be understood. The paragraph could fit easily into a whole composition entitled "My Father." Other paragraphs would be needed, of course, to give a complete picture of the larger subject, and they would each need to be distinct units also.

A paragraph should *not* be a *fragment*. It should not be like part of a conversation that is overheard but not quite understood because the complete conversation has not been heard, nor should it be like a piece from a jigsaw puzzle with shapes or colors that confuse the mind. It should be a whole, complete unit, understandable whether it stands alone or is combined with other parts to form a larger whole.

Remember to *stick to the subject*! One of the easiest ways to destroy the unity of a paragraph is to skip from subject to subject, as in the following example.

Example

My father is very strict with his children, especially me. He won't let me out of the house unless I've done all my homework. Frankly, I don't care whether I go to school or not. School is such a waste of time. There aren't any good jobs, anyway. My mother doesn't agree with my father. They quarrel a lot. Sometimes I wish they would get a divorce, but then who would I live with?

The preceding paragraph lacks unity because it jumps from subject to subject. (Although it has psychological interest, partly because of its lack of unity, the lack is a definite fault in a paragraph.)

Stick to the subject. If you begin a paragraph about dogs, don't switch the subject to parakeets in the middle of your paragraph unless, of course, you must talk about parakeets to clarify what you want to say about dogs.

C. THE PARAGRAPH SHOULD HAVE COHERENCE AND CONTINUITY

The terms *coherence* and *continuity* are closely related. Coherence means that the parts of the paragraph should be logically arranged and connected. Continuity means that the connection of the parts should be smooth. To make a comparison, a coherent paragraph is like a properly assembled motor; with all the parts in the right places, the motor can run. Continuity is like an oil that lubricates the operation, making it smooth and preventing the motor from burning out.

To be coherent, the paragraph must have *order* or *sequence*. The particular order or sequence needed depends on the subject. For instance, people are usually described from head to toe rather than vice versa. On the other hand, photographs are most often discussed from left to right. Recipes usually begin with ingredients and end with the oven. Dressmaking starts with the selection of a pattern rather than the final ironing process. (These subjects illustrate the idea of order or sequence, though some of them are too large to be contained in a single paragraph.) The order or sequence that is logical depends on the nature of the subject to be discussed. The following paragraph is coherent because it has order or sequence.

Example

To get the most out of their textbooks, students should follow several steps carefully. They should make a survey of each book to get a general idea of what the book contains. They should read for understanding and formulate questions. They should make notes of the major points of each chapter. They should test themselves to be sure they can answer questions likely to be raised in class and in examinations. They should review their notes and reread any parts of the book that are unclear to them.

The previous paragraph is coherent, but it is not as smooth as it might be. Let's look at the paragraph again, with added continuity.

Example

To get the most out of their textbooks, students should follow several steps very carefully. First, they should make a preliminary survey of each book to get a general idea of what the book contains. Second, they should read for deeper understanding and formulate questions as they read. Next, they should make notes of the major points of each chapter. After that, they should test themselves to be sure they can answer questions likely to be raised in class and in examinations. Finally, they should review their notes and reread any parts of the book that are unclear to them.

Continuity is added by the underlined words, which provide *transition*. Transitional words or phrases are like passwords. They permit easy passage throughout the paragraph by showing the relationship between one sentence or thought and another. They make the sequence of ideas within the paragraph clearer, and they make the paragraph as a whole more flowing.

A good paragraph is a joy to read. It is not something stumbled through with great labor. It does not stop and start and turn around. It is not jerky. Coherence and continuity, working together, make a paragraph clear and easy to read. For a fuller discussion of coherence and continuity, refer to Chapter 5.

D. THE PARAGRAPH SHOULD BE ADEQUATELY DEVELOPED

The paragraph should do fully what it sets out to do. It should not leave the job half-done. The degree of development depends on the aim or purpose of the paragraph. For example, if the purpose of the paragraph is to explain how to build a bookcase, do not leave the bookcase unfinished. It will probably need paint or stain before you can put books in it, and the paragraph is not complete until it mentions the final part in the building of the bookcase. Do not just end the paragraph — complete it!

Most paragraphs have three basic parts: a beginning, a middle, and an end. These parts are often called the *introduction*, the *discussion*, and the *conclusion*. In the introduction, which may be simply the topic sentence, indicate what you will talk about in the paragraph. In the discussion, talk about the topic. In the conclusion, complete your discussion, often referring to your main point stated in the introduction. Sometimes, the conclusion takes the form of a summary or brief restatement of the main ideas of the paragraph.

To be adequately developed, the paragraph must have *proper proportion* in its three main parts. That is, each part should be a certain length or size. The approximate size of each part is shown in Figure 2 – 7.

The discussion is the biggest part of the paragraph. The introduction and the conclusion are smaller.

Bad paragraphs are sometimes poorly proportioned, as shown in Figure 2 – 8.

The following paragraph is poorly proportioned. As stated in the topic sentence, the main purpose of the paragraph is to tell about a bad automobile accident. However, most of the paragraph is spent on introducing the subject. The discussion, which is underlined, consists of only two sentences.

INTRODUCTION

DISCUSSION

CONCLUSION

FIGURE 2 – 7

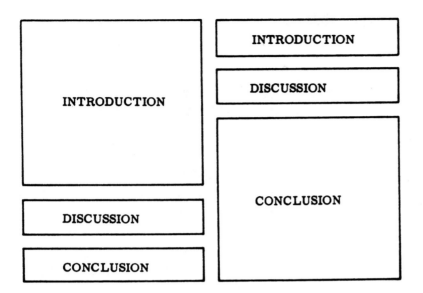

FIGURE 2 – 8

Example

I had one of the worst experiences of my life when I witnessed a terrible automobile accident a little over a year ago. I was on my way to a party with my boyfriend. It was about 8 o'clock at night, and it was raining. Though we were in a hurry to get to the party, my boyfriend was driving slowly because of the poor visibility. We were happily looking forward to seeing our friends, gossiping about some of them, listening to music on the car radio, and humming some of the tunes. We were stopped for a red light at an intersection when the accident occurred. A car in the lane next to us sped through the red light and crashed into a truck, which was just pulling into the intersection from the cross street. There was a terrible crush of metal, splintering of glass, and screaming and moaning of people. We didn't feel much like going to a party after that.

The preceding paragraph has interesting (if horrible) possibilities and could be improved by correcting its proportions. The introduction should be shortened, and the discussion should be expanded.

Expanding the paragraph is not simply a matter of making it longer. Never pad a paragraph. *Do not* just *write* more; instead, *say* more. A paragraph should *not go on and on;* it should go *in and in.* That is, it should be developed by going more and more *into* its subject.

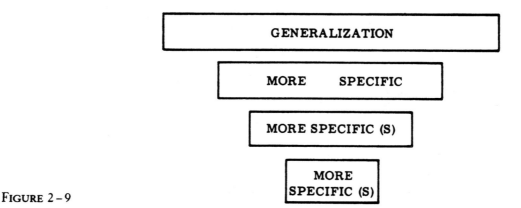

FIGURE 2-9

The best way to develop a paragraph is to be *specific rather than general.* In other words, discuss one thing in definite, exact, precise detail. Do not discuss many things vaguely. Although your paragraph may begin with a statement that is to some extent (within the limits of the paragraph) broad or general, you should develop it by becoming more and more specific, narrowing down your subject, and saying exactly what you mean. Your paragraph should do what is done in the diagram in Figure 2-9, *not* what is done in Figure 2-10.

A general statement should not be developed with a series of further generalizations. A *generalization* is a statement about *all* or *most* of a group or category. It is not definite, not particular, and sometimes not accurate, because it does not allow for exceptions. Moreover, it is vague. It says everything about everything but nothing about anything in *particular.* Your objective in developing the paragraph is just the reverse. You should develop the one central idea of the paragraph with particulars or details that make the idea clear and meaningful.

GENERALIZATION
GENERALIZATION
GENERALIZATION
GENERALIZATION

FIGURE 2-10

Realizing that detail is necessary in your paragraph, you may still wonder *how much detail* is needed. Reconsider the rule of limitation given earlier: The more deeply you go into a subject, the more the paragraph must be narrowed down or limited. Now, add to that rule the following: *The more narrowed down or limited the paragraph is, the more it must go into detail.* Remember that when you stand back from a subject, you see it in less detail, but when you move in close to it, the detail you see in it can become so fine as to be almost microscopic.

Consider the following example of a paragraph that stands back somewhat from its subject, giving an overall view of it. Although it gives some specifics, it does not go into great or fine detail.

Example

City College should have a new campus for three major reasons. First, the present campus is badly overcrowded and there is absolutely no space left for additional expansion. Second, the campus is an ugly improvisation of old high school buildings and flimsy, boxlike portables that fail to create a collegiate atmosphere. Third, the equipment in such departments as science, art, and physical education is completely inadequate for the needs of college students. There are other strong arguments for a new campus, but these are three of the most outstanding.

In the next example, the paragraph moves in a little closer to its subject, making more detail possible and necessary.

Example

City College is completely overcrowded. The lack of space is apparent in all parts of the campus. The classrooms are so jammed that students feel like sardines, and some of them have to sit on the floor. The library and study rooms are so packed that many students must study in the halls and stairways. The cafeteria so bulges with bodies that students often go hungry or lose their appetites. Every inch of the campus is so overcrowded that it looks more like a bargain basement than a place for higher learning.

In the next example, the paragraph moves in still closer to its subject than either of the preceding two examples. Because it narrows down or limits the subject further, it must discuss the subject in greater detail.

Example

The cafeteria at crowded City College is one of the most overworked places on the campus. The service line is frequently so long that a student gives up the idea of eating altogether. If she is patient enough to wait for food, she is lucky if she can find a place to eat it before she wears it. If she is particularly agile, she may work her way through the masses to a spot where she can eat it before it's cold. Once seated, however, she is likely to find the atmosphere so choked with other bodies, noise, and dead air, that she loses her appetite. She cannot easily slip away at that point, either. Wedging her way out of the cafeteria, she discovers, is as miserable a matter as working her way in.

You should keep in mind that the closer you move into or go into a subject, the more the paragraph should be narrowed down or limited and that, likewise, the more the paragraph is narrowed down or limited, the more it must go into detail.

As stated earlier, some of the paragraphs that you will be asked to write may be like the first of the three preceding paragraphs; however, most of your effort should be spent in learning to write paragraphs like the second two.

SUMMARY

Your paragraph will be clear and enjoyable to read if you follow the directions summed up here. First, remember to indent the paragraph—once only! Second, remember that the paragraph should be neither too short nor too long; make it approximately 8 to 12 sentences in length. Third and most important, organize and develop your paragraph carefully. Remember that the paragraph should contain one central idea only, that it should have unity, coherence, continuity, and adequate development. If you follow these directions, your paragraph should be as good as or better than this one.

PART ONE

CHAPTER 3

THE

TOPIC

SENTENCE

WHAT IS A TOPIC SENTENCE?

A *topic sentence* indicates what the paragraph is about, what it will describe or discuss. It is often the first sentence in the paragraph. The following are examples of topic sentences:

Owning a car is expensive.
Going to college requires much more self-reliance than going to high school.
Television is (not) rightly called an "idiot box."
Spring is the most pleasant season of the year.
Parents should (not) spank their misbehaving children.

WHAT IS THE DIFFERENCE BETWEEN A TOPIC SENTENCE AND A TITLE?

Since a topic sentence tells what the paragraph is about, it is a little like the title of a composition. Because the topic sentence serves that function, *the paragraph needs no title*. In other ways, a topic sentence and a title are different.

35

There are several differences between a topic sentence and a title. First, a topic sentence is a sentence *within* the paragraph, *not set off from or above it*, as a title is set off from the main body of a composition. Second, a topic sentence is always a complete thought, whereas a title is frequently a fragment or part of a complete thought. Consider the following examples:

A. TITLE: The Art of Changing a Tire
   TOPIC SENTENCE: Too few drivers appreciate the art of changing a tire.
B. TITLE: In Case of a Flat
   TOPIC SENTENCE: All drivers should know what to do in case of a flat.

Notice the difference in capitalization in the title and in the topic sentence. Several words of a title are capitalized, but only the first word of the topic sentence is capitalized. In addition, of course, if the topic sentence (or any sentence) contains proper nouns, they are also capitalized. Be careful, however, that you do not form the bad habit of capitalizing whenever you feel in the mood for it. Do not go capital-crazy!

EXERCISE E1. IDENTIFY FRAGMENTS AND SENTENCES

Some of the following statements are sentences that could be used as *topic sentences*; some are fragments, groups of words, or sentences that could be used as *titles* (some *are* titles of published works).

Place an "S" in the space next to a statement you think could be used as a topic sentence, and put a period at the end of the sentence. Write a "T" next to a statement you think could be a title. (Note the difference in capitalization of the title compared to the topic sentence, an important clue in distinguishing between the two.)

_____ 1. The Macmillan Handbook of English

_____ 2. Female gymnasts tend to be tiny

_____ 3. Gambling has been referred to as "suicide without the death"

_____ 4. Crime Pays

_____ 5. My dog can read my mind

_____ 6. A Funny Thing Happened on the Way to the Forum

_____ 7. Contact dermatitis is a reaction of the skin to material that comes in contact with it

_____ 8. Poor communication contributed to the disaster of the Oakland-Berkeley fire of October 1991

_____ 9. The Overcompensation of Corporate Executives

_____	10.	An argument can be made for acting on impulse
_____	11.	The Girl Who Was Born with a Telephone in Her Ear
_____	12.	Most politicians running for office resort to negative advertising
_____	13.	Everyone who loves life should be skilled in administering CPR
_____	14.	Cruising the Beautiful San Juan Islands
_____	15.	Haiku Poems: Ancient and Modern
_____	16.	Repotting a plant is a simple procedure
_____	17.	Most people are careless to some degree in their pronunciation of words
_____	18.	What to See in Greece
_____	19.	Some people experience an allergic reaction to the flavor enhancer MSG
_____	20.	The Craft and Art of Dylan Thomas

Another important difference between a topic sentence and a title is that a topic sentence *limits* the paragraph, whereas a title *expands* the composition. Reexamine Figure 2–3 and the explanation given on page 21. You can see that a whole composition covers more ground than a single paragraph. The title of a composition also includes more, suggests more, is broader than the topic sentence of a paragraph. A title of a composition has the effect shown in Figure 3–1. A topic sentence has the effect shown in Figure 3–2.

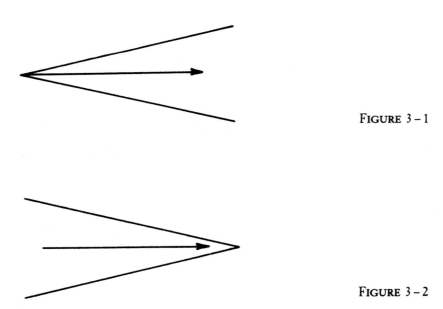

FIGURE 3–1

FIGURE 3–2

A topic sentence must not only indicate what the paragraph is about, it must also make clear what the paragraph is *not* about. It must narrow down or limit the paragraph to an exact point. A good topic sentence controls the paragraph. It sets very clear and definite limits to the topic as well as telling what the topic is.

EXERCISE E2. RECOGNIZE BROAD AND NARROW STATEMENTS

Some of the statements that follow are quite broad and could be titles (some *are* titles of published works); some are narrowed down or limited and could be topic sentences. Place a "B" in the space next to a statement you think is broad. Write an "N" in the space if you think a statement is narrowed down or limited. In addition, put a period at the end of any sentence that is not a title.

_____ 1. All's Well That Ends Well

_____ 2. John Keats died too young

_____ 3. Spelling Improvement: A Program of Self-Instruction

_____ 4. Learning to *see* a word is a means of learning to spell it

_____ 5. Marrying young is a custom in my family

_____ 6. Marriage and Family Life

_____ 7. The Promise of New World Peace

_____ 8. My brother is a pacifist

_____ 9. "The Pasture" is one of my favorite poems by Robert Frost

_____ 10. The Poems of Robert Frost

_____ 11. Growing up in a Big City

_____ 12. Drug dealers operate on the street where I live

_____ 13. My little sister has a vivid imagination

_____ 14. Children of Famous Parents

_____ 15. The Autobiography of Malcolm X

_____ 16. When Malcolm went to a restaurant, he liked to sit facing the door

_____ 17. My aunt's front room is stiff and formal

_____ 18. Home Decoration in America

_____ 19. Joy of Cooking

_____ 20. The secret to cooking vegetables is not to overcook them

IS THE TOPIC SENTENCE ALWAYS THE FIRST SENTENCE IN THE PARAGRAPH?

At first, you should pretend that the topic sentence always begins the paragraph, even though it may not. Advanced or professional writers state the topic at various places in the paragraph. Some writers do not state it at all but rather suggest it with other parts of the paragraph. However, as you begin to practice the paragraph, it is probably a good plan to make your topic obvious. By making the first sentence you put on paper your topic sentence, you remind yourself as well as let your reader know exactly what your topic is.

Be sure your first sentence is your topic sentence. Be sure you take a good look at your topic. Be sure you stick to it!

SUMMARY

Begin your paragraph with a topic sentence rather than a title. Be sure that your topic sentence indicates what your paragraph is about, that it is a complete thought, and that it limits your paragraph.

CHAPTER 4 ⟜

PRACTICING
_____

THE
_____

TOPIC
_____

SENTENCE
_____

REQUIREMENT 1. BE COMPLETE
⟜

The minimum requirement of any topic sentence is that it be a complete sentence. That is, the sentence must contain at least one complete thought. In fact, if it does not contain at least one complete thought, it is not a sentence at all but rather a sentence fragment or part of a sentence.

The first problem in writing a topic sentence is to learn to _write a complete sentence, not a fragment._ Study the following:

1. FRAGMENT: How to change a tire
   COMPLETE: Anyone can learn how to change a tire.

2. FRAGMENT: To change a tire
   COMPLETE: A motorist can learn to change a tire without much difficulty.

3. FRAGMENT: Changing a tire
   COMPLETE: Changing a tire is simple.

4. FRAGMENT: If a driver has a flat tire
    COMPLETE: If a driver has a flat tire, he or she should be able to change it.

5. FRAGMENT: When a driver changes a flat tire
    COMPLETE: When a driver changes a flat tire, he or she should observe three important safety rules.

6. FRAGMENT: A safe way to change a tire
    COMPLETE: There is a safe way to change a tire.

7. FRAGMENT: One of the most important steps in changing a tire
    COMPLETE: One of the most important steps in changing a tire is to set the brake first.

8. FRAGMENT: Five easy steps in changing a tire
    COMPLETE: Five easy steps in changing a tire should be followed by all drivers.

EXERCISE E3. IDENTIFY FRAGMENTS AND SENTENCES

Some of the statements that follow are fragments; some are sentences. Place an "F" in the space next to a statement you think is a fragment. Write an "S" in the space if you think a statement is a sentence, and put a period at the end of the sentence.

_____ 1. Bowling looks boring

_____ 2. Learning to smoke

_____ 3. One of the best parts of the movie is the chase scene at the end

_____ 4. One of the most complex and interesting characters in the entire book

_____ 5. To learn to play poker

_____ 6. To err is human

_____ 7. If I am late for work, my boss frowns

_____ 8. When a player hits a home run

_____ 9. To wear a lava-lava, it helps to have hips

_____ 10. Being a single parent

_____ 11. Attending a high school where students carry guns can be difficult if not fatal

_____ 12. When a man loves a woman

_____ 13. If you want to get along with your mother-in-law

_____ 14. If you have the right hammer, you can make the right rap

_____ 15. One of the first steps in learning to sing

———— 16. One of the first steps in learning to garden is developing pleasure in digging

———— 17. If you want to get good grades, you need to study

———— 18. One of the best ways to pass a course

———— 19. If you want your boyfriend to remember your birthday

———— 20. If a computer virus can be named Michelangelo

EXERCISE E4. MAKE SENTENCES FROM FRAGMENTS

The following are fragments that might become sentences if properly completed. As in the examples given earlier, these fragments can be completed in more than one way. Try to figure out one or more of the ways in which to make them complete.

1. Teaching a child good manners
2. How to carry a gun safely
3. Learning to like grammar
4. If a person wants to be popular
5. To fight the fragment
6. How to avoid an argument
7. If a person wants to learn to style hair
8. Exceeding the speed limit
9. To make elderly people happy
10. Knowing how to select shoes
11. To be a good neighbor
12. When a skier learns to fall properly
13. One of the most important steps in learning to drive
14. To learn to fish
15. If a person wants to learn to dance
16. How to hem a dress
17. If a student wants to pass a course
18. One of the most important steps in learning to swim
19. If teenagers disagree with their parents
20. Learning to paint
21. One easy step in making an interesting flower arrangement
22. When an individual feels lost in a crowd
23. One easy way to get acquainted with strangers
24. To learn to write a paragraph
25. A sensible way to select a career

REQUIREMENT 2. BE CLEAR

In addition to being complete, the topic sentence must also be clear. Keep in mind that the topic sentence announces the idea to be developed in the paragraph and that the paragraph must contain *one central idea only*. Therefore, to be clear, the topic sentence must do the following:

1. State one definite idea
2. Be specific enough for the subject to be discussed within the limits of a single paragraph

The first test for clarity:

> Does the topic sentence state one definite idea?

The topic sentence should make a single topic plain and obvious. It should not confuse the reader with two or more subjects or possible meanings. The following are examples of sentences that *fail* to isolate single topics.

1. Street and highway construction in California is a debatable subject.
2. To play any kind of instrument, one needs to know something about the instrument.
3. House painting should be approached with caution.

The first sentence, "Street and highway construction in California," suggests quite possibly hundreds, perhaps thousands of topics rather than just one. The second sentence lacks even one definite topic, though "To play any kind of instrument" would seem to hint at many. The third sentence *appears* to have a single topic, but exactly what *is* it that should be approached with caution? The topic is slippery, vague, uncertain.

The three sentences might be made clearer if each presented a single, definite idea. Consider the following:

1. Street and highway construction in California is a debatable subject.

POSSIBLE CORRECTIONS:

Many people in San Francisco agree that the removal of the Embarcadero Freeway has improved the view.

Doyle Drive, the approach to the Golden Gate Bridge, is extremely dangerous, but people do not agree on how to solve the problem.

All three-lane highways in California should be abolished.

Widening any freeway is a short-term solution to a long-term problem.

Its one narrow and twisting road makes Panoramic Hill in Berkeley an area where the homes are difficult to save or escape from in case of fire.

2. To play any kind of musical instrument, one needs to know something about the instrument.

POSSIBLE CORRECTIONS:

To play any kind of drum requires a good sense of rhythm.

To play French horn with a mellow tone requires extremely skillful breath control.

To play violin, one needs a good ear.

To play piano, one needs to spend much time practicing finger exercises.

To play trumpet, one needs to develop a strong lip.

3. House painting should be approached with caution.

POSSIBLE CORRECTIONS:

Successful house painting must be preceded by a great deal of patching, sanding, and stripping.

House painting can be a rewarding family project if carefully planned.

Only the most diligent amateur should undertake house painting.

House painting in the hands of an amateur frequently results in unprofessional-looking work.

House painting is an expensive part of home maintenance.

EXERCISE E5.   EVALUATE TOPIC SENTENCES

Some of the sentences that follow *state one definite idea* and therefore have good, clear possibilities as topic sentences. Other sentences (1) confuse the reader with two or more subjects or possible meanings, or (2) lack one definite topic, though they may seem to hint at many, or (3) appear to have a single topic, but what it is, exactly, is not clear.

Place a "C" in the space next to a sentence you think makes one idea definite and clear. Write a "?" in the space if you question a sentence for any of the reasons just given.

_____ 1. Baseball should be approached with caution.

_____ 2. Pitchers are among the most likely baseball players to suffer injuries.

_____ 3. Playing electronic video games continually is a debatable subject.

_____ 4. People who play electronic video games excessively can develop tendinitis.

_____ 5. An animal trainer needs to be skilled in various techniques.

_____ 6. The need for family planning is something people differ about.

_____ 7. The women's movement is controversial.

_____ 8. Marijuana is a debatable subject.

_____ 9. Doctors and others in the medical field question the use of marijuana as medication for people who suffer from cancer, glaucoma, and AIDS.

_____ 10. Harry Houdini, an American magician, specialized in escapes from bonds such as handcuffs and straitjackets.

_____ 11. Magicians always fascinate children.

_____ 12. Exercise is good for people.

_____ 13. Walking is an excellent exercise for most people over 50.

_____ 14. Although noisy, the blue jay is a clever bird.

_____ 15. Bird watchers should be approached with caution.

EXERCISE E6. REWRITE TOPIC SENTENCES

The following sentences are like the three sentences given earlier with possible corrections. They _fail_ as topic sentences because they do _not state one definite idea._ Instead, they (1) confuse the reader with two or more subjects or possible meanings, or (2) lack one definite topic, hinting, instead, at many, or (3) appear to have a single topic, but what it is, exactly, is not clear.

Select _five_ of the sentences that follow and try to determine their faults. Rewrite and correct them in _two_ or more ways.

Example

Going to college is challenging.

TWO POSSIBLE CORRECTIONS:

Attending a daily 8 o'clock class requires consistent effort.

Learning to take good notes is a necessary college skill.

1. Going to college is challenging.
2. To play a sport well, a person needs to know something about it.
3. To do any kind of artwork requires skill.
4. Learning to cook takes patience and practice.
5. Auto mechanics should be approached with care.
6. To raise children, a person needs to know something about child development.
7. Unemployment is hurting society.
8. Crime is worrisome.
9. Sex is a debatable subject.
10. Television can be harmful to children.
11. Motorcycles should be handled with care.

12. The subject of abortion rights is much contested.
13. Drugs should be approached with caution.
14. Health care has become a major issue in the United States.
15. People disagree about the death penalty.

The second test for clarity:

> Is the topic sentence specific enough for the subject to be discussed within the limits of a single paragraph?

When a sentence is sufficiently specific, it tends to be clear. When a sentence is too broad or too general, it tends to be unclear as well. Keep in mind the limitation of a paragraph when considering the topic sentence. The topic sentence must not be so broad or so general that it requires a whole composition or even a book to do it justice. The topic sentence must control the paragraph. The shoe should pinch a little, so to speak, for the topic sentence to fit the paragraph. As a matter of fact, the topic sentence must come to a rather narrow point to be specific.

The following are examples of topic sentences that *fail* to be sufficiently specific:

1. Following the Ten Commandments is difficult.
2. All college students should master the skills of writing good compositions.
3. Teenagers are unsafe, irresponsible drivers.

Each of the three preceding sentences is much too broad or general to be workable as a topic sentence that will be developed in a single paragraph. The first sentence may be too large a topic even for a book or set of encyclopedias. The second sentence calls for many paragraphs of discussion rather than just one. The third sentence is the sort of sweeping generalization that may be false, full of exceptions, or need numerous paragraphs of careful discussion to clarify or support.

The three sentences might be made more specific in a number of ways. Consider the following:

1. Following the Ten Commandments is difficult.

POSSIBLE CORRECTIONS:

The commandment to rest on the seventh day should not be interpreted as meaning *only* the seventh day.

Thou shalt not kill is a commandment the state breaks every time it executes a criminal.

The parent of a starving child is sorely tempted to break the commandment regarding stealing.

"Keeping up with the Joneses" can easily be related to the commandment regarding coveting.

The commandment to work six days a week is out of date.

2. All college students should master the skills of writing good compositions.

POSSIBLE CORRECTIONS:

Writing an outline can be an aid to organizing a composition.

Sentence structure should be varied in a composition.

The thesis statement of a composition can be compared to the topic sentence of a paragraph.

The title of a composition should provoke the reader's interest and give an idea of what the composition is about.

Word choice in a composition should be both exact and imaginative.

3. Teenagers are unsafe, irresponsible drivers.

POSSIBLE CORRECTIONS:

My teenage brother drives carelessly.

Insurance rates are usually higher when the driver is a teenager.

A conscientious teenager takes driver education classes seriously.

When I was a teenager, my friends and I used to race our cars across the San Francisco–Oakland Bay Bridge.

Teenage drivers frequently rely too much on their quick response time.

As indicated in Chapter 2, being specific is sometimes a *matter of degree.* Consider these sentences:

1. My sister wants to devote her life to music.
2. My sister wants to be a singer.
3. My sister is studying to become a soprano in grand opera.
4. My sister's greatest ambition is to sing "Tosca" at the Metropolitan Opera House.

The preceding sentences move by degrees from the general to the specific: The first sentence is the most general; the fourth, the most specific. The first sentence can cover a multitude of activities. The sister may want to be a rap artist, a tuba player, a concert pianist, a research scholar, or a member of a chorus in Las Vegas or Salt Lake City. Her ambition is not very clear because the sentence is so general and vague.

The second sentence is not quite so general as the first but still not specific enough to make the subject clear and easy to discuss within the limits of a single paragraph. *Singer* is a word that has several possible meanings. What kind of a singer does the sister want to be? Country? Rhythm and blues? Gospel? Does she want to sing for local weddings and funerals or be a big international star? The exact nature and scope of her ambition need to be more specific, clearer. The third and fourth sentences are the most exact and therefore the clearest. The fourth sentence, particularly, pinpoints the sister's highest ambition.

Your aim in writing a topic sentence is to be as specific as possible,* to write with the exactness of sentences 3 and 4 in the preceding group of four. However, keep in mind that being specific, to make a comparison, is usually not like flipping a standard light switch, and then the light goes on. It is more like adjusting a "dimmer," bringing the light up gradually until the desired brightness is achieved. You may need to write and rewrite to reach the light you need, that is, to become specific enough to make your idea clear.

EXERCISE E7. IDENTIFY SENTENCES THAT ARE SPECIFIC, TOO BROAD, BORDERLINE

Some of the sentences that follow are *specific enough for the subject to be discussed within the limits of a single paragraph* and therefore have good, clear possibilities as topic sentences. Other sentences are much too broad or general to be workable as topic sentences. Still other sentences, like the first two of the four examples about the sister given earlier, demonstrate degrees of specificity without being specific enough to be entirely clear or discussible within one paragraph. These sentences might be called borderline.

Place an "S" in the space next to a sentence you think is specific enough to be a clear topic sentence. Write a "B" in the space if you think a sentence is borderline. Put a "?" in the space if you question a sentence because it is too broad or too general to be a topic sentence. Be ready to discuss your answers.

    _____   1.   All books are good company.

    _____   2.   Charles Dickens's book *David Copperfield* is loaded with fascinating and entertaining characters.

---

*Remember, being specific is sometimes a *matter of degree*. Keep in mind the rule of limitation stated earlier. The more deeply you go into a subject, the more the paragraph must be narrowed down or limited, and the more narrowed or limited the paragraph, the more it must go into detail. The possible corrections given earlier, and the examples and exercises that follow, are not absolutes or models of perfection. The topic sentences could be made still more specific. Likewise, any paragraphs based on them would then need to be developed with still finer detail.

_____ 3. One of the most fascinating characters in Charles Dickens's book *David Copperfield* is Uriah Heep.

_____ 4. The Korean vegetable noodle *dang myun* is one of my favorite foods.

_____ 5. My favorite meals include some form of Asian pasta.

_____ 6. Pasta is my favorite food.

_____ 7. College students need to know mathematics.

_____ 8. A knowledge of arithmetic should be a part of everyone's survival kit.

_____ 9. Learning a foreign language is very difficult.

_____ 10. Spelling in Spanish is much easier than it is in English.

_____ 11. Philippine women love shoes.

_____ 12. My Philippine cousin Emma loves to run around barefoot.

_____ 13. Homicide is much too common in Oakland.

_____ 14. Crime in many American cities appears to be totally out of control.

_____ 15. The Irish have terrible tempers.

EXERCISE E8. MAKE SENTENCES SPECIFIC

The following sentences are like the three sentences given earlier with possible corrections. They *fail* as topic sentences because they are *not specific enough to be discussed within the limits of a single paragraph.* Instead, they are much too broad or general to be workable.

Select *five* of the sentences that follow, and correct by narrowing down the subject so it is specific enough to be discussible in a single paragraph. Rewrite the sentences in *two* or more ways.

Example

People who live in earthquake-prone areas should make emergency preparations for a major earthquake.

TWO POSSIBLE CORRECTIONS:

People who live in earthquake-prone areas should set aside an emergency supply of food and water in case of a major earthquake.

People who live in earthquake-prone areas should make special arrangements within their families to be able to communicate in case of a major earthquake.

1. People who live in earthquake-prone areas should make emergency preparations for a major earthquake.

2. Drug addiction takes many forms.

3. Being a good parent is not easy.

4. A sense of humor is a vital part of everyone's survival kit.

5. The birth of a baby can spell disenchantment for some marriages.

6. Teenagers sometimes have difficulty surviving their parents.

7. Sexual harassment is a problem in the workplace.

8. Many people feel that vitamins are valuable supplements to their diets.

9. Soul food is some of the best cooking in the world.

10. Contact sports can cause serious injuries.

11. Latins are good dancers.

12. Homelessness is evident in most major American cities.

13. Ambitious people are drawn to the political arena.

14. Being a member of a gang is vital to many American teenagers.

15. Jobs are getting harder and harder to find.

EXERCISE E9. RECOGNIZE DEGREES OF SPECIFICITY

The following sentences in each group of four are like the sentences about the sister, illustrating that being specific is sometimes a *matter of degree*. However, the sentences that follow have been jumbled, and you need to determine their correct order.

Write "1" in the space next to the sentence you think makes the broadest or most general statement of the four. Write "2" in the space near the sentence you think is the next broadest or most general. Write "3" in the space next to the sentence you think more specific than "2." Write "4" in the space next to the sentence you think makes the most specific statement of the group.

Study the following example in which these sentences have been jumbled but correctly numbered:

Example

___2___ My sister wants to be a singer.

___1___ My sister wants to devote her life to music.

___4___ My sister's greatest ambition is to sing "Tosca" at the Metropolitan Opera House.

___3___ My sister is studying to become a soprano in grand opera.

1. _____ Mei Ling is a surgeon.

   _____ Mei Ling has made her career in medicine.

_____ Mei Ling is a doctor.

_____ Mei Ling is an orthopedic surgeon.

2. _____ James is fascinated by the Cooper's Hawk.

_____ James is interested in animal behavior.

_____ James is studying predatory birds.

_____ James is a bird watcher.

3. _____ Matthew is an athlete.

_____ Matthew is a pitcher.

_____ Matthew is a relief pitcher.

_____ Matthew is a baseball player.

4. _____ Yoshi wants to be a homicide detective.

_____ Yoshi wants to join the police force.

_____ Yoshi plans a career in law enforcement.

_____ Yoshi wants to be a detective.

5. _____ Ernesto is in the navy.

_____ Ernesto is in the military service.

_____ Ernesto is a radar specialist.

_____ Ernesto is in the submarine branch of the navy.

REQUIREMENT 3. FIND THE RIGHT WORD

The third requirement of the topic sentence, like the first two, is really a requirement of any good sentence. Because the topic sentence is the first sentence you will write and because it has the important responsibility of introducing the subject of all other sentences in the paragraph, it is given special consideration here. But bear in mind that what is said here and elsewhere about the topic sentence applies to all the sentences you write.

To the first two requirements — being complete and being clear — a third requirement of finding the right word should be added. Finding the right word or choosing words well is probably the most difficult requirement of the topic sentence. Building a good vocabulary from which to select the right word takes time and lots of practice in using words. You should be prepared to put extra effort into expanding your vocabulary and sharpening your ability to find the right word.

First, you should understand that the right word is the word that best communicates your meaning. It is the word that is most exact in saying what you mean. For example, the words _painting_, _drawing_, or _photograph_ are more exact that the word _picture_. The words _play_, _opera_, or _motion picture_ are more precise than the word _show_. You should pay close attention to the exact thought you wish to express and then express that thought with the exact word you need. You may need to ask yourself, "What am I trying to say?" You should then ask, "How can I say that exactly?"

Second, the right word should be vivid. That is, it should be strikingly alive or full of life, lively, colorful, bright, intense, vigorous, fresh, spirited, strong and distinct, imaginative (all synonyms of the word *vivid*). Your aim in writing, once you have mastered the first two requirements of being complete and clear, is to be exciting. You should aim not merely to express yourself but to express the best of you.

You should form the habit (the compulsion, if need be!) of using *two important sources of the right word.* Whenever you write, you should have these references at your fingertips: (1) *a good, up-to-date dictionary* and (2) **Roget's Thesaurus**, a book of synonyms and antonyms. It is likely that the right word, the exact and vivid word you need, is waiting to be discovered by you in one or both of these sources.

Further, in your pursuit of the right word, it may be helpful for you to be able to distinguish between the words **denotation** and **connotation**. The denotation of a word is its precise or explicit meaning that you or anyone else can easily find in a dictionary. For example, the denotation of the word *home* is "dwelling" or "place where one lives." People generally agree about what a word denotes because they accept the dictionary definition that reflects their own usage. The connotation of a word, on the other hand, is what the word suggests to each person as a result of his or her experience or emotional association with the word. Because people differ in their experiences or associations with words, a given word may connote one idea or feeling to one person but have quite a different connotation to another. Consider the word *home* again. It may connote security, love, and protection to one person but instability, neglect, and indifference to another, depending on the experiences associated with the word. If people are to understand each other, they must become aware of these differences in connotation and make them known to each other.

While you are thinking about finding the right word, you should realize that you have had much more practice speaking than you have had writing, and you should understand that *speaking and writing are different.* When you speak, you can express a great deal without words through the sound of your voice, the expression on your face, and body movements. Anger or grief, for example, can be communicated without a word when you are face to face with someone. Writing a letter on either subject, however, takes great effort. How much easier it is to console someone who is mourning the death of a loved one by holding hands in silence or by a hug than it is to write a letter of sympathy.

Keep in mind that writing is different from speaking. *You must fully say in writing what can be half said in speech.* When you write, you do not have your voice, your face, or a gesture of your hand to help you. You have only words on a page with which to express yourself. Choose those words well!

You will need to strike a balance between being afraid to write anything and writing too much. This balance requires first courage and then discipline. At first you must have the courage to try out new words, to experiment, to expand your vocabulary; you will probably make some mistakes that may embarrass or frustrate you but from which you will unquestionably recover. As your writing skill develops, on the other hand, you may fall so deeply in love with words that you may tend to use too many of them. *Your ultimate goal is to be neither wordless nor wordy but to achieve a balance with just the right words.*

The following are some exercises in finding the right word. Preceding each exercise is a brief discussion of a problem to be studied and then dealt with in the exercise. The exercises by no means exhaust the subject of finding the right word, but they introduce some of the problems you will face as you learn to choose words well.

PROBLEM A — AVOID CHEAP SUBSTITUTES

Some words are not words at all, really, but substitutes for words. They are like grunts, and in speech rather than writing they can be meaningful. In writing, though they may be used as crutches, they cripple rather than support communication. The underlined words in the following sentences are cheap substitutes for exact or precise words. Find the words that are needed in place of the underlined words. Rewrite the sentences, eliminating, if possible, words that may become unnecessary when the exact words are found.

1. The <u>thing</u> that makes the car go faster is not easy for an inexperienced foot to control.
2. Those big pointed <u>things</u> in Egypt were all built by slaves.
3. He <u>sort of didn't want</u> to jump from an airplane.
4. He pulled the <u>thing</u> and up billowed his parachute.
5. She didn't want to make a ring on the table with her glass, so she asked for a <u>thing</u> to put her glass on.
6. If a person doesn't know what a word means, he should look it up in that <u>deal</u> in the back of the book.
7. The stranger handed him a paper <u>thing</u> that said he had to go to court.
8. He <u>kind of</u> wanted to go on the trip and he <u>kind of</u> didn't want to go.
9. The rooster-<u>deal</u> that shows which way the wind is blowing fell off the roof of their house.
10. The house was getting too warm, so he lowered the <u>thing</u> on the wall that regulated the temperature of the heater.

PROBLEM B — AVOID TIRED SUBSTITUTES

Some words or expressions are simply worn out or tired from too much use. These words or expressions are called *clichés*. They lack freshness and vitality now, though they may have been quite imaginative when they were first used. Now they fail to challenge the imagination. Instead, they say the same old thing in the same old, tired way.

Clichés are often comparisons; that is, they are expressions that show similarities or differences between one person or thing and another. Although fresh comparisons can be useful in clarifying ideas, comparisons that are clichés are about as helpful as tired blood. They produce dullness and boredom rather than inspiring interest and understanding.

Rewrite the following sentences, replacing the underlined clichés with fresh comparisons or expressions. This is a difficult exercise. As you work with it, you may come to appreciate how original the clichés once were!

1. You can't tell a book by its cover.
2. That man is as strong as an ox.
3. Stretched out in the sun, the old dog looked dead as a doornail.
4. The little girl ran off happy as a lark.
5. In this warm sleeping bag, I feel snug as a bug in a rug.
6. He sat on his hat and smashed it flatter than a pancake.
7. The children were good as gold all day.
8. Her eyes are bigger than her stomach.
9. Last but not least, capital punishment is bad because it is so final.
10. She looks as cool as a cucumber.

PROBLEM C — AVOID WEAK SUBSTITUTES

Similar to clichés are words or expressions that simply lack force and exactness in saying what they mean. They *kinda, sorta* say it, but they do not say it precisely. These inexact expressions might well be replaced by comparisons (but not clichés) or by exact measurements or clear descriptions.

Find more forceful and exact ways of expressing the underlined statements that follow.

1. It is very hot today.
2. That man is good-looking.
3. Everybody likes her because she has so much personality.
4. That movie is just great.
5. We had a nice time at your party.
6. That is an interesting book.

7. Yesterday was <u>cold</u>.
8. He waited a <u>short</u> time and then left.
9. She was <u>sorry</u> she had lost the contest.
10. That award was a <u>really big</u> surprise.

PROBLEM D — AVOID WORDINESS*

Your search for the right word is a special kind of treasure hunt. You should not look for a pot full of the fanciest words in the dictionary. Instead, you should hunt for the one perfect gem you need to express your thought. Look for quality, not quantity.

Keep in mind that the purpose of language is to communicate, not to call attention to itself. The reader should not notice the words you use but rather what you say with them. Do not decorate! Communicate!

Eliminate the repetitious or unnecessary words in the following sentences. If needed, rewrite the sentence, using words that express the idea with greater force or exactness.

1. He was certainly a very old man, and he never went out in his little boat with anybody at all but rather always went fishing alone way out in the Gulf of Mexico off Cuba, and he had spent all of eighty-four long days now without catching any fish at all, not even one fish. (The first sentence of Ernest Hemingway's *The Old Man and the Sea* illustrates his economy of words as well as his exact though simple word choice: "He was an old man who fished alone in a skiff in the Gulf Stream and he had gone eighty-four days now without taking a fish.")
2. She was a funny little old lady who had no sense of humor at all but was still funny or strange or something because she never came out of her house in the day at all but rather she came out of her house only at night to go to the store or to go to see people or to go anyplace.
3. He was really very tired and weary of working or going to work and he planned to quit or stop working and retire.
4. He couldn't think of the word he needed even though he needed that word and not some other word he didn't need.
5. That painting of Picasso is really very unusual, but then it doesn't really look like what it is, or what it is trying to be, or what I think it is trying to be, if I understand what it is trying to be, and I'm trying.

*See Chapter 15 for a fuller discussion of this topic.

PROBLEM E — AVOID "THIS, THAT, AND IT" ERRORS

One weakness in word choice might be termed the "*this, that,* and *it*" problem. Although the weakness is actually a grammatical error, it is frequently the result of careless word use. As a general rule, *this* and *that* (and *these* and *those*) are words that should not stand alone but should be attached to other words. Most often *this* and *that* are used as modifiers — that is, as adjectives and adverbs — and should be combined with the nouns or other words they modify.

Examine the following sentences to determine how errors in the use of *this* and *that* make meaning vague and sometimes impossible to understand.

1. Advertising that associates smoking with the freshness of ocean surf and forest glen is questionable. This increases sales desirably but misleads the public.
2. Home buyers are becoming younger despite the enormous cost of real estate. There are two reasons for this.
3. Too many clothes are made from synthetics rather than cotton or wool. These are harder to find.
4. Some people think of animals only as objects designed to feed them, clothe them, and amuse them. That is gross.

POSSIBLE CORRECTIONS:

1. This method of advertising increases sales desirably but misleads the public.
2. There are two reasons for this trend.
3. These fabrics are harder to find.
4. That attitude is gross.

It is also often abused or misused. When there is no noun or noun phrase in the same sentence or in the sentence preceding the one in which *it* is used as a substitute, what *it* refers to is either unclear or may even be nonexistent, as in the following example.

Athletes and top sportsmen are used by advertising companies. *It* is giving the public a false impression of the product.

POSSIBLE CORRECTION:

Athletes and top sportsmen are being used by advertising companies. *Endorsements and testimonials* by athletes are giving the public a false impression of the products advertised.

As seen in the correction given, what is often needed in place of the pronoun substitute *it* is a noun or noun phrase that makes clear what *it* really is! Unless *it* has a clear reference, use an exact noun. Avoid *it* whenever *it* is confusing.

Other pronouns such as *they* and *them* also are often abused. As in the case of the pronouns already discussed, care must be taken in using *they* and *them* to make certain that the nouns for which these pronouns substitute are obvious and clear.

Rewrite the following sentences, using nouns with or in place of the underlined *this*, *that*, and *it* errors.

1. When the value of the dollar rises, the price of gold tends to go down. There must be a reason for this.

2. He argued with me, insulted me, and then he tried to hit me. That did not make me happy.

3. Stella yawned as she looked at the ruby ring, the pearl necklace, and the diamond bracelet. These bored her.

4. Dogs chase cats and cats chase mice. Sometimes they catch them.

5. Why are the children running into the house, screaming at the top of their lungs, and then running out again, slamming the door? I don't like it.

6. He was told to rewrite all of his compositions. He didn't like that.

7. She liked the short man better than the tall man. However, they didn't know it.

8. He failed the examination but was admitted to the college anyway. It was a good thing.

9. During winter Dennis has to stay inside the house much of the time or wear very heavy clothing when he goes outside. He gets tired of it.

10. A person can lose a lot of time worrying about nothing. This is not good.

PROBLEM F — BE CAREFUL OF MANY MEANINGS

Words are slippery. They can mean many different things to people. A word intended to be a compliment can result in being insulting. A word intended to convey one meaning may result in suggesting another or several others. You must be aware of the ambiguous nature of words — that many words have two or more possible interpretations — in your search for the right word.

A single word can stand for many different things, such as the word *show*, for example, which can mean a play, a review, an opera, a motion picture, and so forth. On the other hand a single thing can be referred to with many different words. A *couch*, a *sofa*, a *davenport*, a *chesterfield* are examples of different words that refer to the same thing.

When different words can be used to refer to the same thing, the particular word chosen sometimes reflects an attitude or feeling the user of the word has about the thing. The same play, for example, can be called a *triumph* by one person and a *flop* by another. Words can be classified into three categories: neutral, positive, and negative. When people have no strong feelings one way or another about a thing, they refer to it with a neutral word. If they like the thing, they use a positive word for it. If they dislike the thing, they refer to it with a negative word. Consider the following:

NEUTRAL	POSITIVE	NEGATIVE
1. police officer	officer of the law	cop
2. thin	slim/slender	skinny
3. jail	correctional facility	slammer

Being aware of the neutral, positive, and negative effects that some words can have is vital to successful communication. Obviously, if you want to communicate in a positive manner, you cannot achieve success by using negative words. Neither can you succeed in being negative by using neutral or positive words. Imagine complaining about an unfair bill in positive words or writing a letter to a prospective employer using negative words!

Consider the following words. Determine their various meanings and decide whether they are neutral, positive, or negative. Be prepared for discussion and disagreement concerning this exercise.

1. work	11. family	21. flag
2. party	12. divorce	22. computer
3. budget	13. fidelity	23. apology
4. debt	14. home	24. beauty
5. arrest	15. parent	25. vacation
6. convict	16. chef	26. soul
7. music	17. waiter	27. joke
8. student	18. fashion	28. news
9. average	19. college	29. fat
10. millitary	20. friend	30. poor

━

S U M M A R Y

The three requirements of the topic sentence are that it be complete, clear, and well worded. These requirements apply not only to the topic sentence but to all good sentences. Remember that words used well are the material from which good sentences are made. Good sentences, in turn, make good paragraphs if the paragraphs are properly organized and developed. With these considerations in mind, you should be ready to practice writing the whole paragraph.

━

CHAPTER 5   ⟍

PICTURE A PUZZLE

Picture a smooth wooden ball just a little larger than a tennis ball. As you look at the wooden ball more closely, you can see it is a puzzle, composed of interlocking pieces that can be taken apart. (See the puzzle on page 60, for example.) Bound together, the pieces form a single entity, a perfect little ball that is a pleasure to hold in your hand. When the ball is taken apart, each separate piece looks unique, and it is a challenge to reconstruct the ball, which is the point of the puzzle. You are guided in that effort by the fact that each piece of the puzzle is unmistakably a part of the ball. Though notched and angled differently, the pieces are all made of the same wood, and each piece is curved so you can see in it some part of the round ball. Keeping the shape of the ball in mind, you begin to fit the pieces together again.

COMPARE THE PARAGRAPH AND THE PUZZLE

A well-organized paragraph is like that puzzle. It is a *unified* whole, a single entity, made from interlocking pieces. Its purpose gives it its distinct shape, like the roundness of the ball, and all its parts or sentences are formed and fitted to that purpose. When they are properly assembled, the sentences have *coherence* and can lock together into one *continuous* unit.

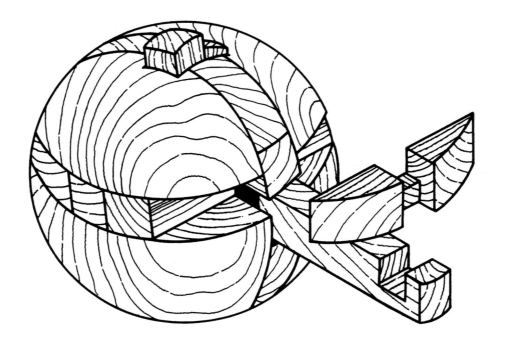

MAKE THE PARAGRAPH COHERENT

A coherent paragraph is one that hangs together because it is planned and arranged deliberately to have *order* or *sequence*. First things come first, second come second, and so on. To create this order within your paragraph, you must plan your course with care, deciding first what the main topic of your paragraph is. Then you may wish to make a simple list of main ideas and supporting points of your discussion, which at first need be no more complicated than the kind of list you take with you to the grocery store. However, when you make your grocery store list, as a rule, you jot things down as they occur to you, at random. You may do the same with your paragraph list, too, at first, so your mind is free to wander and snag ideas as they pop into your head. Ultimately, however, you must impose *order* on this list. After all, even when you go to the grocery store or supermarket, you do not actually follow your random list, scrambling back and forth through the store picking up things as you have listed them. The store is organized, even if your shopping list is not, and you proceed through the store in an orderly manner, selecting what you need from each of its departments. When you return home from the store and think in terms of the dinner you will serve, you organize your thoughts in yet another way. Compare the following two lists and decide which is the random list you might take to the store, and which represents the dinner as you might serve it.

I. Dinner for friends
  cake
  asparagus
  tomatoes
  coffee
  lettuce
  ice cream
  wine
  cucumbers
  roast
  potatoes
  rolls
  scallions

II. Dinner for friends
  A. salad
    1. lettuce
    2. tomatoes
    3. cucumbers
    4. scallions
  B. main course with wine
    1. roast
    2. asparagus
    3. potatoes
    4. rolls
  C. dessert with coffee
    1. cake
    2. ice cream

It is quickly apparent that the first list is made at random. Obviously, the meal will not begin with cake and end with onions! The order of the meal is shown in the second list. You may notice another difference in the two lists. The second is organized into categories with main headings (A, B, C), and under them are subheadings (1, 2, 3) that show what each category contains. This systematic scheme makes the second list a clearer plan or *outline* than the first, and as a result, the total meal as well as its component parts can easily be seen. As you begin to think about your paragraph, you may start by making the first kind of list, but you should end by organizing your thoughts into the more coherent form shown by the second list or outline.

WRITE A SIMPLE OUTLINE

You may find an outline useful in the beginning of your writing process, or you may use it to check the end result. Just as contractors use or follow blueprints to build a house, so you may use an outline to plan and develop your paragraph. On the other hand, you may favor a freer, more spontaneous creative process, using an outline only as a means of testing and revising what you have written after you have written it.

If you are a freer spirit, you may begin writing, as suggested in Chapter 1, by clustering in order to generate ideas. You may find that listing thoughts at random primes the pump, so to speak. Start by jotting down this idea and that in words, phrases, or full sentences, stopping, thinking, and starting up again. You may change your mind, go back to revise an earlier idea, possibly even become stuck but then muddle through and move on. From this process you may see emerging a controlling idea (possibly becoming your topic sentence) and sufficient supporting material to begin to develop this idea meaningfully and effectively. Many experts in the writing field hold that this is how the creative process works: Writing does not necessarily follow a linear, logical, forward moving pattern but may be a fitful process that moves about in a haphazard, unpredictable manner that is difficult to control.

Ultimately, however, the creative process must evolve into an orderly arrangement of ideas — into a presentation of your thoughts that anyone, friend or stranger, can perceive and understand. When your controlling idea becomes clear to you, it is probably time to think about making it clear to others by writing it out in a full topic sentence. Write your supporting ideas in full sentences also, and arrange these sentences into what, at this point, seems to be a logical sequence. In other words, write the first draft of your paragraph. Then stand back to analyze your work.

Check to see if all the ideas come together in a thought pattern that is smooth and clear, that there is a natural flow between one idea and the next, that each idea readily dovetails into the next with no abrupt breaks in the flow of the thought process (and with no reader of your paragraph left to wonder, "How did this writer get from there to here?") as it moves from sentence to sentence. You may need to rearrange what you have written in order to get your various ideas into their proper sequence. You may even need to add an idea or sentence to keep the progress or flow of ideas clear and smooth.

At this point making a simple outline of your paragraph may help you. Remember that an outline is an organized sketch, or blueprint, so to speak, of the principal ideas in your paragraph. An outline allows you to see how well your ideas fit together into an organized, whole unit. *If you are able to put what you have written into outline form, your paragraph is probably well organized. If your paragraph is not outlineable, chances are its organization needs repair.**

Your sense of order will likely sharpen as you work on your outline, and you will probably begin to see how to organize not only your main ideas or headings (A, B, C, and so on), but how to arrange their supporting points or subheadings (1, 2, 3, and so on), as illustrated in the following example. Notice that the subheads indicate both *content* and *order*.

(TOPIC) Giving a good party
    A. Early evening
        1. Welcome guests at door
        2. Attend to introductions
        3. Serve and maintain beverages
        4. Circulate among guests

---

*This rule generally holds for expository writing. Certain other kinds of writing, for example some narrative and descriptive paragraphs, do not require such a tightly organized structure.

B. Middle evening
  1. Begin buffet dinner by 8 P.M.
  2. Serve dessert and coffee about 9:30 P.M.
  3. Present special event such as musical performance
  4. Play parlor games if guests in mood
  5. Serve after-dinner drinks and offer more coffee
C. Late evening
  1. Depending on mood of party, dance, sing, or converse
  2. See guests to door

If your topic is a process that takes place within a time period, as in the preceding example, you will probably want to organize your outline *chronologically*, that is, to arrange the events within the time period in the order in which they occur. The main headings of your outline can show the major divisions of the time, and subheadings can indicate specific activities within each major division as well as the order of their occurrence. If your topic is *spatial* or *geographical*, then your main headings will likely divide that space in some way such as north, south, east, west, or left, right, top, bottom, and so forth. Examine the following outline, which is organized geographically.

(TOPIC) My messy study
A. West side of room
  1. Cluttered desk
  2. Dirty windows
  3. Mishmash of cards and pins

B. North side of room
  1. Disarray of books
  2. Crowded collection of toys, other objects
  3. Paper, letters falling to floor

C. East side of room
  1. Closet doors busy with posters, photographs, museum magazine cover, cartoons
  2. Old thermometer jammed next to door to room
  3. Door to room almost concealed by posters

D. South side of room
  1. Books, artifacts stacked every which way
  2. Bed, table, chair covered with books and papers
  3. Typewriter table overcrowded with papers

Notice that the outline describing the room is divided into four geographical sections. However, the purpose of the outline is not simply to describe the room but to show the room is messy. Therefore, the subheadings select only those aspects of the room which focus on that topic. Thus, although the main headings of the outline are *geographical*, the subheadings are *topical*. That is, they all support the (messy study) topic. You will often experience just such a mixture of structures, but try not to be confused by it. Your topic and supporting points or subheadings are always closely related, regardless of how your support is packaged by main headings or divisions of the support. Remember, your primary aim is to make your thoughts hang together or cohere, and that objective may require an outline which is purely chronological (organized by time), strictly geographical, completely topical, or that uses some other entirely consistent structural scheme. Or, you may need to use some combination such as the preceding example.

The following outline is *topical*. That is, it is organized by topics. The order or arrangement of ideas in a topical outline depends on both the subject and the writer's approach to the topic. As with the chronological and geographical outline, related ideas are generally grouped together. For example, an outline on birds might group water birds under one main heading and shorebirds under another. However, a particular writer might approach the subject of birds in terms of his or her favorites, beginning with those liked best — hawks, for instance — and then proceeding to others that are not as well liked. Examine the following outline, which divides the topic into four main headings (see p. 94 for the paragraph on this topic).

(TOPIC) My biggest problem in college: lack of self-confidence
    A. Others seem more capable than I.
        1. They are more knowledgeable.
        2. They are more articulate.
        3. They are wiser.
    B. I avoid speaking in class.
        1. I try to make myself invisible.
        2. I sit in the back of the classroom.
        3. I never volunteer.
    C. If I am forced to speak, I feel very uncomfortable.
        1. My throat feels squeezed.
        2. My words feel disconnected.
        3. I feel out of control.
    D. Terrified that I will expose my inadequacies, I withdraw into silence.
        1. I fear the ridicule of my classmates.
        2. I fear my instructors and counselors will lose respect for me.

You may have been exposed to outlining before and therefore know that it can be much more complicated than the examples given to you in this chapter. However, these outlines are enough to help you think through your paragraphs in a coherent manner. They will permit you to organize your paragraphs, to line up your ideas from beginning to end.

STUDY TWO PARAGRAPHS AND OUTLINES

Read the two paragraphs that follow and compare them to the first two outlines (Giving a good party; My messy study) in this chapter.

Example 1

When I give a party, I try to make it a good one by being both careful and casual. As the evening begins, I am careful to meet guests at the door and welcome them, not just let them slip into my house unnoticed and unsung. If some of my guests do not know each other, which is possible, as I believe new faces help to spark a party, I see to introductions next. After that, I serve my guests beverages and then keep an eye on their glasses to see that no thirsty person lacks refreshment. Before dinner, I try to circulate among my guests, sharing their interests, breaking the ice, and doing what I can to generate lively conversation and good will. By eight o'clock most people are hungry, and I serve dinner then, which I like to make a casual buffet. My guests select what they like, and they arrange themselves, having got acquainted by that time, in informal groups around my living room. After a leisurely dinner, we have dessert and coffee around nine-thirty, and then one of my guests might entertain the group with piano music for a brief period, which I hope gives the evening a quiet focus and a change of pace. Next, if the mood of the guests is agreeable, we play charades or some other parlor game, which I follow with after-dinner drinks and more coffee. Later in the evening the mood of the party often peaks with dancing and singing, but sometimes it simply mellows out with more conversation. I don't push the party in any particular direction. I like it to flow wherever it goes naturally. The party ends as it began, at the door of my house, where my guests and I part with much reluctance and with promises to "do it again soon."

Example 2

My study is an almost uncontrollable mess everywhere I look. Beginning on the west side of the room, where I sit at my cluttered desk and look through dirty windows to a tangle of trees that almost conceals the beautiful bay, I can also see a mishmash of picture postcards tacked to the wall and buttons declaring such mottos as "Support Your Right to Arm Bears" attached to the drapery above the desk. Turning north in this smallish room, I can view one of the two floor-to-ceiling bookcases the room contains. Besides a disarray of books, the bookcase is crowded with antique toys, paperweights, bottles, seashells, and photographs. Reams of paper, assorted envelopes, bills, and old letters are also stuffed into the bookcase, though they are almost falling to the floor.

The east side of my study contains closets, and the closet doors are busy with old Dutch shipping posters, the photograph of a French cathedral, the cover of a museum magazine picturing reclining Holstein cows, and some of my favorite cartoons. An old thermometer is jammed next to the door to the room, also located on the east side, and the door itself is almost concealed by museum posters. The south side of the room contains the second bookcase, where the only semblance of order is in the uniform rows of encyclopedias and Great Books. Otherwise, books are stacked every which way, together with assorted artifacts such as a teddy bear squashed against two volumes of folklore, a bud vase leaning perilously, and the figurine of "Speak No Evil, Hear No Evil, See No Evil" about to sail out at me where I sit at my typewriter. There are also a single bed, a low table, and a canvas chair on the south side of the room, all covered with books and papers. The one sometimes clear space in my study is a second chair that I now occupy, turned to the typewriter table next to my desk. As I type this paragraph, I must constantly reassemble the papers beside my typewriter lest its movement jiggle them to the floor.

COMPARE THE OUTLINE AND THE PARAGRAPH

It may be useful to think of the outline as the skeletal frame of the paragraph and the paragraph itself as the fleshed-out body. Remember that your outline may be written first and serve to guide the organization of your paragraph, or your paragraph may be written first, and then its organization proven by trying to write the paragraph in outline form. If you choose the latter course, you should soon discover whether or not your paragraph is well organized. If you can easily outline the paragraph you have written, if its content lines up in an orderly manner, first things first, second things second, minor supports following major ideas properly, and so on, then you should be confident it is well organized. If you have to struggle to outline your paragraph, if you find parts out of kilter, if ideas jump around, are suddenly dropped or mixed into places where they do not logically fit, then the structure of your paragraph needs repair. An outline, written before or after your paragraph is composed, makes *seeing* your organizational scheme and its flaws, if any, much easier. The paragraph is a dense pack of words. But the outline is sparse, a clearer track that points up the progression of thought within the paragraph.

Although the outline and the paragraph are similar in some respects in their basic form, they are quite different in other ways. The main ideas and supporting points in the paragraph are approximately the same as those in the outline, and the order or sequence in each is identical. However, the outline only *suggests* what the paragraph must fully *explain*. Therefore, the paragraph contains more words than the outline and sometimes even some supporting ideas that do not appear in the outline. In addition, the paragraph begins with a topic sentence. Although a topic is given at the beginning of the outline, it does not (though it may) contain a topic sentence. That is, no sentence in the outline indicates what its exact point will be or what will be said about the topic, only what the topic is.

As you may have noticed, there is a striking difference between the outline and the paragraph in their *written style*. The outline is often written with fragments and in a telegraphic style — that is, in the concise style of a telegram, including only the most essential words — whereas the paragraph is written with standard sentences and complete wording. There are also marginal differences. The left margin of the paragraph, as you know, moves down the page in a straight line except for the indentation with which it begins. However, the left margin of the outline begins without an indentation for main headings (A, B, C), but beneath these headings are subheadings (1, 2, 3), which are indented, as in the repeated example that follows.

EXERCISE E10. BEFORE OR AFTER WRITING A ROUGH DRAFT PARAGRAPH, ORGANIZE AN OUTLINE

Think about the following topics. As you let your mind wander, thinking of ideas at random, you may wish to try clustering the thoughts that occur to you. Then you might make up a grocery list of your ideas. When you are ready, either before or after you try writing a rough draft of a paragraph on the topic, organize your thoughts into an outline with main ideas or headings (A, B, C) and under them supporting points or subheadings (1, 2, 3) that indicate both the *content* and *order* or sequence of that content. Use the following example to guide you. (Notice that the example makes use of the first topic but this topic is by no means used up and can be used over and over with different results, depending on the opinions or tastes of the particular writer.)

(TOPIC) Giving a good party
  A. Early evening
    1. Welcome guests at door
    2. Attend to introductions
    3. Serve and maintain beverages
    4. Circulate among guests

  B. Middle evening
    1. Begin buffet dinner at 8 P.M.
    2. Serve dessert and coffee about 9:30 P.M.
    3. Present special event such as musical performance
    4. Play parlor games if guests in mood
    5. Serve after-dinner drinks and offer more coffee

  C. Late evening
    1. Depending on mood of party, dance, sing, or converse
    2. See guests to door

1. What does a good party, one that you give or attend, contain? How should the party proceed from beginning to end? Organize your outline chronologically.

2. Describe a room in your house, organizing your outline spatially or geographically.

3. What is your idea of a good date or a perfect evening out? What does it require and what should it include? Organize your outline chronologically.

4. You have a beautiful day off, and there are many things you would like to do with it, but there are also commitments you have made to study, do chores around the house, pay bills, visit a sick relative or friend in the hospital, and so forth. Organize your outline chronologically into three parts, morning, afternoon, and evening; divide each part topically, showing first what you would like to do, but second, what you will do instead.

5. People who are important to you are coming to your area for the first time, and it is your job to show them around. They will be with you for only one day, and you want them to see the most striking sights and most interesting places. How do you plan the day to make the most of it? Organize your outline chronologically, indicating what you will do with each part of the day.

6. Is your diet wholesome? On a typical day, what do you eat for breakfast, lunch, and dinner, and if you snack, what do you normally consume? Organize your outline topically, indicating what each meal consists of, and then decide if your diet is nourishing or primarily junk food.

7. Recreate the high points of a film, play, or concert that has impressed you. What were the most memorable features? Organize your outline topically or chronologically.

8. Describe an outdoor area with which you are familiar, such as the yard around your house, a nearby park, or your college campus. Organize your outline geographically.

9. Recreate a frightening, embarrassing, maddening, or amusing moment in your life. For example, have you experienced a burglary; had your car, purse, or wallet stolen; been clumsy or fallen down in front of a lot of people; waited in a long line and failed to achieve your goal; been the perpetrator or target of a practical joke? What happened and how did you handle the experience? Organize your outline chronologically.

10. Are you and your best friend alike or different? Consider such points of comparison as appearance, personality, activities, and interests, and use these or other subjects to organize your outline topically, deciding how you and your friend should be described in each category.

EXERCISE E11. REASSEMBLE JUMBLED PARAGRAPHS

Think back (or see pp. 59–60) to the comparison of the puzzle with which this chapter begins. When the ball is taken apart, as already stated, it can be a challenge to reconstruct it. However, that is the point of the puzzle. It is also the purpose of the exercises that follow. The paragraphs have been purposefully mixed up or jumbled. Your task is to assemble them again in their correct order. Rewrite the paragraphs so they have *coherence*. It may help you to locate the topic sentence and then to proceed from that point. There are no superfluous sentences. Each sentence is "a part of the ball." In other words, each fits somewhere in the paragraph. (Note that the sentences, though they are numbered for easy identification and classroom discussion, are *not* in the correct order.)

A. [1]As soon as her dog hits the night air, his automatic response is to howl and bark, which he does for a full half hour. [2]An example is my neighbor's dog across the street from me. [3]My neighbor lets her dog out for about a half hour every night around midnight. [4]If there's one thing I dislike, it is dogs that bark late at night. [5]I want to be a good neighbor, so I try not to complain too much, but I am getting very tired of that midnight serenade. [6]Instead, barking seems to be his form of nightly exercise. [7]He does not seem to bark at anything in particular.

B. [1]Pressing my remote control, I survey the available channels, looking for my "sleeping pill." [2]I begin that process generally around eleven or so at night, right after the news. [3]I must, of course, reject the most action-packed movies, though their repetitious violence is often monotonous enough; however, car crashes, gunshots, and scream-filled stabbings do not make the best background music for my tentative trip to Nod. [4]I perversely try to follow the speaker for at least ten minutes before my eyelids get in the way, my mind grinds down to zero, and I gradually flunk the class. [5]Instead, I must find something more tranquil. [6]If I am lucky, I discover someone droning on about a topic in which I have little interest or aptitude, such as one of the finer points of auto repair, a complex mathematical problem, or some subtle insight into stocks and bonds. [7]One way I use television is to put myself to sleep.

C. [1]Cars weren't locked, either. [2]After that, I go up the stairs to my car, where I use one key to turn the alarm off before I insert another to open the door. [3]I have joined the paranoid ranks of Americans who, of necessity, have become fully security minded, but I did not grow up that way. [4]It was not uncommon to leave the key in the switch, where it was handy and ready to go. [5]With what nostalgia I think of those sweet old days as I leave my house in the city now, after first pressing out the code on the panel of my electronic security system and double-locking the front door. [6]I drive off to work, remembering the sounds of lowing cows grazing in fields, as yet another neighbor's house alarm rings out, fire, fiend, or false alarm! [7]In fact, I doubt if anyone had a house key, though one might have existed and been lost somewhere in a drawer full of old string and rubber bands. [8]Where I grew up in the country, nobody in my family ever thought of locking our front door.

D. [1]Related to the problem of energy are other crucial environmental issues such as clean air and water, the preservation of the wilderness, and endangered species. [2]However, they are working hard to change the apparent fate of the earth. [3]Another problem concerning environmentalists is human dependence on nonrenewable energy sources and people's need to develop alternative energy programs that will preserve the natural ecosystems on which their survival depends. [4]Perhaps the most threatening is the danger of nuclear war. [5]Humankind is beset with profound environmental problems. [6]According to a report by one environmental organization, there are 50,000 nuclear warheads stored in silos, submarines, bombers, and warehouses around the world. [7]These and other problems worry conservationists, who feel that time is running out. [8]The touch of a button or the turn of a key could end the world as we know it.

E. [1]You want to get a head start on the day, so you leave home early in the morning, but that is a mistake because you must contend with rush-hour traffic on the freeway. [2]By noon you are exhausted and hungry, and you line up at a restaurant where, afterward, you line up again to pay your check. [3]The pressure of increasing population is easy for anyone to feel in both auto and pedestrian traffic. [4]Suppose you plan to leave your suburban home (where there are more houses than there used to be) to spend a day in the city. [5]In the afternoon you think of going to a movie, but the line is so long that you decide to line up for your car instead, to get a jump on the evening traffic going home. [6]Even with carpools, the morning and evening freeway rush is a bumper-to-bumper snarl that is tedious and time consuming. [7]Once again you edge your car into the bedlam of the city streets, but when at last you find the freeway, you are appalled by how many others have had the same idea as you and are also very slowly heading home. [8]Finally parked, you wend your way through crowded streets into crowded department stores, where you elbow your way to what you want and then wait in line to pay for it. [9]You feel worn out before you reach the city, and when you get there, you must devote more time to finding a parking space.

GIVE THE PARAGRAPH CONTINUITY

Turn your thoughts again to the puzzle with which this chapter begins. Imagine that you are holding the smooth wooden ball in your hand. You can, of course, feel that there are slight spaces between the interlocking pieces that compose the ball, but the pieces are so well fitted together that the narrow spaces are hardly noticeable. So it should be with your well-organized paragraph. A *coherent* paragraph, although made of a number of pieces or sentences, hangs together as one unified piece that has continuity; that is, it moves without interruption in one unbroken course.

To have continuity, the puzzle and the paragraph must first have the right pieces in the right places. Imagine trying to assemble the puzzle with a stray piece in it or with a piece in the wrong place. The puzzle couldn't cohere and would most likely fall apart. Similarly, if an unrelated idea is introduced into the paragraph or if its ideas are jumbled or out of order, it falls apart for lack of unity, or it becomes incoherent. If the paragraph is neither one unit nor an orderly progression of ideas, it lacks continuity as well. Continuity is the result, in large measure, of both unity and coherence. These essential elements move the paragraph in one continuous direction (not stop and start and turn around) and make it easy to follow.

USE TRANSITIONS

If your paragraph is put together well, with all its pieces or sentences in their right places so that it hangs together as one coherent unit, it may nonetheless have slight spaces or gaps, as with the puzzle, between its sentences. Even though these gaps may be hardly noticeable, you may want to bridge them to ensure that continuity is not lost or to reinforce it. You can bridge these gaps with *transitional* words or phrases that permit easy passage from one sentence or idea to the next. A transition is a little like a road sign that alerts a motorist to what lies ahead along the road, if there is a curve coming up or a downhill grade, for instance. Although you may not have been as aware of transitions as you will now become, you probably depended on them to help you reassemble the mixed-up paragraphs in the exercises beginning on page 69. You may remember (or want to look back at) such expressions as *an example, but, instead, after that, another,* and *finally,* which helped you see the correct order of the sentences in those paragraphs. Of course, you relied still more on figuring out the logical progression of ideas within the paragraphs, but these transitional expressions helped you do that. Transitions help to point the way, to keep the direction clear, to reinforce the continuity of the paragraph.

Transitions are frequently used at the *beginning* of a sentence, to link or relate that sentence to the one that precedes it, but they are also used *within* a sentence, especially one that is a bit long or complicated, to relate ideas within it to each other. There are a number of ways transitions relate sentences or ideas: (1) They may show that something is being *added, repeated,* or *intensified*; (2) they may *compare* or *contrast* two things or *contradict* something; (3) they may show a *time* or *space* relationship; (4) they may *limit* something or prepare for an *example*; (5) they may signal *cause* or *result*; (6) they may assert that the *truth* of something is *obvious* or *grant* an *opposing* argument or position. The following list is by no means comprehensive, but it includes some of the most commonly used transitions. (Note that some of the words in one category may also be used in another and there are some duplications to suggest these various uses.)

1. Transitions that *add, repeat,* or *intensify*:

and	moreover	first, second, and so on
also	indeed	to conclude
in addition	in fact	to sum up
besides	as a matter of fact	again
too	to put it another way	once again
another	nevertheless	usually
in other words	finally	habitually
further	after all	anymore
furthermore	to repeat	

2. Transitions that *compare, contrast,* or *contradict*:

similarly	unlike	in spite of,	on the contrary
like	on the other hand	despite	nevertheless
likewise	however	but	nonetheless
in like manner	though	yet	then again
by comparison	although	whereas	to put it another
as	regardless	even when	way
as well as		rather than	in fact
as, as if		instead	either . . . or
		instead of	neither . . . nor

3. Transitions that show a *time* or *space* relationship:

before	earlier	beside
now	at first, last	between
next	then, just then	beyond
after that	until	across
after so much time	soon	over
in time	the next day, night	at
later	while	from, to
following	meanwhile	into
finally	then	outside, inside

eventually	from then on	up, down
since	during	near, far
ever since	beginning, ending	within
even when	still	when

4. Transitions that *limit* or prepare for an *example*:

if	that is
unless	namely
when	for example
provided that	for instance
in case	to illustrate
in particular	such as
that	

5. Transitions that signal *cause* or *result*:

because	thus
for	so, so that
for this, that reason	as a result
therefore	consequently

6. Transitions that *assert obvious truth* or *grant opposition*:

no doubt	of course	in fact
doubtless	naturally	granted that
undoubtedly	surely	conceding that
without a doubt	certainly	

EXERCISE E12. UNDERLINE TRANSITIONAL WORDS OR PHRASES

Underline the *transitional* words or phrases that help to give the following paragraphs *continuity*.

A. [1] The two old friends were happy to meet again after such a long separation; however, the meeting was a strain for both of them. [2] It was an effort, after so much time, to find common ground for comfortable, easy conversation. [3] In addition, they had not parted on the best of terms, so that they each needed to labor to rise above old wounds. [4] At first they stuck to safe topics such as the weather, the health of those they knew, and ordinary events in each of their lives. [5] At last they approached the problem that had led to the break in their relationship. [6] How painful it was to stir that up again.

[7]In fact, they experienced the same old impasse, but they discussed the subject for about an hour before they gave it up, both frustrated by the effort to communicate. [8]Finally they parted, each one wondering what had become of their friendship.

B. [1]I am suspicious that anyone who uses the expression "women's lib" is not very liberated. [2]To illustrate, there was an article in the newspaper the other day that asked if women were better off before "women's lib." [3]Of course, the way the question was put evoked biased answers. [4]For example, one woman said, "Women shouldn't be allowed to be boss. That's what women's lib comes down to . . . being the boss or equal. It's not right. The man is supposed to be the head of the house." [5]Although that woman may be happy with her husband, she is nonetheless denying herself full citizenship and rights equal to his. [6]However, if she had been asked if she enjoyed being a second-class citizen, her consciousness might possibly have been raised enough to answer differently.

C. [1]One of the reasons the violin is difficult to learn to play is that its fingerboard contains no visual or tactile aids to help the beginner acquire competence in fingering. [2]Unlike the banjo or guitar, for instance, the violin has no frets, that is, no small metal bars or ridges to guide the fingers. [3]Therefore, the novice must learn exact positions and literally feel his or her way, unaided, from position to position up the fingerboard of the instrument. [4]That precise process is demanding and painful to the fledgling violinist, who must contort fingers and arm into unnatural and unfamiliar angles while pressing the strings at the correct places and with enough force to get a clear tone. [5]If the beginner is a hair off, the note will be sharp or flat, that is, sour. [6]Until the novice develops skill, many notes are painfully out of tune. [7]Even when skill increases, the fledgling player may still sound off key unless he or she has a good ear. [8]Thus, not only does the novice suffer, he or she can also torture those listening, as many a stoic parent or sacrificial sibling can affirm.

D. [1]What a drab place the culinary world would be without onions! [2]In fact, losing any member of the onion family would be an international disaster to the world's great chefs, the gourmet cooks, the slingers of hash, and the heaters-up at home. [3]For instance, how could the Dutch manage without leeks? [4]What would the French do for onion soup? [5]How would the Italians make spaghetti sauce? [6]Moreover, how could any part of the world get along without garlic? [7]Regardless of the tears shed over these bulbous plants, the smells that are endured, the deodorants and mouthwash that are spent on them, onions and their kin are vital to the gustatory pleasures of this world.

[8]Surely fine restaurants would lose their stars without the onion family, and great chefs would lose their flair. [9]The zing would go out of even hamburgers and hot dogs, as well as the freedom of those hard choices one must make when ordering them. [10]Besides, think of holidays and children growing up without the familiar smell of turkey stuffing wafting from the oven; and who would have the heart to toss a salad anymore? [11]Indeed, it would be a depressed and dreary world without onions.

E. [1]Most people like to talk, but few people like to listen, yet listening well is a rare talent that everyone should treasure. [2]Because they hear more, good listeners tend to know more and to be more sensitive to what is going on around them than most people. [3]In addition, good listeners are inclined to accept or tolerate rather than to judge and criticize. [4]Therefore, they have fewer enemies than most people. [5]In fact, they are probably the most loved of people. [6]However, there are exceptions to that generality. [7]For example, John Steinbeck is said to have been an excellent listener, yet he was hated by some of the people he wrote about. [8]No doubt his ability to listen contributed to his capacity to write. [9]Nevertheless, the results of his listening did not make him popular. [10]Thus, depending on what a good listener does with what he hears, he may pay a price for his talent or go unappreciated in his lifetime.

EXERCISE E13. WRITE IN TRANSITIONAL WORDS OR PHRASES

Write in the blank spaces the *transitional* words or phrases you think are needed or appropriate in the following paragraphs to help give them *continuity*. Note that your choice of transition will depend on how you interpret the statements in the paragraphs and that there may be more than one way to fill in the spaces correctly. Therefore, prepare to explain or defend the transition you choose.

A. [1]The problem with an old car is that it is always needing something replaced or repaired. [2]_____, about the time the fourth tire is replaced, the first one begins to wear thin again. [3]_____, if the front brakes are renewed, _____ the rear brakes start to go. [4]_____ common problem is that some kind of pump is always breaking down and needing replacement. [5]_____ the air pump may develop trouble, _____ the fuel pump may go bad, and _____ the water pump may give up. [6]These pumps _____ require new hoses. [7]_____, everything under the hood seems to need a new hose or a new valve. [8]_____ the car needs a new transmission or a new engine. [9]There seems to be no end to the trouble and expense of keeping up an old car.

B. ¹The homes of the two friends are very different. ²One is situated in the United States on a hill in Seattle, _____ the other is located in The Netherlands by a canal in Amsterdam. ³There is a generous yard around the hill house, _____ there is no space at all around the canal house _____ canal houses are built right next to each other, wall to wall. ⁴The Seattle house has only one floor, _____ some of its rooms are spacious; _____, the Amsterdam house has five floors, _____ most of its rooms are small. ⁵The differences in these homes _____ reflect differences in lifestyle. ⁶The American house is casual and opens to a patio for outdoor living. ⁷_____, the Dutch house is more formal, and _____ of hard winters, is closed against the cold outside. ⁸_____ the two homes are different, each one suits its location.

C. ¹Some of my older relatives amaze me with their vitality. ²_____, one of my cousins is in her eighties; _____, she has the vitality of someone much younger and is as active and interested in what goes on around her as anyone I know. ³Her quick wit, _____, is a match for the sharpest, most alert of people. ⁴_____ illustration is my aunt, who is in her nineties. ⁵_____ she recently broke her hip and suffered a small stroke, she is _____ still driving her car _____ playing cut-throat bridge. ⁶_____ my cousin, my aunt is _____ a dynamo. ⁷_____, these two ladies put some of their younger relatives to shame with their vigor.

D. ¹Most people who live in the San Francisco Bay Area appreciate the night and morning fog. ²_____, they like the fog _____ it controls the temperature naturally, keeping the nights and mornings cool _____ disappearing _____ for the day to warm to a comfortable degree, _____ in the sixties or low seventies _____ the summer months. ³Just a few miles _____ the Bay Area, suburbanites may be sizzling in temperatures ranging _____ the mid-eighties _____ the upper nineties and higher _____ people near San Francisco keep their cool in the mild climate of the Bay. ⁴The _____ reason San Franciscans and their immediate neighbors like the fog is _____ its beauty. ⁵They love to see it tumbling _____ the hills, enveloping the Golden Gate Bridge, and _____ creeping _____ the Bay itself _____ it touches its eastern shore, where it climbs _____ the hills again. ⁶Few people dislike the fog. ⁷_____, most people depend on it and admire it.

E. ¹Contentment is the one emotion that daytime television dramas cannot long endure. ²*All My Children*, _____, draws its life breath from discontent, misery, and pain. ³Erica Kane, the central character, may fall in love innumerable times and even get married repeatedly. ⁴_____, she must never settle down. ⁵_____, some mishap or dire complication must interfere with every relationship. ⁶_____, she may even need to recycle her lovers to sustain her anguish. ⁷Adam Chandler, _____, comes in handy when she is running low on lovers, or a new one, _____ Dimitri Marick, is revving in the wings. ⁸_____, after a great deal of high and low drama, Erica may have her heart's desire. ⁹_____, her bliss must be short lived and terminate in some manner, _____ quickly from disaster, _____ slowly, drip by drop, _____ she is _____ her wretched _____ indomitable self, poised for the _____ heartbreaking chapter in her tantalizing life.

SUMMARY

A well-organized paragraph is a single entity, a unified whole made of a number of parts or sentences so well ordered and fitted together that they cohere or hang together in one continuous unit. A simple outline of the main ideas and supporting points of your paragraph, written before or after the paragraph is written, can serve to guide the structure of your paragraph or to ensure its organization and coherence. In addition, if you make good use of transitional words or phrases when you write your paragraph, you will make sure it has continuity as well.

CHAPTER 6 ⟍

The paragraph models in the exercises in this chapter are purposely rigid in their form and organization, which may prove frustrating to you in the beginning. You may wish to express yourself more freely than the exercises permit. Your thoughts may be forced into unfamiliar or unnatural patterns of organization, and you may suffer the way a dancer suffers learning the fundamentals of dance. Yet it is impossible to dance without knowing the steps, or swim without knowing the strokes, or play tennis, football, chess, or anything requiring skill without laboring through the necessary training period. Similarly, it is impossible to communicate in writing without learning form and organization.

The strict order of the exercises in this chapter is planned to give you a sense of the form and order necessary to communication. Once you get used to using the organizational patterns discussed in Chapter 6 and the more advanced patterns presented in Chapter 7, you should be ready to go on to the exercises in Chapter 8 that encourage you to express yourself with greater variety and imagination.

The particular patterns of organization used in this chapter are not the only acceptable forms through which to communicate, but they have proved to be among the best. You will find they are clear and not too difficult to imitate. They make your subject obvious from the beginning. They should also help you to stick to the subject and develop it to a conclusion.

Keep in mind that the emphasis in this chapter is on form and organization. Your primary aim is to be orderly and clear. However, you should make every effort to be imaginative and thoughtful. To stimulate your imagination as well as to assist you with structure, you may find it helpful to precede each of the following exercises with clustering. Return to Chapter 1 if you need to review the clustering process.

EXERCISE 1. EXPLAIN HOW TO DO OR MAKE SOMETHING

Directions

Write a paragraph in which you explain how to do or make something; that is, clarify a process, step by step. Organize your paragraph chronologically, following the structure in the example that follows. Notice how the transitional words that are underlined show sequence and provide continuity within the paragraph.

Example*

(TOPIC SENTENCE) To wash your dog properly, you should follow several steps with the utmost care. (DISCUSSION) First, you should make sure that your dog knows nothing, in advance, of your plan to wash him. After quietly preparing his tub of lukewarm water, you should plunge him into it tenderly but firmly. Then, keeping his head well above water, you should soap his whole body, proceeding from his neck to his tail. Work the soap throughout his hair and skin until it lathers and saturates his body. After your pet is completely covered with soap, be sure to rinse him thoroughly.

*Note that in most situations in formal college writing, the second person *you* is not preferred or acceptable. It is easy to substitute a noun for the pronoun *you*, for example, *an owner, a person, a builder*. There are some cases, however, such as when giving specific instructions, as in Exercises 1 and 2, when this form of direct address is permissible and may be called for. Further note that it may be wise to avoid the subject of recipes for Exercise 1, unless they are carefully written in complete sentences, because recipes are often written in fragments.

For your dog, being washed is an experience that cannot end soon enough. (CONCLUSION) Therefore, as soon as possible, you should both enjoy the <u>final</u> step of his bath — the vigorous sport of drying him.

EXERCISE 2. EXPLAIN HOW TO BUILD SOMETHING

Directions

Write a paragraph in which you explain how to build something. Organize your paragraph <u>chronologically</u>, as in the example that follows. Notice that the necessary equipment and materials need to be presented before the process is described, so be sure to show their use in your discussion. Be careful to discuss the process in the correct order, using <u>transitional</u> words such as those italicized and underlined to make the sequence clear.

Example

(TOPIC SENTENCE) Building a low stone hillside retaining wall without mortar can be a satisfying and worthwhile project, especially if you follow a specific procedure that should guarantee its sturdiness. (DISCUSSION) <u>First</u>, you need to assemble the necessary tools and materials: a shovel, hammer, trowel, tape measure, two 2 × 2-inch stakes about 18 inches long, a heavy string, and an adequate supply of stones, the exact number of which will depend on the length of the wall and the size of the stones. If plants are to be worked into the crevices of the wall, include them as well. The <u>first</u> <u>step</u> in the building process is to hammer the stakes about 10 inches into the ground at each end and at the front line of the proposed wall site. <u>Next</u>, tie the string to the stakes at ground level, pulling the string taut to establish a straight line. <u>After that</u>, using the string as your guide, dig a trench with the shovel for the first row of rocks, making the trench 4 to 6 inches deep and as wide as your stones. <u>As</u> you dig, slope the trench slightly downward into the hillside. <u>Then</u> lay the largest of your stones into the trench with the back of each stone tilted down and into the bank of earth to be retained. The secret to building a strong retaining wall is to be sure the weight of the stones is supported by the bank. The <u>next</u> <u>step</u> in your wall building is to place the second row of stones on top of but slightly behind the first row so the finished wall is slanted back at least 2 inches per foot of height. Thus, a 3-foot high wall should slant back 6 inches from the bottom to the top. <u>As</u> you lay each row you may need to use your trowel to scrape away some of the hillside as well as to fill in crevices with loose soil, where you may also work in any desired plants. Remember to use your tape measure frequently to maintain the necessary slant as you proceed to lay the stones row by row until you finish the wall. (CONCLUSION) If you follow this procedure, especially regarding the slope of your wall, the finished product should reward you by being strong enough to retain tons of earth!

EXERCISE 3.   DESCRIBE SOMEONE'S FACE

Directions

Write a paragraph in which you describe the face of someone, preferably someone you do not know well, so you have not formed prior impressions of the person but must observe him or her carefully for the first time and record exactly what you see. A likely candidate for your portrait is a classmate you have just met or someone in class you turn to for the purpose of this exercise. Look at your subject carefully (he or she may be doing the same with you simultaneously) and begin to make quick notes at random of what you see. Note your overall impressions and then look for details that will sharpen your portrait. Next, organize your observations spatially or geographically into a paragraph. Perhaps the easiest procedure is to work from the top to the bottom of your subject, as in the following example, although you may find other ways to proceed. Try to be objective. Do not flatter or insult your subject. Just write about what you see. You may wish to draw a tentative conclusion about your subject at the end of your paragraph. If so, be sure your discussion supports your conclusion. Do not introduce a new or unrelated idea at the end of your paragraph. Note the use of the name John Smith in the example and replace it with the name of your subject.

Example

(TOPIC SENTENCE) John Smith's face inspires study and description. (DISCUSSION) He has a thin oblong face. Under his light brown hair, which is thick and straight, his forehead is smooth, tanned, and slightly sunburned. His heavy eyebrows are darker than his hair, but they have reddish blond tips, as if bleached by the sun. His eyes are a pale sky blue, fringed with short brown eyelashes. One eye looks a little smaller than the other from habitual squinting. His long straight nose is sunburned and peeling. There is a large mole on the right side of his high-boned, tanned cheeks, about midpoint between the tip of his nose and his short sideburns. There is also a noticeable scar on his upper lip just under his nose. His mouth is fairly wide, but his lips are thin, and they smile slightly, even in repose. He has a clean-shaven, chiseled chin. (CONCLUSION) John Smith is apparently an outdoorsman.

EXERCISE 4. DESCRIBE A ROOM IN YOUR HOME

Directions

Write a paragraph in which you describe a room in the house or building where you live. You may select any room that interests you or you think you can describe well, such as the living room, dining room, kitchen, bedroom, or hall. Study the room carefully. As you look at it, what overall impression does it give you? Find a <u>theme</u> or <u>central idea</u> around which you can focus your description, as in the following example, which describes a kitchen in terms of its dominant color scheme. Other such themes might show that a room is formal or informal, warm or cold, colorful or drab, ugly or beautiful, orderly, large, small, congested, spacious, airy, sunny, or dark. Regardless of your approach, the basic structure of your paragraph will need to be <u>spatial</u> or <u>geographical</u>. Decide on what point in the room you should begin your description, and proceed from there around the room. If the ceiling and floor are remarkable, you may want to include them in your paragraph as well.

In this exercise be careful not to make your paragraph a mere listing of what the room contains. Your objective here is not to take inventory but to make the room interesting. Begin by making the theme or central idea clear, and build interest as the description proceeds. Keep the paragraph relatively simple; be specific but do not get lost or tangled in too many details. Try to find a lively or novel way to end the paragraph.

Example

(TOPIC SENTENCE) The dominant color scheme of my kitchen is black and white. (DISCUSSION) The plan is most noticeable in the floor, which is a checkerboard of alternating 12-inch squares of black and white vinyl tile. The walls continue the theme: Three of them are white, the north wall black (actually a charcoal color). Many of the cabinets, also charcoal, are fixed to the north wall, but some of them follow along the west side of the room, where the building material is either white brick or glass. The dark cabinets there stand out in sharp contrast to the brick as well, providing continuity from the dark north wall to the light west wall. The east wall, also white, contains a closet with a large black door punctuated by a white porcelain doorknob. The south wall and the ceiling are also white. All the appliances are white as well, though their handles and knobs are dark. (CONCLUSION) Overall, my kitchen is a room of sharp black and white contrasts — an appropriate setting for the high drama that sometimes takes place in it.

EXERCISE 5. DESCRIBE A MEMORABLE INCIDENT

Directions

Write a paragraph in which you describe a memorable (exciting, funny, tragic) incident or moment in your life. The incident you write about is one that must have taken place in a matter of minutes or hours, not in days, weeks, or months. Do not try to tell the story of your life in this one paragraph! Limit yourself to one brief event in your life. Study the example that follows. Notice that the topic sentence gives three important informational cues — the age of the writer (or time period) when the incident occurred, a characterization of its impact (frightening), and an indication of what happened or almost happened (suffocation). Your topic sentence should give these cues without giving away the entire incident, and thus it will serve not only its usual function as a topic sentence, but it will also become a teaser to interest the reader. In addition, notice that the <u>chronological</u> discussion is in two parts. Observe the function of each part.

Example

(TOPIC SENTENCE) One day when I was a little girl about nine years old, I had a frightening experience during which I almost suffocated. (DISCUSSION 1: <u>set scene, give background, introduce characters</u>) The incident occurred on the ranch in California where I grew up. Pestering the hired hands working there, my brother and I had been playing in the barn where baled hay was stored, stacked high for winter feed. Between the bales there were sometimes spaces, like tunnels, which my brother and I liked to explore. (DISCUSSION 2: <u>present problem, develop action</u>) That day I discovered an unusually long, dark hole in the haystack and crawled into it. I had crawled several feet into the hole when I realized, with a shock, that I could not get back out. I was trapped in the middle of the huge haystack! I screamed for help. My brother and the hired hands ran to my rescue, but it was some time before they could discover where the small voice in the haystack came from. After a seemingly endless period of waiting in the dark and dusty spot where I was caught, I was finally dug out by my rescuers. (CONCLUSION) I will never forget the first clear breath of air or the wonderful sight of summer sunshine I experienced when I was lifted from my tomb.

EXERCISE 6.   DESCRIBE A PICTURE IN A MAGAZINE

Directions

Write a paragraph in which you describe a picture or photograph you find in a magazine. Before you choose your picture, look through several magazines so you realize the tremendous variety of possibilities for this exercise. Then narrow down your choices to a few with which you feel most in touch or that you think you can describe well. You might choose something quite simple or touching, a picture that is amusing, dramatic, strange, poignant, tragic or horrifying, something ugly, fashionable, plain, or beautiful. You may want to try writing about two or three different pictures before you settle in your final choice, which should be interesting but not too complex to cover well in a single paragraph. The example that follows describes a fairly small (approximately 3 × 5 inches) though relatively complex photograph; you may want to choose a less difficult subject. Look at your final choice very carefully and decide, first, what it is saying, so you can make that point clear in your topic sentence and carry it throughout your paragraph. Next, plan your discussion so you describe the picture <u>spatially</u> or <u>geographically</u>, moving from left to right, top to bottom, or in some other clear order, such as in the example.

Example

(TOPIC SENTENCE) At first glance the scene looks picturesque, a study in dramatic contrasts, but the photograph in *Time* magazine is of West Beirut, a city being destroyed by war. (DISCUSSION) The upper portion of the picture shows a cloudless blue-gray sky, but just a little below, massive clouds of smoke billow across the city and rise hundreds of feet into the air. The smoke surges to its highest point on the left side of the photograph, and under that mass the tops of the buildings in closest camera range are barely visible, while much of the city nearby has disappeared from view. Arid ground slopes down from the buildings on the left to cliffs that dip abruptly into the blue-green shore of the Mediterranean, and this lower left corner of the picture is its only calm area on land. From left to right, the lower half of the photograph is shared by land and sea, the land so devastated that the vibrant sea beside it seems out of place, an intruder frolicking upon a tragedy. Just right of the picture's center, the eye is struck by a huge building located by the shore. It might be a large tourist hotel, for the view of land and sea from its many stories of balconies and picture windows must normally be breathtaking. However, the view is now the panorama of the war exploding almost everywhere in the city, and the focal point of the picture is a great flash, probably a bomb or rocket blowing up, not more than a mile down the coast, to the right of the large building. The upper-right corner of the photograph, balancing the lower left, is filled with placid-looking sky, the fresh air no doubt blowing from this direction, carrying the smoke to the center of the city, where it appears to be most dense. (CONCLUSION) Alas, what a lovely old city this must have been without a war, the sea skirting its length, its buildings looking out on the water and catching the breezes as they climbed the hills behind. Now strangely illuminated by fire and setting sun, what is left of the battered city is fast becoming rubble.

EXERCISE 7.   DISCUSS AN ANIMAL

Directions

Write a paragraph in which you tell about an animal: a pet you have had, or an animal (pet or wild) you have had experience with that belonged to someone else, lived in a zoo, a stable, or elsewhere. Think of some way in which to characterize or identify the animal (the animal is/was clever, mischievous, stubborn, friendly, difficult in some way, faithful, etc.), and make that characteristic the focus or topic of your paragraph, first expressed in your topic sentence. Then develop that topic by presenting a series of incidents which illustrate your point. Thus, while your paragraph should begin topically, it may proceed either chronologically or topically, or a mixture or blend of the two structures.

Among the animals you might choose to write about are the following: dog, cat, horse, bird (parrot, canary, pigeon, quail, etc.), raccoon, snake, pig, rabbit, mouse, whale, or cow.

The example that follows may be useful as a guide.

Example

(TOPIC SENTENCE) Teddy resisted us in every way he could. (DISCUSSION) Above all, that Shetland pony did his best to avoid being caught or ridden. In our attempt to catch him, various members of my family and I used every deceit we could think of, such as offering grain with one hand while hiding the rope in the other, acting uninterested by walking away, perhaps even sitting down on a nearby rock, pretending to gaze at the scenery until curious Teddy came up to us, but he was generally quick to duck and run before we managed to put the rope around his neck. When we were able to catch him, he resisted the bridle by clenching his teeth and the saddle by expanding his girth so that the cinch was hardly ever tight enough. As I had to ride Teddy to school, the loose cinch made me an easy target for the first downhill trail where he would put his head down to try to dump me and the saddle from his back. (He succeeded several times.) During the winter, when the rains had filled the creeks we had to cross, Teddy liked to get rid of me by hunkering down and almost rolling over in the water. More than once I arrived at school with my shoes and socks and the lower parts of my clothes soaked from the bath Teddy had given both of us. Finally, after several years, that pony got up and left us, simply disappeared from the ranch where we lived, slipped away somehow. We looked for him for a long time because he was old by then, and we were worried he was off sick somewhere or might have fallen and broken a leg or something. (CONCLUSION) However, we never saw him again, and we concluded that Teddy had resisted us to the end.

EXERCISE 8. SUPPORT A GENERAL STATEMENT WITH PARTICULARS

Directions

Write a paragraph in which you make a general statement and then support it with particulars, examples, or illustrations. Organize your paragraph topically. That is, decide on the topic of your general statement, and then think through or outline a number of subtopics or particulars to support the general statement. Finally, arrange that support in your paragraph in the manner you think most effective. You might present your strongest support first, and having won your audience, add other points that are also convincing. On the other hand, you might begin with moderately convincing points, then top them by placing your strongest support last; or you may discover some other effective way to proceed. In addition, you may use illustrations from particular situations you have experienced, or you may wish to invent or create illustrations representative or typical of your general experience, as in the example that follows. Among the general statements you might use for this exercise are these: applying for a job can be frustrating; telephone solicitations are annoying; people in supermarkets can be pushy; waiting in line is tiresome; people can (not) be trusted; doctors are not gods; high school is (not) a waste of time; it is not safe to be out alone at night; parents are not perfect; children grow up too fast; crime does (not) pay; no one takes pride in his or her work anymore; women are (not) underpaid; the pen is mightier than the sword; discrimination is (not) a thing of the past.

Example

(TOPIC SENTENCE) Some people go crazy when they get behind the wheel of an automobile. (DISCUSSION) For example, to save a few seconds, otherwise sane people may race through city streets as if they were competing at the Indy 500. They may also run red lights and ignore stop signs, putting pedestrians in jeopardy or even hitting them. When traffic is congested, temporarily insane drivers may lean on the horn, as if its blast could clear the way instead of making everyone around miserable. On the freeway, mad drivers can be supreme in first one lane and then another, swerving in front of other cars, never looking back or signaling, getting ahead of the pack at any cost. Heaven help the car that blocks their way, for they specialize in tailgating at high speeds, even if they must lock bumpers with the car ahead. On the other hand, with an out-of-town guest in the car, daffy drivers may travel very slowly in the fast lane, oblivious to the traffic snarl and near accidents they may be causing as they gesture toward some interesting vista. When it comes to parking, such drivers are short on manners and stars at stealing base. (CONCLUSION) However, when these crazed persons step out of their vehicles, they magically become their docile selves again.

EXERCISE 9. DISCUSS YOUR NEIGHBORS

Directions

Write a paragraph in which you discuss your neighbors. Since you cannot write about all your neighbors in a single paragraph, select one family or household that is most remarkable, enjoyable, difficult, or obnoxious. Be selective in your discussion, also, focusing on your neighbors' most noticeable features and limiting your discussion to only those qualities or points. You may choose to discuss your relationship with your neighbors, as in the example that follows. Organize your paragraph topically, though some chronology may also be needed.

Example

(TOPIC SENTENCE) My nearest neighbors and I began our relationship with great difficulty, but we have gradually developed into a friendly and "peaceable kingdom." (DISCUSSION) In the early years of our relating, my neighbors and I were anything but friendly, and for a long time we viewed each other with suspicion and distrust. We had many bones of contention, and we fought over such matters as parking (which is at a premium where we live), over trees (to be cut down or not to be cut down?), over the property line (was my fence over the line or not?), over building codes (did they have a right to convert their garage into living space or not?). Whether we simply exhausted ourselves with feuding, or whether little by little we began to appreciate each other is not entirely clear to me. I know I always liked them, despite our differences, and wished for a better relationship, and possibly they had similar feelings. It is not easy to live side by side and not get along. Now that we have become friends, I'm very grateful for the easy interdependence and warmer atmosphere we have developed. We have also been steadfast during crises such as unusual winter freezes causing havoc with water pipes, threat of devastating fire and earthquake, standing guard for each other, in addition, against criminal peril including burglary and property damage. We have even taken to being guests in each other's homes! (CONCLUSION) My neighbors and I have mellowed over the years, and our difficult past has given way to a more compatible, happier present.

EXERCISE 10.
DISCUSS YOUR HOBBY IN A SPECIAL WAY

Directions

Write a paragraph in which you discuss one of your hobbies or pastimes in a special way. That is, try to discover why you need the hobby or what it does for you psychologically, not simply why you "like" it. Look beneath the surface and discuss your hobby honestly, with feeling and insight. After you decide on your main topic, dig into it and list or outline what you find, and then develop your paragraph topically. Use the example that follows to guide you.

Example

(TOPIC SENTENCE) I like to garden under most circumstances, but gardening when I am upset emotionally is especially therapeutic. (DISCUSSION) When my day has been particularly hectic, when I have been frustrated, when people have hurt me or made me mad, then, especially, I like to work in the yard. When I weed, I not only clean up my garden, I clean away the ugly parts of my day. When I dig, I imagine what I would like to have said to some people but didn't or couldn't. Sometimes I pulverize the soil with my thoughts! Releasing my pent-up energy of the day on weeds and soil, I am ready to recreate it with bulbs or new plants. I relax completely when I water my garden and then sit and look at it. (CONCLUSION) I see in my weedless, freshly dug, newly planted garden my day as I wish it had been or the next as I hope it will be.

CHAPTER 7 —

Having mastered the exercises in Chapter 6, you are now ready to go on to the more complex patterns of organization in this chapter. The exercises that follow pose special problems which will require extra concentration for you to master them. In addition, you may find it useful to practice clustering before you write your paragraphs. Each exercise is preceded by a discussion designed to help you through the exercise.

DISCUSSION OF EXERCISE 11

Your main purpose in Exercise 11 is to discuss or describe something *in detail*. Earlier in this book you considered the need to develop the paragraph by being

89

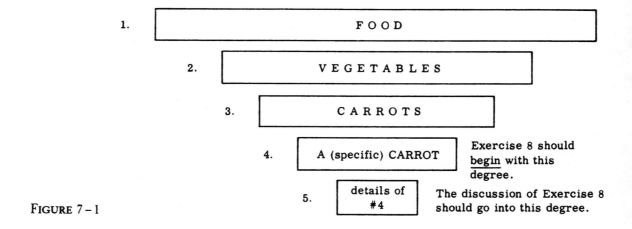

FIGURE 7-1

specific. This exercise is designed to emphasize that point. You should concentrate most on going into detail, on being specific or particular (these terms have basically the same meaning).

Being specific is a matter of degree, as mentioned earlier, and you may wonder what degree is required of you in this exercise. Figure 7-1 may make the degree clear to you.

The illustration begins with a generalization or general category and proceeds by degrees to specifics. As noted previously, your paragraph in this exercise should begin at the fourth level or degree of being specific and should progress still further into details. In other words, you should be very, very specific in this exercise.

Your choice of topic for the exercise should be guided by the degree of detail you are asked to discuss. The "food" level, for example, is much too broad or general a topic for the exercise, nor can you discuss "vegetables," nor even the third level, "carrots." You must narrow down to one specific such as a single particular carrot, and discuss or describe it in detail.

Organize your paragraph *geographically* or *topically*. Or you might mix the two schemes, as in the example that follows, which focuses on simplicity and age as it describes an antique clock from top to bottom.

Other topics you might use for this exercise include manufactured objects such as a lamp, table, chair, plate, flowerpot, hat, ring, shoe, gate, or birdbath, or natural objects such as a rock, flower, or branch of a tree.

EXERCISE 11. DISCUSS SOMETHING IN CLOSE DETAIL

Directions

Write a paragraph in which you discuss an object in close detail. Because you must go into detail, be careful to limit your topic. Use the following example as a guide.

Example

(TOPIC SENTENCE) The antique clock in my living room is appealing to me primarily because of its simplicity and age. (DISCUSSION) It has a plain round oak case and a large easy-to-read face. It has black, handpainted Roman numerals, and its brass hands are also handmade. Protecting the face of the clock is a simple glass cover that is opened once a week when the clock must be wound. A plain, unencased pendulum of brass, fastened to a short piece of wood, swings from beneath the face of the clock. From a distance, the clock appears to be in perfect shape, but when I approach it closely, I can see that time has worn away some of its original appearance. The hands are bent a little out of shape, the white of the face is cracked, and the black numerals are chipped in several places. (CONCLUSION) The old clock was once a school clock, and as I watch the slow swinging of its pendulum and listen to its regular ticktock, I can imagine how it must have lulled the pupils of some country school to sleep a century ago.

DISCUSSION OF EXERCISE 12

Exercise 12 resembles Exercise 11, for you are again asked to discuss or describe an object in close detail. There are, however, two differences in this exercise. First, Exercise 12 calls for a fresh and more immediate response to the object. The exercise requires you to complete it within a fairly restricted time limit such as a class period and to make careful observations of an object you have *never studied before*. The second difference is that the exercise should provoke a more complete sensory reaction. You will need to observe and write about not only what you *see* but also whatever you are able to *touch* or *feel*, *hear*, and *smell* about your object. (If it is safe to do so, taste your object also.)

You should begin the exercise with a 10- to 20-minute walk around the campus of your college, preferably, perhaps, in the vicinity of your classroom. Take a pen or pencil and a notebook with you to jot down ideas before you return to your classroom to write your paragraph, or if space and weather permit, you may even want to write your paragraph outside the classroom wherever your object, especially if it is not portable, is located.

Look around you carefully as you walk. Stand and stare at something. Touch it. If possible, pick it up. Turn it over. Smell it. Rub it. Crinkle it. Listen to it. Notice how it catches or reflects the light. Get in tune with it (or be jarred by it). Study it. If it bores you, put it down or go on to something else. Try out objects until you find one that you can really relate to, one from which you get the right vibrations.

Record your impressions. You might begin by making miscellaneous notes about your object. As you write you will probably come upon some scheme to organize your paragraph. For example, you might write about your object as you perceived it in time; that is, what you noticed about it first, then second, and so on. You might organize your observations according to what your senses dictate. Your sense of smell may be most powerful, and after that your sight, and then your touch. You might give your overall impressions and then proceed to details. Let your imagination wander a bit, as in the example that follows, finding comparisons between your object and other objects that may be surprisingly like it.

Your choice of subject matter will, of course, vary with your own taste and with what is available in your surroundings. You might choose a natural or a manufactured object such as the following: a blade of grass, a stone, a leaf, a door, a windowsill, a section of a wall with or without graffiti, a section of pavement, a faucet, a doorknob, a gum wrapper, a paper cup, a can, an apple, a feather, a handful of sand, a hubcap, a nail, a seed, an ocean wave, a coin, a drainpipe, a piece of candy, a piece of string.

EXERCISE 12. DESCRIBE YOUR SENSORY REACTION TO AN OBJECT

Directions

Write a paragraph in which you describe your fresh and immediate sensory response to an object you have never studied or thought about before. The object may be natural or manufactured. Use the preceding discussion and the following example to guide you.

Example

(TOPIC SENTENCE) The fresh new leaf that I hold in my hand I have just picked from a nearby oak tree. (DISCUSSION) The leaf pricks my palm with its jagged edges that curve in tight symmetrical swoops to short stiff points, like tiny needles or delicate cat claws. Veins lead back from each of the points to the center stem of the leaf. When I hold the leaf up against the sky by the end of the stem, I can see that the shape of the leaf is like the shape of the tree from which it came, the stem like the trunk of the tree, the veins its branches. When I turn the leaf over, it becomes a little boat. The veins are the ribs of the boat, the stem an inverted keel. The leaf is not dark green and brittle, like the old growth on the tree, nor have caterpillars crawled over it, leaving holes. It is a bright avocado color, unspoiled in any way, a light and pliant little boat such as a child might play with on a pond. (CONCLUSION) It smells faintly like an acorn.

DISCUSSION OF EXERCISE 13

In Exercise 13 you are asked to discuss your biggest problem in college. Your problem may or may not be the one discussed in the model paragraph that follows, though you may organize your discussion in a similar way and should give details like those in the model.

Suppose your biggest problem is a particular subject you are taking, such as mathematics or biology or English. If you are having trouble with everything about the class, you will need to select two or three representative problems to discuss, because you cannot write about everything without making your paragraph too long or without destroying its unity. After selecting the two or three representative problems, you will need to connect them in some way, such as showing a common difficulty you have with them. Also, be sure to give specific examples or details to make your discussion clear.

If you are having trouble with only one part of a class, such as speaking before it or participating in class discussions, you will need to discuss the problem in considerable detail. You might first describe situations in which the problem generally exists, and then you might settle on one particular example in which it has occurred, telling what happened and how you felt about it.

Perhaps your problem is not knowing how to study or being easily distracted from your studies. Your discussion should make clear, then, what your study habits are like. You might describe the environment in which you study, telling about distractions such as television, phone calls, family traffic, or street noises.

Your problem may be adjusting to some aspect of college life, such as learning to think for yourself, meeting new people, getting along with your instructors and classmates. Make clear what you are used to, what is unfamiliar, what is painful or confusing. Give an example or illustrate your thoughts.

Your problem may be something personal that interferes with your academic life, such as illness in the family, financial worries, a part-time job, a hobby that consumes much of your time, or an overactive social life. Take stock of what it is and discuss it realistically. Make your discussion meaningful by giving particulars.

EXERCISE 13. WRITE ABOUT YOUR BIGGEST PROBLEM IN COLLEGE

Directions

Write a paragraph defining or discussing your biggest problem in college. The example that follows may be helpful as a guide.

Example

(TOPIC SENTENCE) My biggest problem in college is my lack of self-confidence. (DISCUSSION) I tend to feel that everyone else in class knows more than I do, has a better background, is sharper, more articulate, wiser. I hate to be called on by the instructor. To prevent having to speak up in class, I try to make myself invisible, hide behind heads, lower my eyes "to study my notes," sink down in my chair (of course, I sit in the back of the room). Very often I know the answers to the questions being asked, but I never raise my hand, never volunteer, never open my mouth willingly. When I am forced to speak, I feel as if there are hands around my throat squeezing the words out. When I hear my words rattling in the air, I feel disconnected from my voice and out of control. Often I think I am as bright as others in the class, but I'm afraid to assert myself. If I even think about speaking up, I begin to blush, my heart begins to pound, and I can imagine a room full of eyes turning and staring at me with contempt and ridicule. I become paralyzed with self-doubt and conceal my shame in silence. (CONCLUSION) Sometimes I think about discussing my problem with my instructors or counselors, but I'm afraid I'll lose their respect if I open my mouth.

DISCUSSION OF EXERCISE 14

In Exercise 14 you are asked to define an important word by first giving its dictionary meaning and then discussing your interpretation of it. The first part of the exercise is easy, but the second part is not. In the second part you may move from a consideration of what the word *denotes* to what it *connotes* (see p. 52) — that is, you may need to think about your experience or emotional association with the word. Your paragraph should not be a mere parroting of the dictionary or other sources outside yourself (remember to use quotation marks wherever quoting, and take care that your quotation(s) do not become too long). You must do some original work in this paragraph. Put your personal stamp on it. To do the second part well will require quite a bit of thought and effort on your part.

As stated earlier in this book, words are slippery and can have many different meanings, depending on who speaks them and to whom they are spoken. After you have selected your word for this exercise from the list on page 96 or from suggestions your instructor may give you, and after you have looked it up in one or more dictionaries, you should formulate a plan by which to make your own special study of the word. This study should result in your discovering many meanings and applications of the word that you may never have thought of before.

Your plan for studying the word might first consist of going to written sources in addition to the dictionary. For instance, you might consult an encyclopedia, or you might ask your librarian to help you find essays, newspapers, magazine articles, or books that discuss the word. After you read about the word, or while you are reading about it, you should also discuss it and listen to other people who discuss it. You may learn enough about the word by using it in casual conversation with various people you know. If not, your plan may require more of a system.

You might systematize your plan by working up an interview with people concerning the word. You should interview as many people as possible and people from as many walks of life as possible. Interview your family, your friends, your neighbors, your instructors, even the person on the street, whom you may not know. Your interview might include the following questions:

1. What does (the word) mean to you?
2. When and how do you use the word?
3. Do you like the word? Do you think it is complimentary, insulting, or neither?
4. Whom do you hear using the word and where and how?
5. Does the word mean to you today what it did in the past?

If you have followed this procedure carefully, you have generated some ideas of your own and have shared them with or tried them out on people you have interviewed, in order to test your perception of the word. Little by little, or in a flash of realization, you should come to a plan or an approach to the second part of the paragraph, your original statement or personal stamp. This is the more interesting part of the paragraph, the part your reader is looking forward to and will weigh more heavily. In it you will reveal your feelings or share your ideas about the word as they have evolved during the course of your study.

Your study of the word should result in your having too much to say about it for one paragraph. You will need to boil down what you have discovered and thought about the word or you will need to select what you consider to be the best possible statement you can make about it. Remember that you can develop only one central idea.

LIST OF WORDS

self-confidence	friend	fundamentalist
conservative	alcohol	mistake
home	sleaze	death
homeless	music	automobile
suicide	noise	civility
fashion	drought	bliss
job	hurricane	walk
work	listen	college
play	crime	enemy
hero	fantasy	humid
addiction	green	beach
adultery	bread	horse
sexism	food	dog
harassment	disability	patriotic
racism	rap	photography
abortion	child	jog
polyester	parent	lifestyle
panhandler	abuse	sports
maturity	sex	intelligent
poverty	identity	respect
wealth	brainstorm	computer
family	lust	input
earth	cruel	access
planet	coffee	business
punishment	dining	ambition
expert	baby	pollution
happy	brave	wilderness
fire	gossip	forest
baseball	teacher	slang
women	artist	graffiti
men	competition	poetry
vote	trust	vegetarian
imagination	guilt	amateur
art	comedy	justice
science	tragedy	law
wife	pathos	bad
husband	class	wedding
garden	left	ritual
exercise	right	ceremony
language	smoking	space
manners	entertainment	machine
style	amplifier	

EXERCISE 14. DEFINE AND DISCUSS A SIGNIFICANT WORD OR TERM

Directions

Write a paragraph in which you define a significant word or term according to its dictionary meaning(s) and then proceed to an original discussion of its meaning(s) or applications. Your discussion should reveal your personal feelings or ideas about the word. The following example may help to guide you.

Example

(TOPIC SENTENCE) The word *tolerance* is an ambiguous term worth thinking about. (DISCUSSION) To tolerate others, according to *The American Heritage Dictionary*, means, on the one hand, to recognize and respect them, their beliefs or practices, without necessarily agreeing or sympathizing with them. On the other hand, the word can mean to put up with or bear with others, though you may despise them, because some force, such as the law, requires that you do so. It seems to me that people often pretend to use the first meaning of the word when they really have in mind the second meaning. In such cases, people are hypocritical when they use the word, and I do not admire them. They pretend respect for others, but in reality they are merely putting up with them. It is as though they were saying: Behave yourself and I will be gracious enough to permit you to exist. Has anyone the right to be that gracious, I wonder? The idea can be expressed in another way: If you will accept my superiority, I will tolerate you. With such an attitude, the word *tolerance* implies a sense of inequality that is unacceptable to me. (CONCLUSION) Because the word is ambiguous and often used in a hypocritical if not an insulting manner, I often wonder what people mean when they use it, and I sometimes think we would be better off without the word.

DISCUSSION OF EXERCISES 15 AND 16

In Exercises 15 and 16 you are asked to make comparisons. In Exercise 15 you must show how two things are similar. In Exercise 16 you need to contrast two things or show how they are different.

Think about what a comparison (including the idea of contrast) is. The word *compare* comes from a Latin word that means "to pair" or "to match." Keep this meaning in mind when you think about and try to decide on topics you will use for comparison. The two things you choose to compare must have enough in common to make them comparable. You cannot compare, or pair, and antelope with a rock, for instance. There is insufficient common ground between the two. The two things you compare or contrast must be matchable or mismatchable rather than totally unrelated to each other.

Examine Figures 7–2A and 7–2B, which are overlapping circles. The circles in Figure 7–2A overlap (see the shaded area) more than those in Figure 7–2B. That is, they have greater common ground. Figure 7–2A represents two things that should be compared to show *similarity*. There is less common ground (but enough in common to make the two circles comparable) in Figure 7–2B. This figure represents two things that should be compared in terms of their *differences*.

FIGURE 7–2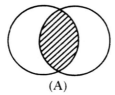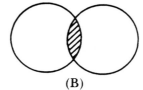

(A)   (B)

One of the primary problems in making a comparison is *sustaining both parts* of the comparison. That is, you must discuss equally the two things being compared, keeping a balance between the two. A paragraph that promises (the topic sentence is a promise that must not be broken!) to compare *two* things must not end in discussing only *one*. You must not merely mention one of the two things and then spend most or all of your discussion on the other, nor should you spend the first half of the paragraph all on one thing and the second half all on the other. The first mistake is a matter simply of failing to fulfill half of your promise. The second mistake causes your paragraph to split into two parts, thus destroying its unity. Exercises 15 and 16 should look like Figure 7–3, not like Figures 7–4 or 7–5.

Before you write your paragraph for either Exercise 15 or 16, make a preliminary list summarizing the similarities (differences) you see in your comparison. This list will guide you in the development of your paragraph. You might work out a scheme or plan similar to either of the two examples that follow.

Mary and Anne are alike as follows:

1. girls/sisters
2. similar age/teens
3. look and act alike
   a. tall/slender
   b. brown hair/eyes

c. olive complexions/warm smiles
d. dress alike
e. talented/friendly
4. popular

```
                                              X O X O X O

                                              X X X X X X

                                              X X X X X X

X O X O X O          X O X O X O              X X X X X X

X O X O X O          X X X X X X              O O O O O O

X O X O X O          X X X X X X              O O O O O O

X O X O X O          X X X X X X              O O O O O O
  FIGURE 7 – 3         FIGURE 7 – 4             FIGURE 7 – 5
```

Standard cars and compact cars are different as follows:

	STANDARD	COMPACT
1. purchase price:	higher	lower
2. operating expense:	higher	lower
3. repairs/maintenance:	higher	lower
4. comfort/room:	greater	lower
5. maneuverability:	less	greater
6. power/performance:	greater?	less?
7. prestige:	?	?
8. safety:	?	?

Suggested topics for Exercises 15 and 16 include the following: two people, famous or otherwise; two sports; two types of food; two neighborhoods; two ethnic customs; two kinds of music; two kinds of dance; two different times or periods in the same place (see the example in Exercise 16); two cars; two jobs; two trees; two ways of walking; two college classes; two teachers; two kinds of weather; two buildings; two characters in fiction; two kinds of crime; two pieces of furniture; two hobbies; two types of tires; two tools; two objects of art; two ways of relating to people; two forms of greeting or leave-taking; two attitudes.

EXERCISE 15. MAKE A COMPARISON BY SHOWING SIMILARITIES

Directions

Write a paragraph in which you show that two things are similar. Because your comparison will be about similar rather than identical things, inevitably you will notice differences as well as similarities; but your purpose is to focus on the likenesses, not the differences. Because you do not want to lie or distort the picture, you must choose your comparison carefully, selecting two things that have more in common than they have at odds with each other. Use the preceding discussion and the following example to guide you.

Example

(TOPIC SENTENCE) My two cousins Mary and Anne are very similar in appearance and personality. (DISCUSSION) In fact, some people think the two girls are twins rather than sisters because they are close in age, both of them in their early teens, and because they look and act a good deal alike. They are both tall for their age and slender, and they both wear their dark-brown hair long and straight. Mary, who is 15, has stunning large brown eyes with long dark eyelashes; and Anne, who is 14, also has beautiful dark eyes. They both have lovely olive complexions, and when they smile, they radiate warmth and happiness. They even dress alike. Mary sews almost all of her own clothes, and Anne is also learning to sew. Because they are almost the same size, they can borrow each other's patterns as well as each other's clothes. What is most noticeable about the two girls is that they are both talented, outgoing, and friendly. Mary is the vice president of her class and active in dance and drama. Anne, who is also a good student, is a star member of the tennis team as well as an accomplished guitarist. (CONCLUSION) As might be guessed, my two cousins are both very popular.

EXERCISE 16. MAKE A COMPARISON (CONTRAST) BY SHOWING DIFFERENCES

Directions

Write a paragraph in which you contrast two things or show how they are different. Because the two things you choose to write about must have something in common to be comparable, you will recognize that they have similarities as well as differences, but your aim in this paragraph is to concentrate on their differences. Select your subject matter carefully so that it is easy, without distorting the facts, to focus on differences. The example that follows is a discussion of two different times or periods in the same place. Other suggested topics are given in the discussion preceding Exercise 15. Use that discussion and the following example to guide you.

Example

(TOPIC SENTENCE) Orinda is a more sophisticated town today than it was a few years ago. (DISCUSSION) In a fairly short time the town has been transformed from a small country village where everyone knew each other to a large suburban community where people who rush home each night from city offices barely have time to get acquainted. Just a few years ago the children of Orinda walked to one small school through pear orchards and tomato patches. Now they ride to several schools in cars and buses, driving past well-trimmed lawns and swimming pools. Orinda used to be a quiet rural town. Now it is bustling and sophisticated. The rocking chair has been replaced by the aluminum recliner. Community suppers have given way to country club parties. The horsedrawn plow has been replaced by the tractor and rototiller. The two-lane road through town has moved aside for a wide new freeway. (CONCLUSION) There are a few old-timers left in Orinda who probably wonder whether all the changes that have taken place rightly deserve to be called progress, but most of the people are caught up in the new life and seem to be satisfied with it.

DISCUSSION OF EXERCISE 17

The purpose of Exercise 17 is to summarize a short story or, as in the case of the model exercise that follows, a short novel. Think about a few of the problems this exercise poses before you begin to write.

First, your purpose is simply to give the plot or to tell what happens in the story. To do this task well, you must be objective. You must keep your own ideas or opinions out of what you write. Whether you like the story or not is not the point of the exercise. No personal comments should appear in your paragraph.

Perhaps the most difficult part of this exercise is to condense, or boil down, the story to approximately 10 sentences. The complete story is probably many pages long, but you must tell it in one short paragraph. The paragraph will thus test not only your ability to write clearly, but also your understanding of the essential parts of the story. You can give only the skeletal outline of the story in one paragraph. You must leave out much in the way of incidental background, minor points in the plot, and minor characters in the story.

As you shave away the story to its barest minimum, be careful not to distort the story or misrepresent it. Do not fall in love with one part that, though it may be a meaningful sidetrack, is not essential. Do not blow it up and out of proportion. You must spend your 10 sentences most carefully to represent the story fairly and clearly in summary form.

You should also realize that a story, if it is fiction, neither lives nor dies but is always present whenever you read it or discuss it. Therefore, when you write about it in your paragraph, use the simple present tense. That is, you should write, first, this *takes* place, then such and such *happens*, after that something else *occurs*, and finally the story *ends*. In most cases no other tense is needed. To use the model paragraph that follows as an example, the main character *fishes* alone rather than *fished* alone. Though the story itself may be written in the past tense, when you talk about it, your discussion is present and requires the present tense.

This exercise, though difficult, is worthwhile. Being able to condense a story in your own words (you should use few quotes, if any) gives you a better understanding of the story as a whole. Once you have mastered this exercise, you will be ready to go on to the next, in which you are asked to give your opinion of the story. Because of this exercise, you will be in a better position to do the next.

EXERCISE 17. SUMMARIZE A PLOT

Directions

Write a paragraph summarizing the plot of a short story or novel. Remember that your object is to <u>condense</u> the story. Try to tell it in no more than <u>10</u> sentences. Use the following example to guide you.

Example

(TOPIC SENTENCE) *The Old Man and the Sea* is a short novel by Ernest Hemingway. (DISCUSSION) The novel is about an old Cuban fisherman, Santiago, who fishes alone in the Gulf of Mexico. Friendless except for a young boy named Manolin, Santiago has only one remaining purpose in life—to catch a big fish in order to prove to Manolin and to himself that he is still a good fisherman. After eighty-four days of unsuccessful fishing, on the eighty-fifth day Santiago goes far out into the gulf, where he hooks a giant marlin. He struggles with the fish for two days and nights and finally kills it. Lashing the fish to his skiff, he sails for home. Soon sharks appear and attack his prize. The old man fights them off with all his strength but fails to protect his catch.

(CONCLUSION) Only the skeleton of the great fish remains as proof of Santiago's courage and endurance when he returns with it to the harbor in Havana.

DISCUSSION OF EXERCISE 18

For Exercise 18 select a character from a short story or novel to discuss in a paragraph. You know, of course, that the paragraph must be limited and that any interesting character is too complex to be contained fully in a single paragraph. Therefore, focus on *one limited aspect* of the personality or appearance of the character.

Although your paragraph will be *your view* of the subject, be careful to base your discussion on what the *author tells you* about the character. Examine the evidence in the story before you draw your conclusions. Notice the details the author gives about the appearance of the character and observe the cues given about the character's behavior, thoughts, fears, and desires. Note how the character interacts with others in the story. Pay attention to what he says and how he says it.

If you study the character carefully, you will probably become fascinated with some special facet of personality or appearance. Something in particular will catch your eye. Having studied the character (and story) as a whole, you will begin to form an opinion about the particular aspect of the character that interests you most. You will then be ready to try to express your opinion or conclusion in the topic sentence of your paragraph.

Remember that your topic sentence must be sharply focused and your paragraph limited. Suppose you conclude that the character you choose to write about is a cruel, bitter person. It will be impossible for you to deal with every aspect of the character's cruelty and bitterness. Instead, write about one part, for example, the way he mistreats his animals. If you think your character is appealing, say, because she is a sincere and thoughtful young girl awakening to the complexities of adult life, you might demonstrate one aspect of this larger theme by showing that her relationship with her mother is questioning rather than totally submissive and obedient. If the appearance of your character strikes or repels your fancy, you will need to restrict yourself to some particular feature such as the character's fashionable dress. Discuss one part rather than the whole of what you see in your character.

Your topic sentence is a conclusion, a claim or assertion you make about the character. How will you support, substantiate, or prove your claim in your discussion? You will need to cite the evidence in the story that justifies your interpretation of the character. You will need to build a convincing case, something like a lawyer in court, that proves your position. You must present the evidence and interpret the evidence so your reader will view it your way and respect that view.

Bear in mind that it is essential to keep a *sharp focus* in the development of your discussion. Do not be sidetracked or lured away from your primary objective. You may need to discuss fragments of the story to get your point across, but do not become immersed in the storytelling. Move quickly from the story fragment to the point you are making with it. Brief quotations, as in the example that follows, may help to clarify your position, but keep them brief. Do not allow your paragraph to turn into a summary of the story (you have already done that in the preceding exercise) and do not let it become one long quote. *Your* ideas are what matter here. Develop *them*. Be in control of your paragraph. Keep an eye on your topic sentence. Let it remind you of your objective, and stay on course!

EXERCISE 18. DISCUSS A CHARACTER IN A STORY

Directions

Write a paragraph in which you discuss one limited aspect or element of a character in a short story or novel. Notice that the following example examines a very small part of the character. Limit your paragraph accordingly.*

Example

(TOPIC SENTENCE) The laughter of the tinker in John Steinbeck's short story ''The Chrysanthemums'' is one sign of his deceitful personality. (DISCUSSION) When the tinker first meets Elisa, the main character of the story, he appears to appreciate the humor she sees in the cowardly behavior of his mongrel dog. He echoes her laughter with his own. His attitude changes abruptly, however. ''The laughter had disappeared from his face and eyes the moment his laughing voice ceased.'' The fact that his expression becomes suddenly so humorless suggests there is something false about his laughter or that there is actually little humor in him. The moment in which Elisa has been caught up has not really involved him. Perhaps he has merely turned on and off the required social response needed to gain Elisa's approval. Similar behavior can be seen a little later when Elisa tries to rekindle the wit she believes they have shared. He smiles ''for a second'' before artfully shifting the subject. (CONCLUSION) The tinker's laughter and his fleeting smile convey the impression that, although he is a skillful salesman, he is underhanded and dishonest.

*This exercise can be expanded into a short composition if two or three aspects of the character or the character as a whole is discussed.

DISCUSSION OF EXERCISE 19

In Exercise 19 you are asked to propose some change in the existing state of affairs on the local, national, or international scene. In other words, you must present an argument.

The discussion part of Exercise 19 poses a special problem in logic and in presenting proof in support of the topic sentence or proposal. Notice the verbs used in this paragraph. *Should be* is used only in the topic sentence. In the supporting sentences in the discussion, the verbs *is* or *are* should be used.

CORRECT VERBS IN DISCUSSION: *is* or *are*

INCORRECT: *should be, would be, might be, could be*

The purpose of the discussion part of Exercise 19 is to give *partial* support of the topic sentence by discussing the evils, faults, or flaws of *present reality*. It is *not* to guess about the *future*. Whenever anyone proposes a change in the way things *are*, he must *first* show there *is* something wrong with the way things *are*. Naturally, it is wise to look ahead and wonder what would happen, or might happen, or could happen if the proposed change became a reality in the future. But pondering the future is not the task of the discussion part of Exercise 19.

To provide more complete support of the change proposed in the topic sentence of Exercise 19, a fairly long composition would be needed. In the long composition it would be necessary to show, for example, the benefits of the proposed change, that the proposed change is the best among possible changes, that the change would not bring about additional problems, that the change would not be too expensive, and so on.

You should think of Exercise 19 as only *part* of an argument. In fact, it is a *summary* of part of an argument. The example in the exercise is not a typical paragraph, nor is it an especially good paragraph, because it is quite general rather than specific, and it is much too short and underdeveloped as well. Its main purpose is to give an overall view in summary form. You will see that it is a means to an end rather than an end in itself. Exercise 19 is really a condensed composition. Before writing a composition, it can be helpful to write an outline or summary first to guide the organization of the composition. Exercise 19 serves this purpose.

Notice that the exercise does not go into much detail in the discussion but rather gives only main ideas with a few supporting clues. Later, in Exercise 20, you will be asked to go into more detail. Here in this exercise only a few details are needed.

You should think about the order or sequence of ideas that is best to use in the discussion of Exercise 19. Most often, it is best to present the strongest supporting idea or reason for the proposed change first, and to present ideas of less importance after that. In some cases, it is more dramatic or effective to begin with the weakest support and then to build to the strongest. Think about your topic carefully before you decide on the order that is best for your paragraph.

Your choice of topic for this exercise, as indicated in the directions, is broad. You should, however, choose a topic about which you are informed. If you are not well informed about topics of international or national importance, then you had better write about a problem close to home.

The topic of the model paragraph that follows is billboard advertising. This topic may or may not be a problem where you live. Look around you. What needs a change? Is there a curfew where you live you think is unreasonable and would like to see abolished? If so, show the faults of the curfew. Is there a course at your school you are required to take which you feel has little value? If so, you might propose it should not be required, and in the discussion part of your paragraph, you should show what is wrong with the course. Do your parents impose a rule on you that you think is unjust? Propose a change and discuss the injustice of the rule. Does your school need a new campus? See the arguments regarding this topic on pages 31 – 32.

While you search for a proposal to write about in this exercise, bear in mind that you must be reasonable. Do not propose that your allowance should be raised to $1,000 a week unless your parents can afford it, or that you should get A's in all your classes unless you merit them. Your proposal might be debatable, but it should be capable of being debated by reasonable people.

You will see that the model paragraph in Exercise 19 does not have a conclusion. Keep in mind the special nature of the exercise: It is a *summary* of *part* of an argument. No conclusion, therefore, is possible. The whole argument would need to be presented, and that would require many paragraphs before it would make sense to come to a conclusion.

EXERCISE 19. PROPOSE A CHANGE IN THE EXISTING STATE OF AFFAIRS

Directions

Write a paragraph in which you propose some changes in the existing state of affairs on the local, national, or international scene. Your paragraph should contain two or three reasons in support of your proposal. Follow the pattern of organization given in the following example.

Example

(TOPIC SENTENCE) Billboard advertising should be abolished along public highways for three reasons. (DISCUSSION) First, billboards are ugly and hinder the enjoyment of natural roadside beauty. Second, billboards are a distraction and therefore, I believe, a danger to motorists, who should keep their eyes on the road. Third, the purpose of billboards is to promote private business; therefore, they do not belong along public tax-supported highways.

DISCUSSION OF EXERCISE 20

Look at the topic sentence of the model paragraph of Exercise 20 and then look back at the first sentence of the discussion part of the model paragraph of Exercise 19. You will see that they are the same except that the first word of the sentence in Exercise 19 has been dropped in Exercise 20. The sentence in Exercise 20 is as follows:

Billboards are ugly and hinder the enjoyment of natural roadside beauty.

From this sentence, you should be able to conclude that the purpose of Exercise 20 is to illustrate or explain the first point made in the discussion part of Exercise 19. You need not be restricted in your paragraph to the first point, but you should limit your paragraph to *one* of the points made in Exercise 19.

Organize Exercise 20 in one of two ways. One way is through illustration. The model paragraph that follows should guide you if you elect this method. Another way to organize the exercise is by explanation. If you choose this method, turn back to pages 31–32 for guidance. The paragraph beginning "City College is completely overcrowded" should be particularly helpful.

Using either method of organization, develop Exercise 20 with as much detail as possible. Your experience with Exercise 11 in which you discussed something in close detail should be of value to you here. In fact, it might be worthwhile to turn back and review the discussion of that exercise before you begin this exercise.

You should see that Exercises 19 and 20 are related to each other. Consider how they could be used as exercises preliminary to writing a short composition. A composition usually consists of several paragraphs that are related because they discuss the same subject. The subject of the example paragraphs in Exercises 19 and 20 is billboard advertising. Exercise 20 develops the first argument given in Exercise 19 against billboard advertising. If the two remaining points against billboard advertising made in Exercise 19 were also developed into paragraphs, the result would be three paragraphs that could form the main body (discussion section) of a short composition. To complete the composition, two additional paragraphs, one an introduction and one

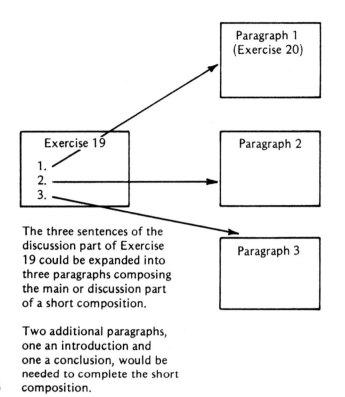

Exercise 20 is an expansion or development of the first point of the discussion part of Exercise 19; hence, it could serve here.

Exercise 20 could be used again to develop the second point of the discussion part of Exercise 19; hence, it could serve here.

Exercise 20, if used to develop the third point of Exercise 19, could serve here.

The three sentences of the discussion part of Exercise 19 could be expanded into three paragraphs composing the main or discussion part of a short composition.

Two additional paragraphs, one an introduction and one a conclusion, would be needed to complete the short composition.

FIGURE 7–6

a conclusion, would be needed. The total of five paragraphs would comprise a short composition that might be titled "What's Wrong with Billboards?"

Figure 7–6 illustrates how Exercise 19 might be expanded into a short composition if Exercise 20 was used three times, each time developing one of the three points made in the discussion part of Exercise 19.

Your instructor may ask you to write Exercise 20 three times to prepare you to write the short composition. Whether you write it one or more times, the exercise should help you see the relationship between one paragraph and another and between a paragraph and a composition.

Exercises 19 and 20 are among the most difficult exercises in this book and have therefore been placed last among the exercises that emphasize form and organization. Though difficult, the exercises should prove useful in helping you to think and to organize your thoughts about countless topics of importance to you.

EXERCISE 20. GIVE ONE REASON IN SUPPORT OF YOUR PROPOSED CHANGE

Directions

Write a paragraph in which you illustrate or explain one reason in support of a proposed change in the state of affairs on the local, national, or international scene. Use the following example as a guide.

Example

(TOPIC SENTENCE) Billboards are ugly and hinder the enjoyment of natural roadside beauty. (DISCUSSION) To illustrate, suppose a person is tired of the city — the smog and the hurry — and he decides to get away for a while. He gets into his car and travels away toward freedom and relaxation. Along the way, he pulls over to the side of the road to enjoy the quiet beauty of a country scene. What does he see? Billboards! One billboard shows giant dice dripping dirty motor oil; another billboard displays huge slices of bread falling on an immense plate; still another shows pastel toilet tissue, spelling out the name of the product he should buy. These and numerous other billboards are ugly substitutes for the trees and meadows, rivers, lakes, deserts, hills, and mountains he is seeking. (CONCLUSION) These eyesores spoil his enjoyment of natural roadside beauty.

CHAPTER 8   ⟵

PROBLEMS

OF

VARIETY

AND

IMAGINATION

The paragraph models in the exercises in this chapter are organized in a variety of ways. Although some are the same as or similar to those in Chapters 6 and 7, others are quite different. For example, in some of the models that follow, the topic sentence is the first sentence. In others, the topic sentence appears elsewhere. In still others, the topic is not stated at all but is implied or suggested by other parts of the paragraph.

There are other differences in organization in the following paragraphs. One of the most noticeable, perhaps, is the lack of obvious form in some of them. Freer form, however, does not mean formlessness or disorganization. You should remember that all paragraphs must contain unity, coherence, continuity, and the other essentials discussed earlier. Without these ingredients, a paragraph cannot communicate clearly.

You will see that no parenthetical guides to organization like those in the exercises in Chapters 6 and 7 are given in this section. It is assumed by now that you will recognize the form in the following exercises or that you will have achieved the sense of form needed in the exercises. You are free now to use the models only as cues rather than as exact patterns of organization to imitate. You should read them primarily to stimulate you to form your own ideas. If you have learned to discipline yourself in writing a paragraph, by now you should be free to do as you wish.

The emphasis here is to encourage you to express yourself with variety and imagination. Here you will be asked to be creative and to express your feelings. Expressing your feelings with imagination and clarity, as you may know, is not easy. How many times have you said, even to your closest friends, "I know what I mean, but I can't express it"? Understanding that you have difficulty expressing yourself to those who know you well, you can imagine how much harder it will be to write the paragraphs in this chapter, which will be read by your instructor, who probably knows relatively little about you. How will your instructor, a comparative stranger, know what you mean?

Think about how you are going to make your feelings clear. Strangely enough, you cannot come right out with your feelings. You cannot write, for example, "That night it was very quiet." Your instructor, reading your paragraph, will wonder what you mean by "very quiet." *Like what?* he or she will wonder. To make the quietness clear, you will need to tell your reader what you could hear or not hear that very quiet night. Shakespeare had this problem in the beginning of his play *Hamlet*, and he solved it by writing, "Not a mouse stirring." It was so quiet that even the tiniest of nighttime creatures, mice, could not be heard. With such exact detail, Shakespeare made the quietness of the night clear.

To make your feelings clear, you must write about the *cause* of your reaction, *not the result*. You should not write "I felt afraid." Instead, you should make the cause of your fear so clear that the reader too can feel the horror. When you can make the reader feel what you have felt, then you can communicate your feelings successfully.

Your job, then, is to recreate your experience in order to convey your feelings about it. Examine the following paragraph.

Example

Often during my young life I had galloped my horse down hills, chasing cows, and I had never been afraid. Suddenly I experienced a moment that terrified me. I was on a narrow ledge of rock on one of the highest points of the ranch, and I could see the treetops on the plateau below, like tiny shrubs, racing beneath the hoofs of my horse. The cow was getting away from me! I urged my horse to go faster and then, to gain distance, I made him jump to a steep slope below. He skidded in the winter mud to the edge of the slope and hung for an instant, balanced precariously, half falling into the deep canyon hundreds of feet below. Miraculously, he got his footing again. Shaking with fright, I got off him and sat down in the wet grass, trembling with the thought of what had almost happened. Then, slowly and carefully, I led my horse back down the steep hill, wondering how we had ever got up so high in the first place. "Somebody else is going to have to get that cow," I said to my father. "I'm not going up there again."

The experience described in this example is one of sudden and unusual fright. Very little is said about the emotion inspired by the experience. Instead, the paragraph recreates the experience in such a way that the emotion can be felt without discussing it outright.

Consider how the example expresses the feeling of fear. First it discusses height, fearsome to most people, not only by talking about it but by giving a comparison of the trees to small shrubs, which makes the sense of height clearer. It also relates speed of movement not only to height but also to a minimum of space that suggests the risk involved in the experience. At the moment of greatest fear in the experience, the emotion is not discussed at all. Rather, the action is given — "skidded . . . half falling" — causing readers to use their own imaginations, to draw back from the edge of the slope and balance precariously, too.

You must get readers to participate in the experience you write about, to share it with you, if you wish to express your feelings to them. To cause their participation, you must *appeal to their senses*. You must make it possible for them to see what you have seen, hear what you have heard, taste what you have tasted, touch what you have touched, smell what you have smelled, and in every way have the same experience you have had. When you appeal to readers' senses, you must be as *exact* as possible. If they cannot quite see what you have seen, for example, they will be unable to participate in your experience, and hence you will have failed to convey your feelings.

Being exact requires finding the right words, so it might be worthwhile for you to review the section on words beginning on page 51 before you begin to write the exercises here. Remember when you write the exercises that follow to have a good dictionary and also *Roget's Thesaurus* at hand. Remember, also, to avoid cheap, tired, and weak substitutes for the right words you need, to be neither wordless nor wordy in expressing yourself, and to be careful of the many meanings some words have.

Remember the value of comparisons and use them whenever they will make your meaning clearer. Be creative in your use of comparisons. Avoid clichés. Find your own fresh comparisons. Surprise readers with your imagination. Make them sit up and notice you. Show them who you are, what you have experienced, and be so clear as well as clever about it that they cannot help but appreciate your effort. Above all else, make readers understand your experience as you do; after reading your paragraph, every reader should be able to say, "I know what you mean."

Finally, think about the difference between well-expressed sentiment and gushing sentimentality. Sentiment, when expressed well, consists of feeling or emotion that is both powerful and controlled. It is neither overstated nor understated. It is just right when it is sincere and when it leaves a little to the imagination of the reader. Do not pour it on! On the other hand, do not be afraid to show your feelings. If they are imaginatively expressed and carefully restrained, they can be the most beautiful statements you are capable of making.

At the end of this chapter there are notes on each of the exercises. These notes may be helpful to you in writing the exercises.

Remember that these exercises may be easier and more enjoyable to do if you practice clustering before you write the paragraphs.

EXERCISE 21. DESCRIBE AN UNPLEASANT SENSORY EXPERIENCE

Directions

Write a paragraph in which you describe an unpleasant sensory experience that you have had. In other words, tell about something that has happened to you which has involved, in an unpleasant way, your sense of taste, touch, sight, smell, hearing, or any combination of these senses. Choose an experience that you know or remember well, and write vividly, selecting words that will make the reader feel what you have felt. The example that follows may be a helpful guide.

Example

Each time I reached the front door of the nursing home, I thought I had prepared myself for the heat, the lack of air, and the odors, but I was never ready. It was always a shock, something to get past, that opening of the door. I tried to hold the door open as long as possible to let in a little fresh air, but someone usually called out, "Close the door! It's cold!" When it closed, the door seemed to seal out freshness, and everyone inside became hot house plants, shielded from anything resembling weather. I understood the chill of the patients with their thin skin clinging delicately to bony arms and legs, but what about the nurses? How could they stand the close atmosphere, much less work in it? I took off my sweater and walked toward the nurses' station, adjusting as I went to the odd mixture of smells that permeated the place. The noonday meal was being prepared, but its aroma was overpowered by the pervading odor of disinfectant doing battle with incontinence. The charge nurse looked up, smiled and said "Hello," and I could tell by her expression that she had long since withdrawn from the outside world and was satisfied with the way things were running.

EXERCISE 22. DESCRIBE A PLEASANT SENSORY EXPERIENCE

Directions

Write a paragraph in which you describe a pleasant sensory experience. The directions are the same here as for the preceding exercise except that in this case there is a change from an unpleasant to a pleasant experience. Notice that the difference between a pleasant and unpleasant experience is not necessarily in the subject matter itself but in the way it is viewed by the writer. For example, the experience in the following example might easily be regarded as unpleasant by some people, but the writer does not present it that way.

Example

The smell of alfalfa in the tightly packed bales of hay I sat on was strong and fresh. With my knees tucked up, my arms curled around my legs, I watched the cows come into the open barn for their evening meal. It was twilight, my favorite time of day. The summer air was quiet. The burnt hills were turning from dark amber to a darker grayish brown, becoming faintly magenta where the last sun streaks had recently left them. When the cows had settled into their stanchions, the only sounds left were the shiftings and breakings of dry hay as twenty-five big tongues reached out and wrapped up large mouthfuls to chew, and then the chewing itself, which was strangely peaceful to watch and listen to. I sat as though mesmerized, and only dimly did the day's struggles or my life's ambitions enter my mind. When thoughts did come, they came effortlessly, like the gentle rustling of the birds in the nearby trees, and they were as comfortable as the birds, sleeping peacefully with room to spare in the generous oaks for all of them. I could easily have sat on top of the haystack for the rest of the night, but then the dinner gong sounded in the distance. I got down from my perch in the cow barn and walked back to the house, reluctant to close the front door on the sights and sounds I had been enjoying outside. It seemed a shame to me that people lived in houses on summer nights, and I thought that maybe after dinner I would take my sleeping bag back down to the barn and sleep there.

EXERCISE 23. DESCRIBE AN EXPERIENCE IN FLASHBACK FORM

Directions

Write a paragraph in which you tell about an experience in flashback form. Begin with the conclusion in which you state the most outstanding feature(s) of the experience and then proceed to tell what happened leading up to the conclusion. Use the following example as a guide.

Example

What I remember most is running down the driveway to our house, clutching my back and screaming with pain, and then feeling the agony of my hands soaked in iodine. This experience was the result of my childhood habit of collecting stray dogs and bringing them home. It began one dusty day in the middle of summer when I introduced a stray dog to our family of five dogs, calling the five by name, petting the stray, and trying to make everybody feel at home. Nobody was very happy about the situation but me, and soon a fight started, with my hands on the stray dog in the middle of it. In seconds my hands were riddled with dog bites. Because the shock was so great, I didn't feel the pain in my hands right away. Instead, my back jerked out of shape, and I ran down to the house humped over, like an old lady. My frantic mother looked to see what was wrong with my back as I screamed to her, "No! My hands! My hands!" Blood gushed from the punctures the dogs had made. My mother ran for the medicine chest, grabbed a bottle of iodine, and poured the whole bottle over my hands.

EXERCISE 24. DESCRIBE A MOMENT WHEN YOU FOUND OR LEARNED SOMETHING NEW

Directions

Write a paragraph in which you describe a moment in your life when you found something or learned something you had never known about before. Use the example that follows to guide you.

Example

It was a rainy day and there was nothing for a child my age to do, so I went down into the basement of our house to investigate some of the mysteries that were stored there. My favorite diggings, a musty old trunk, smelling of camphor and mildew, in which my mother stored old clothes, held no fascination for me that day. Looking for new excitement, I tried on an old raincoat that was hanging on a hook. It was miles too long for me, and I almost hanged myself with it when I fastened the top snap, for the rubber in it had grown stiff with age. Next I read some old magazines that oozed moisture, and it became a game to separate the pages without tearing them. Finally I came across my prize, a book that held me spellbound. I could barely understand a word of it. Yet the words themselves captivated me. "What wild heart-histories seemed to lie enwritten upon those crystalline, celestial spheres," I read. I spent hours reading that book, and I was still absorbed in it, treasuring each word, as I carried it back up into the house. I was like a sleepwalker moving in a dream, unaware of existence outside of the biggest discovery of my life, a book of poetry by Edgar Allan Poe!

EXERCISE 25. EXPLAIN HOW OR WHY YOU ASSOCIATE ONE THING WITH ANOTHER

Directions

Write a paragraph in which you explain how or why you associate one thing with another. Perhaps a certain sound or smell calls to mind something you remember at some point in your life. Or perhaps an object, an animate or inanimate thing, reminds you of a particular experience. Use the example that follows as a guide.

Example

I have always associated the stone turquoise with my first trip to Lake Tahoe. I can still see myself as I was then, eight years old, sitting next to my brother in our family sedan. My mother and father had been talking about the Donner party, and as we approached the summit, my brother and I imagined we could see skeletons in the shadows of the tall trees. The sharp granite cliffs and brisk air of the mountains seemed in sharp contrast to the heat and haze of the Sacramento Valley, which we had passed through not long before. My father stopped the car somewhere near the summit, and we went into a shop that sold Indian things. It was like walking into a jewel box.

Everywhere I looked I saw the sky-blue stone. It was in rings and bracelets inside glass cases; it was in necklaces hanging from hooks; it was in other ornamental objects spread out on brightly colored blankets. My mother went up to the shopkeeper and asked the price of something she had seen in one of the cases. It was a tiny silver cross with a little round turquoise stone set in the center of it. "How would you like that?" she asked me. "Oh, could I?" I responded eagerly. Looked at through adult eyes, the event might seem unimportant, but I can remember well what a thrill it gave me when my mother placed the little cross on its silver chain around my neck and how proud I felt as we walked out of the shop and climbed back into the car.

Exercise 26. Discuss a Quotation

Directions

Do you have a saying in your family or is there a famous quotation that you have wondered about or found particularly meaningful? Present it and discuss it in one paragraph. Use the example that follows as a guide.

Example

An aunt of mine has often said, "Youth is wasted on the young." This statement has piqued my curiosity for years. People usually smile when she says it, and I have always smiled, too. But I think I'm just now beginning to understand the meaning of the saying. Quite recently I thought how close in meaning it is to a statement Thornton Wilder made in his play *Our Town*. Toward the end of the play, Emily, one of the main characters says, "I didn't realize. So all that was going on and we never noticed! . . . Do any human beings ever realize life while they live it — every, every minute?" Older people, looking back, can appreciate youth, its real meaning and significance, but young people, while they are in the middle of their youth, never fully realize what they have. An older person recognizes his increasing age by making comparisons to his youth. "I'm not as young as I was. Better slow down," he says to himself. The vitality of youth, the energy and excitement of it, is realized, ironically, only after it is gone. Thus, it seems to me, my aunt is right. Youth is wasted on the young. Babies should be old and gray-haired when they're born. Only after many years should they be permitted to enjoy their youth.

EXERCISE 27. WRITE WHAT WOULD HANDS HAPPEN IF . . .

Directions

Write a paragraph in which you express what you imagine would result if something we all take for granted in our lives were to end, to stop, or to die. For example, suppose there were no more police officers, suppose all the rivers or lakes dried up, suppose all schools closed permanently, what would happen? Remember, you cannot discuss everything in one paragraph. Limit your subject. The example that follows may be a helpful guide.

Example

Suppose the sun were to die. What would happen then? Could people find a way to survive? Perhaps they could split atoms for heat. Perhaps they could manufacture synthetic foods to eat. Perhaps they could create a new sun. Maybe there would be many new suns, one for each city, and some man-made stars along the freeways so that people could get from one place to another. Just think, the world would fill with people who had never seen the sun. Grandparents would be revered for their tales of what it was like before the sun died. Then they would drop away, like old war veterans, and the reality would become a legend. If the story got into books, would people believe it? Or would they, except for the most devout, believe there had never been a sun at all?

EXERCISE 28. DESCRIBE SOMEONE YOU SEE OFTEN

Directions

Write a paragraph in which you describe someone you see often, but do not know, in your neighborhood, or on your way to school or to work. Describe the aspects of appearance or behavior that cause you to notice this person, and also explain your reaction to the person. Use the example that follows as a guide.

Example

Her hair is white, like her face. Her eyes are sunken into her head. They look opaque; I wonder what they see? She mutters to imaginary companions as she wanders about in the garden. Crazy old woman, I think, who is she talking to? Her legs are frighteningly thin. I wonder how they can carry her to and from the nearby store for groceries. When she walks by my house, I see her hesitate before the tiniest bit of water that spills down onto the sidewalk from my front lawn. She talks to herself for a moment, then moves carefully out into the street, then back onto the sidewalk again. I feel guilty for having turned the water on. This cadaverous creature is my neighbor. She lives in a room and has kitchen privileges in the house next door to me. She has visitors once or twice during the year, I think, for I see her come to the front porch, waving them off with her thin fingers. I stand at a window in my house watching her, and I wonder how pity and repulsion can become so intertwined. There seems so little left of her, so little left for her. This ghost of a woman is a haunting vision.

EXERCISE 29. DESCRIBE A FAMOUS PAINTING

Directions

Write a paragraph in which you describe a famous painting. Discuss what you think is most striking about the painting, and then describe whatever else seems most noticeable to you. Use the example that follows as a guide.

Example

The most striking feature about van Gogh's famous painting *The Bridge at Arles* is the sense of calm it projects. The light blue sky behind the bridge is clear; the nearby trees are straight and unmoving, suggesting there is little or no wind blowing; and a man in a horse-drawn cart is leisurely crossing the bridge. Even the women scrubbing clothes in the stream beneath the bridge seem to be working contentedly. The half-sunken boat in the foreground invites the mind as well as the eye to a peaceful submersion in the gently rippling water. The colors in the painting are noticeable, too, and contribute to the calmness of the whole. Although all parts of the painting are bright and clear, nothing is glaring. Various shades of yellow strike the eye in pleasant contrast to the blues of the sky and water. A third predominating color, green, is distributed about the painting, mixed with burnt orange in places and flecks of brown. This rural scene, it is easy to tell, was done when van Gogh lived in Arles, the happiest, most peaceful period in his life.

EXERCISE 30. DESCRIBE YOUR REACTIONS TO ILLNESS

Directions

Write a paragraph in which you describe your physical and/or emotional reactions to injury or sickness. You might discuss a particular time when you have been hospitalized or ill in bed at home. Or you might, as in the following example, describe a recurring feeling that you experience whenever you are ill. See the discussion on page 124, which explains the use of the third person in the example that follows.

Example

The most depressing thing about an illness is the sense of being left out or brushed aside by it from the mainstream of living. When a person is ill, he cannot keep up with the world of healthy people. Life begins to occur without him. Even language seems to change. What is said to a sick person does not involve him, and therefore he begins to interpret it differently. He loses touch with the outer, healthy world. "It's affected his mind," the outside world murmurs, shrinking back from him kindly, gently imprisoning him more deeply in his own thoughts. His sense of isolation is increased rather than lessened by the doctor's regular visits. The doctor labels the sick person's disease and confines him to his special place. With tact and skill, the doctor completes the patient's helplessness and makes final his separation from the world of strong arms, sound legs, clear skin, and lungs that breathe deeply. The sick person's only hope is to return to life again, and he clings to the thought of getting well. He thinks of sick people who will not get well, and he thinks of old people who will soon die. He discovers a compassion he hopes he will not lose when he is well again, and he feels gratitude that he, unlike some others, will get well.

NOTES ON EXERCISES IN CHAPTER 8

EXERCISE 21

To do this exercise well, you should write at least two or three drafts of it. In your first rough draft, do not worry about organization or mechanics such as grammar, sentence structure, and spelling. Free your mind of such matters. Concentrate instead on remembering the experience just as it happened and getting it all down on paper. Write everything about the experience you can think of, even seemingly unimportant details. Details are especially important in this exercise. The more exact you are with details, the more reality your paragraph will have. Remember, in this paragraph you must make it possible for your reader to see what you have seen, feel what you have felt, and hear what you have heard.

When you write your paragraph for the second or third time, you will need to organize it and polish it. Probably you will need to cut parts of your first draft as you get a better idea of what you want to say and how it is best said.

Do not decorate your paragraph. Do not put anything in it that is not real. Tell about the experience just as it happened, and tell it exactly.

Suggested topics: listening to a boring lecture; seeing an accident; being sick; trying to cross a busy intersection; traveling on a crowded bus on a hot afternoon; experiencing severe cold or frostbite; listening to your younger sister practice the cello; feeling stage fright; forcing yourself to eat something terrible or to take bitter medicine; trying to stay awake or to go to sleep; being punished; being hungry or thirsty; trying to diet.

EXERCISE 22

Details are as important here as they are in Exercise 21. It may be even more important in this exercise not to decorate. Do not try to paint a pretty picture. Instead, be exact and real. If you are realistic, the pleasantness of your experience, whatever it is, will be felt by the reader.

Suggested topics: enjoying Thanksgiving dinner; walking in the park or country; sailing; attending a party; dancing the last dance at the senior prom; picnicking on the beach; receiving unexpected money; buying new clothes; traveling; meeting someone famous; buying your first car; seeing an unusually beautiful sunrise or sunset; enjoying a day in spring; hearing, seeing, or tasting something exciting for the first time.

EXERCISE 23

The first sentence should make a clear and definite impression, even though the facts leading up to it are not explained until later. The first sentence should tease the reader into wanting to know more about the "how," "when," "what," and "why" of the experience to be explained in the paragraph. The paragraph should then proceed to explain everything that must be known to make the first statement fully understood. The paragraph should not leave noticeable gaps in the experience; neither should it be too long.

Suggested topics: narrowly escaping some kind of danger; taking or refusing a dare; missing an important plane or train; saving someone's life or being saved; waking up after an accident or operation; meeting a shark, bear, tiger, bull, mad dog, or thief; being injured while hunting or playing a sport; winning or losing a race; running for your life or a political office; having an embarrassing moment; learning a lesson. Notice that rather dramatic topics are best suited for this exercise.

EXERCISE 24

Be careful to set the right mood in this exercise. Notice that the mood of the model paragraph is rather playful, indicating the content is not to be taken too seriously. If you wish to present your discovery more seriously, then you will need to establish quite a different mood. Build an element of suspense into your paragraph, carefully leading up to the moment of discovery.

Suggested topics: realizing your parents are human; discovering hidden talent in yourself or someone else; realizing the truth or falsity of an old saying; discovering music or art or beauty in something unrealized before; seeing your first view of a foreign country; feeling strange in familiar surroundings or feeling familiar in a situation that is actually strange; suddenly feeling unafraid in previously fearful circumstances; sensing your own maturity or immaturity; achieving humility.

EXERCISE 25

Allow your mind to be free to make emotional as well as logical associations in this exercise. Consider how you feel, for instance, when you hear a popular song that reminds you of that summer two years ago, or that time you visited Uncle Joe in South Dakota, or that moment you met a very special person. You can make associations with things you see, smell, or taste as well as with things you hear, such as music. Free your mind to be imaginative, to wander at will, to make the association that is needed in this exercise.

You should make a rough first draft of this exercise before you worry about organizing your thoughts into a good paragraph. Your rough draft may consist of nothing more than a series of fragmentary thoughts scribbled on paper. Let your ideas flow freely before you try to give them order.

Suggested topics: chocolate ice cream may remind you of your tenth birthday; the scent of gardenias may call to mind your first formal dance; the odors of an old house might remind you of someone who has died; camel's hair coats may make you think of football in the fall; a particular food such as cole slaw or codfish might bring back a moment of discipline when you were a child. Other associations might be made with the following: the smell of newly mown grass or freshly cut lumber; the sight of sunshine on a blade of grass or a gold filling in a smiling mouth; the sound of glass breaking, brakes screeching, or music in a minor key.

EXERCISE 26

"That's life," the saying goes, but what does it mean? In this exercise you should think of an old saying, examine it, and decide what it means, if anything. No doubt you have grown up listening to countless quotations, some of them more meaningful than others. Think of one that stands out in your mind because it has affected you in some way, made you happy or sad, made you wise or thoughtless, or simply because you have heard it used so many times that it might be interesting to study it and write about it.

Suggested topics: "All work and no play makes Jack a dull boy"; "It is better to have loved and lost than never to have loved at all"; "Nothing is right or wrong, but thinking makes it so"; "Judge not, lest you, yourself, be judged"; "Do unto others as you would they did unto you"; "He's a penny-saver and a pound-loser"; "Take a stitch in time and save nine"; "A penny saved is a penny earned"; "Shirtsleeves to shirtsleeves in three generations"; "Turn the other cheek"; "He who hesitates is lost"; "Neither a borrower nor a lender be"; "Familiarity breeds contempt."

EXERCISE 27

Here you can and must be wild. Be as daring in using your imagination as you can be. Look around and think about the many things you are used to, the many things you count on, the many things you could not do without. Then imagine life without one of them. What would it be like? Your guesses should make some sense, of course.

Suggested topics: suppose there were no more gravity; no more babies born; no more deaths; no more wars; no more birds; no more means of communication such as telephones, radios, television, newspapers; no more entertainment such as television or movies; no more major cities such as New York or Washington; no more grass; suppose people could no longer laugh, or cry, or feel sorry for others; suppose you were the last person on earth; suppose you could find nobody who knew you; suppose you could not suppose.

EXERCISE 28

There are always people at the edges of your life whom you notice but do not really know. When you shop in the grocery store, for instance, you begin to recognize faces you see there often, or when you go to school or work, you pass the same people over and over again. You may nod, but you never or rarely speak. Why do you notice one person in particular? Does she remind you of someone you know? Does he look strange? Do you wonder what that person is thinking? Do you wonder what makes that person happy or sad or what he or she is really like? When you do not see that person for a day or two, do you wonder why? Select one of the people at the edges of your life to write about.

Suggested topics: someone who waits with you for the same bus; someone who drives or walks to school or work when you do; a customer where you work; someone who plays the flute in the symphony orchestra concerts you attend; someone who walks his or her dog past your house in the evening; an elderly person you see in a wheelchair through a window of a convalescent hospital; a person who looks mysterious, funny, sinister, distinguished.

EXERCISE 29

When you really look at a painting, you see much more in it than you can at a casual glance. The subject matter means more, whether it is exciting, interesting, amusing, or confusing. The composition is more meaningful because of its shapes, colors, contrasts, and variety. The mood of the painting may be impressive. If the painting is famous, you may wonder why and linger over it to try to find out why so many people admire it.

Your instructor may select a painting for you to study and write about in this exercise, or you may need to make your own choice. Look at the painting carefully. What do you see? What is most noticeable? What else is impressive? Study the painting and then write about it.

Suggested topics: Mona Lisa by Leonardo da Vinci; *The Harvesters* by Pieter Bruegel; *Northeaster* by Winslow Homer; *Stone City* by Grant Wood; *The Flower Vendor* by Diego Rivera; *Vegetable Gardens* by Vincent van Gogh; *Tahitian Mountains* by Paul Gauguin; *Woman at the Mirror* by Pablo Picasso; *The Dancer on the Stage* by Edgar Degas; any good painting, either old or modern.

EXERCISE 30

Consider your emotional and physical reactions to illness or injury in this exercise. Although you will be discussing your innermost feelings, try to be objective. Keep in mind that readers who do not know you very well will be reading your paragraph and you must make yourself clear to them. You may find comparisons useful. Your readers will understand you better if you can tell them your reaction was *like* something they know.

Neither underplay nor overstate your feeling in this exercise. Be sincere. Be as exact as possible.

The model paragraph uses the third person (he, she, they) as a means of objectifying the content or avoiding sentimentality. This technique is an experiment that you need not use unless you want to. If you find it simpler to use the first person (I), go ahead and use it. The point, however, is still the same: to show feeling without becoming so involved in it that you lose objectivity or discipline.

Suggested topics: feeling like a queen for a day in a hospital after minor surgery; feeling like a prisoner in solitary confinement with a contagious disease; waiting for a cast to be removed; getting bored with ice cream after a wisdom tooth extraction; being embarrassed to have your friends see you with your face swollen from poison oak; sharing an illness with your hospital roommate; not being able to live like others because of some permanent physical disability.

PART TWO

WRITING

THE

SHORT

COMPOSITION

CHAPTER 9 —

THE

SHORT

COMPOSITION

WHAT IS A SHORT COMPOSITION?

A short composition, also called a *theme* or *essay*, has already been partially defined elsewhere in this book. The word *composition* means putting together a whole by combining its parts. Thus defined, the word applies to art and music as well as to literature. Here the word is applied to a form of writing done by students. It is an exercise in putting together words, sentences, and paragraphs — the parts of the composition that are combined into the whole. The word *short*, of course, is relative. *Short composition* here means a composition of about four to eight paragraphs or two to five pages in length.

WHAT DOES A SHORT COMPOSITION LOOK LIKE ON THE PAGE?

The first page of a short composition might look like Figure 9 – 1. The appearance of the composition on the page depends, of course, on whether it is typewritten or handwritten. Figure 9 – 1 contains more paragraphs than could probably be handwritten on one page, at least by the average hand.

129

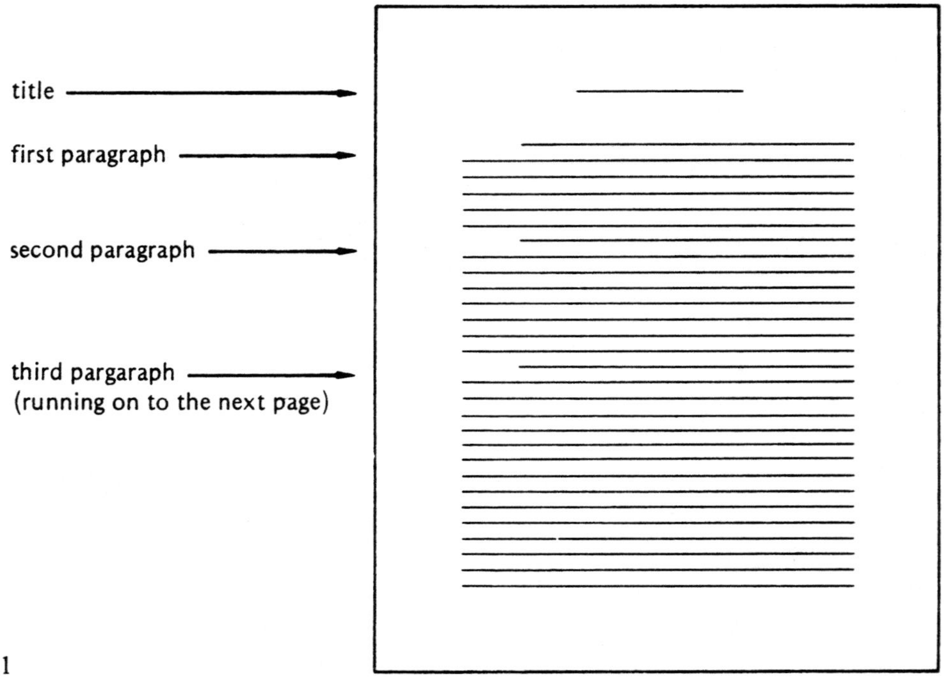

title ————————————▶

first paragraph ————————▶

second paragraph ————————▶

third pargaraph ————————▶
(running on to the next page)

FIGURE 9-1

WHAT IS A TITLE?

Notice that the title is the first thing written on the page in Figure 9-1. It is written in the upper part of the page and centered.

A title should do the following:

1.   Indicate what the composition is about.
2.   Provoke interest in the composition.
3.   Be as brief as possible.

A title is often a fragment rather than a complete sentence. The first and last words of a title are always capitalized. Unless they are the first or last words of the title, prepositions and articles are not capitalized, though some people prefer to capitalize prepositions of five or six letters or more. Examine the capitalization in the following titles:

The Grapes of Wrath

A Passage to India

The Return of the Native

For additional discussion of titles, see Chapter 14.

WHY SHOULD A COMPOSITION BE ORGANIZED?

Understanding *why* can make *how* easier. Appreciating the importance of organization is a key to better organization. Take a quick look at Figure 9 – 2. How many dots are there in each group? You must count the dots in Figure 9 – 2A carefully to determine their number, but you can tell at a glance that there are four groups of three, or a total of twelve dots in Figure 9 – 2B. There is no readily discernible pattern or arrangement in Figure 9 – 2A, whereas Figure 9 – 2B is clearly organized and its pattern is easy to recognize.

A disorganized composition is like Figure 9 – 2A. The words, sentences, and paragraphs of the composition, like the dots in Figure 9 – 2A, fly off every which way in no easily recognizable pattern. An organized composition is like Figure 9 – 2B. The words, sentences, and paragraphs line up easily to form a clear pattern.

"But I like Figure 9 – 2A better!" you might say, finding it more interesting or imaginative than the seemingly dull and monotonous Figure 9 – 2B. However, you should keep two points in mind. First, remember that you are a beginner and your primary objective is to be organized and clear. Second, do not misinterpret the two drawings. Figure 9 – 2B is intended to represent order, not monotony. Once you can achieve order, then and only then can you free yourself to be imaginative, and your imagination will make sense because it will be organized and clear.

HOW IS A COMPOSITION ORGANIZED?

The composition has a central purpose or objective that controls the whole composition. The purpose is expressed in the beginning paragraph of the composition in a sentence called a *thesis statement* or *thesis sentence*. The thesis statement gives the plan for the composition, and the composition must follow that plan. No matter what

Figure A   Figure B

FIGURE 9 – 2

the thesis or plan of a particular composition is, all compositions have in common three major parts.

The first part of any composition is the *introduction*. In a short composition the introduction is usually quite brief. It may consist simply of the thesis statement, or it may contain additional sentences. (For further discussion of the introduction, see Chapter 14.)

The second part of the composition, the *discussion*, is the main part. In a composition of five paragraphs, for example, the discussion normally consumes the three longest paragraphs. The proportion is similar in longer compositions, with the discussion part being three fifths to four fifths of the total composition.

Among the problems that most frequently arise in the discussion part of the composition are the following:

1. Getting the correct order. The correct order depends on the purpose of the composition. If the purpose is to narrate or tell a story, the correct order might be *chronological*. In other words, you should tell what happened first, second, third, and so on.

If the purpose of the composition is to explain something, the correct order might be *cause and effect* or vice versa. In other words, you should tell first what causes A and describe the results of A, then tell what causes B and describe the results of B, and so on. Or you might show the results first and then the causes.

If the purpose of the composition is to argue for or against something, the correct order is a matter of what is *logical*. For instance, in an argument against capital punishment, the first task would be to show what is wrong with capital punishment. The next job might be to show the benefits of abolishing it. If the purpose of the composition is to show both sides of an argument, then it is logical to discuss first one side and then the other.

If the purpose of the composition is to discuss several related things or a group of things, the order might be simply *topical*. In other words, one topic would be announced and then discussed and then a second topic would be introduced and discussed, and so on with the remaining topics. Of course, you would need to show a unifying relationship among the topics to maintain the necessary order or organization of the composition. For example, if the purpose of the composition were to discuss dogs, you might divide your subject into the various species of dogs, the various purposes served by dogs, or the various sizes and shapes of dogs. You must make certain that a central purpose controls the whole while you divide the whole into intelligible parts. There must be unity in your topical arrangement.

If the purpose of the composition is to describe something, the correct order might be *spatial* or *geographical*. You might move your description from north to south or from west to east, for example, or from top to bottom or from side to side.

Whatever the correct order is for the particular purpose of the composition, make it clear to readers and maintain it throughout the composition.

2. Keeping a balance.   Keeping a balance among the parts of the discussion, like putting them in correct order, depends on the purpose of the composition. If the purpose is to show two sides of an argument, for example, you must show both sides equally. If the purpose is to discuss the life work of an author, a poet, or a painter, you should not leave out or slight major events in your subject's life. Because no composition can fully describe anything or anyone, the limits of the composition are set in the introduction, but the composition must live up to those limits. You must not fall in love with only one part of your subject, for example, after you have promised to discuss two or three parts. You must achieve a balance, and that balance depends on the purpose you state in the thesis sentence of the introduction.

3. Providing signals.   Provide signals to readers at all important points in your composition, particularly at major turning points. These signals, like road signs to the motorist, help keep readers moving in the right direction in following your thoughts in the composition. The easiest direction for you to take to avoid losing readers is a straight line, but turns are often inevitable, as well as interesting. Such turns must be announced with phrases like "Going back, for a moment, to 1910" or "In England, as well as in America, the problem exists" or "Ten years from now" or "The argument against this proposition is more reasonable than the one that supports it." Readers will be happy to follow you in any reasonable direction you care to take, but your direction must be made clear to them.

4. Paving the way.   Reading the composition should not be an unpleasant experience for readers. In addition to providing them with signals along the way, you should pave the way for them. Make your word choice, your sentence structure, and the organization of your paragraphs smooth and readable. You should do everything possible to make the composition a pleasure to read. If readers must struggle to get your point, if they must stumble, go back, read parts over and over again to understand your meaning, if they must, in effect, work harder at the composition than you have, the result is disastrous. Readers become frustrated, irritated, and antagonistic rather than sympathetic. On the other hand, if you pave the way for your readers, your composition can provide you both with the exquisite joy known as communication.

(For a closer examination of the discussion, see Chapters 12 and 13.)

Finally, the third part of the composition is the conclusion, which, like the introduction, is usually brief. (See Chapter 14 for further discussion of the conclusion.)

CHAPTER 10

THE

THESIS

STATEMENT

WHAT IS A THESIS STATEMENT?

A *thesis statement* or *thesis sentence* (the terms are synonymous) states the purpose of the composition. It conveys the central or main idea of the composition and often indicates how you will support the main idea. Ideally, it is a one-sentence summary of the whole composition.

WHAT IS THE DIFFERENCE BETWEEN A THESIS STATEMENT AND A TOPIC SENTENCE?

A thesis statement governs the content and structure of a whole composition, whereas a topic sentence guides only one of its parts or paragraphs. Both sentences are signals of what is to come. The thesis statement plans the trip, as it were; the topic sentence shows one of the places that must be passed through to get to the destination.

WHERE SHOULD THE THESIS STATEMENT BE PLACED WITHIN THE COMPOSITION?

The best place for the thesis statement is at the beginning of the composition. It should be written in the first paragraph and may be the first and only sentence of that paragraph, or it may follow an introductory sentence or two and then come as the climax of the first paragraph.

ARE ALL THESIS STATEMENTS ALIKE IN CONTENT AND FORM?

Thesis statements vary in a multitude of ways with respect to content (who knows how many subjects there are to write about?); they also vary in their form.

In your college courses, you will frequently be called on to formulate thesis statements in response to assigned reading. You will read, and then you will be asked to react in writing. To some degree, therefore, both the content and the form of your thesis statement, which is your reaction in a nutshell, will be determined by your reading and by the nature of your particular assignment. In all cases, however, *a thesis statement* is a statement of *position*, of *belief*, or of a *point of view*, either your own or that of someone else, such as the author of your assigned reading.

The form of the thesis statement is important not only in making a clear statement but in making it in such a way that it governs or controls the organization of the whole composition. A good thesis statement tells not only where the composition is going but how it is going to get there. Much like a good outline, the thesis statement gives the plan for the composition.

The following suggestion may aid you in making the thesis statement not only a clear sentence but a good plan: *Divide the thesis statement into two or three parts.* Dividing your thesis statement gives both you and your reader a more precise preview of the composition as a whole.

Compare the following sentences. The first of each pair is an undivided thesis. The thought is expressed in one vague lump that gives no indication of the way in which the composition will proceed or how it will be organized. The second sentence of each pair is divided into two or three parts that suggest the organization of the composition.

1. People who live in the suburbs are alike. (UNDIVIDED)
   People who live in the suburbs are alike in *age*, *race*, and *politics*.
   (DIVIDED INTO THREE PARTS)
2. Capital punishment should be abolished. (UNDIVIDED)
   Capital punishment should be abolished because it is *useless* and *inhumane*.
   (DIVIDED INTO TWO PARTS)
3. The essay is a satire. (UNDIVIDED)
   The essay satirizes *younger* as well as *older* people. (DIVIDED INTO TWO PARTS)
4. Pollution constitutes a serious problem to humanity. (UNDIVIDED)

Air and *water* pollution constitute a serious problem to humanity.
(DIVIDED INTO TWO PARTS)

5. Life on this earth may soon be wiped out. (UNDIVIDED)
Plants, *animals*, and *people* may soon be wiped out. (DIVIDED INTO THREE PARTS)

The second sentence of each pair is a brief summary that tells not only where the composition is going but how it will get there. Consider the first example: *People who live in the suburbs are alike in age, race, and politics.* One can tell at a glance not only the subject of the composition but also how the composition will be organized. The subject, the similarity of suburbanites (that you may disagree is perfectly all right; the point is that you know the subject), is divided into three parts: age, race, and politics. One knows what to expect in the composition. Your reader knows and you know (if this is your subject). The division is as useful to you as it is to your reader. Suppose you lost track of your subject and the way in which you wanted to present it. Look back. There it is, all spelled out in the thesis.

IS IT ALL RIGHT TO CHANGE THE THESIS STATEMENT?

Yes! The thesis statement is not a sacred oath nor is it written in concrete. It is simply a way to think through and organize your discussion. As you write your composition, you may realize your thesis is not working out, that your plan is faulty, doesn't make sense, or makes writing the discussion too difficult. Perhaps you come up with a better idea, a better plan. In that case, rewrite or rearrange your thesis statement.

However, keep in mind that the **thesis** and **discussion must match:** Whatever the content and order in one is, so must be the content and order in the other. In the example given about the similarity of suburbanites, the discussion must begin with *age*, proceed to *race*, and then turn to *politics*. That is the content and order promised in the thesis statement. Don't promise one thing but deliver another. Of course, you might decide you prefer a different content or a different order in your discussion. In that case, rewrite or rearrange your thesis to agree with your discussion. However, be sure your thesis and your discussion line up and move in the same direction.

ARE THE DIVISIONS OF THE THESIS DESIGNED SIMPLY TO ORGANIZE THE DISCUSSION?

The division of the thesis statement is sometimes simply for the purpose of breaking down the thought into areas or aspects that make the discussion more orderly and manageable. However, more often the division is for the purpose of *supporting the thought*. The position, belief, or point of view you present in your thesis statement is more meaningful or convincing when it is supported. *Proof* is needed, in other words. *Why* do you think such and such? What is your *evidence*? What are your *reasons*? When you summarize or outline your major points of proof by stating them in your thesis statement, you straighten out your own thinking and you permit your reader to see in advance of your discussion not only what it is that you want to prove but also how you plan to prove it.

Compare the following pairs of sentences. The first of each pair makes an unsupported claim. That is, no proof, evidence, or reasoning is offered to support the position, belief, or point of view presented. The second sentence of each pair offers support.

1. It may rain today. (UNSUPPORTED)
    It may rain today because there are dark clouds in the sky and my barometer is falling. (SUPPORTED)

2. Mr. X thinks he has a cold or the flu. (UNSUPPORTED)
    Mr. X thinks he has a cold or the flu because he has a sore throat, a headache, and a fever. (SUPPORTED)

3. Ireland is a tourist's delight. (UNSUPPORTED)
    Ireland is a tourist's delight for three reasons: The country is beautiful, the people are friendly, and the prices are reasonable. (SUPPORTED)

4. Rachel Carson's thesis in *The Silent Spring* is that the indiscriminate use of chemical insecticides should be abolished. (UNSUPPORTED)
    Rachel Carson's thesis in *The Silent Spring* is that the indiscriminate use of chemical insecticides should be abolished, as it is unnecessarily poisoning wildlife and as there are better controls, such as the use of natural predators. (SUPPORTED)

5. Real estate, though it promises work and worry, is a good investment. (UNSUPPORTED)
    Real estate, though it promises work and worry, is a good investment in that it is substantial and relatively secure, it generally appreciates, and it offers tax advantages. (SUPPORTED)

The second sentence of each preceding pair, because it gives proof or reasons, is the more meaningful or convincing of the two. As a thesis statement, it would also be a better guide than the first. It would suggest both the content and the order of the whole composition.

Do Compositions Always Contain a Thesis Statement?

Compositions that are *expository* — that is, explain or discuss ideas and facts — require a thesis statement. Argumentative compositions demand a thesis statement also. These are the two types of compositions you are most often asked to write in college courses; therefore, it is important that you master and learn to think in terms of the thesis statement. You should be aware that there are other types of compositions, however, such as narrative and descriptive compositions, and these types may or may not require a thesis statement. If you learn to write so well that you decide to take a course in creative writing, for example, you should then be in a position to decide whether your composition needs a thesis statement. Meanwhile, assume it does.

Is the Thesis Always a Single Sentence?

In some cases, it may be simpler or clearer to break the thesis down into more than a single sentence, especially if the main idea of the composition is unusually complex or if the composition is long. In most cases, at least in the exercises in this book, you should be able to state the purpose or main idea in a single sentence.

Is the Division of the Thesis Statement Always Limited to Two or Three Parts or Supports?

In a short composition of four to eight paragraphs, which is the approximate length expected in your compositions, it is a good plan to limit the parts or supports of the main idea to two or three. Additional parts or supports would likely result in insufficient development of each part within the relative brevity of the composition as a whole. In a longer composition, however, the parts or supports might well exceed two or three.

SUMMARY

Begin your composition with a thesis statement that is precise in conveying the purpose or central idea of the composition. It is best to divide your thesis statement into two or three parts, in order to make clear not only what your composition is about, but exactly how it is organized or developed. You thus give a preview or overview of the entire composition.

CHAPTER 11   —

PRACTICING

THE

THESIS

STATEMENT

Before you begin to practice the thesis statement, it may be helpful for you to consider it in a way that has not yet been discussed. Another way to view the thesis is to see it as a condensed form of the paragraph. Take another look at Exercise 19 on page 107. As already stated, Exercise 19 is a special paragraph, in fact a summary in several sentences, capable of being expanded into a short composition. Condensed into one sentence, Exercise 19 could consist of a thesis statement with a three-part support, as follows:

Billboard advertising should be abolished along public highways because it is ugly and hinders the enjoyment of natural roadside beauty, because it is a distraction and therefore a danger to motorists, and because, since its purpose is to promote private business, it does not belong along public tax-supported highways.

Just as Exercise 19 can be expanded into a whole composition, so the preceding thesis statement can function in the same way. Notice that the argument in the sentence is supported. An unsupported version of the argument follows:

Billboard advertising should be abolished along public highways.

The unsupported version is useful in that it presents a subject capable of being developed into a composition. However, because of the lack of supports, it does not show how the subject will be developed, argued, or proved. It does not summarize the composition as a whole. Remember that a good thesis statement tells not only where the composition is going but also how it is going to get there. The first sentence, in which the argument is supported, is a far better guide than the second sentence. It makes the total plan of the composition clear.

THE MOST COMMON FORM OF THE SUPPORTED THESIS STATEMENT

Probably the most common form of the supported thesis statement is the one that *first states the subject and then presents the supports*. The supports are often introduced by words or expressions such as the following: *because, for, since, as, due to, by, in, in that*. A punctuation mark, the colon (:), may substitute for these words and serve the same purpose.

Examine the following:

1. Deems Taylor calls Richard Wagner a monster <u>because</u> Wagner was conceited, unstable, and selfish.
2. Attending a community college makes sense, <u>for</u> the quality of instruction is high and the cost is low.
3. Two years in the army provided me with valuable experience, <u>as</u> there, for the first time, I learned the value of discipline, neatness, and respect for authority.
4. Christmas is an exhausting experience <u>due</u> to the extra energy and tension it inspires.
5. *The Forsyte Saga* is an outstanding television experience <u>in that</u> it is a good old-fashioned story of an English family from 1879 to 1926, the many characters are all various and interesting, and the acting is superb.
6. The profession of law demands three important qualities of mind<u>:</u> the ability to analyze ideas, an interest in people, and patience with details.

EXERCISE E14. DEVELOP THESIS STATEMENTS WITH TWO OR THREE SUPPORTS

The following are unsupported thesis statements: They contain no proof, evidence, or reasoning to support the position, belief, or point of view expressed. Try to develop them into thesis statements with two or three supports. Use the common forms just given—that is, make the supports *follow* the subject and introduce them with words such as those in the preceding examples or with the colon (:) punctuation mark.

1. The Surgeon General has determined that cigarette smoking is dangerous.
2. A compact car is a wise purchase.
3. A career in nursing offers rewarding opportunities.
4. Writing a good composition can be an exhausting experience.
5. A good marriage depends on three important qualities in a couple.
6. Daytime television dramas are emotionally draining.
7. Men as well as women suffer from sexual stereotypes.
8. Four years of high school were (not) of great value to me.
9. Being a good police officer demands three important qualities of mind.
10. This world today is a dangerous place in which to live.
11. A dictionary is a good book to study.
12. Tennis (football, baseball, and so on) is a challenging sport.
13. Whales and other endangered species are important to protect.
14. Cooking and eating at home make sense.
15. A good vacation has three important ingredients.

OTHER FORMS OF THE SUPPORTED THESIS STATEMENT

The supports or breakdown of the subject sometimes precede it in the thesis statement for reasons of style or for the purpose of emphasis. Examine the following sentences, which illustrate the reverse order the thesis statement can take:

1. The bore, the brag, the flirt—these people typify most cocktail parties.
2. A grain of achievement, an avalanche of failure and frustration, and then the shroud of oblivion—these elements constitute the human condition.
3. To love and honor—these vows may be altered by circumstances.
4. Hunger and poverty plague a great portion of the world today.

The thesis statement sometimes announces a composition that aims to compare or contrast two or more subjects. Such a sentence requires special consideration with respect to form. Examine the following sentences.

1. Mr. X is short, fat, and outgoing, whereas Mr. Y is tall, slim, and shy.

2. Mr.. X and Mr. Y are similar in two ways: They are both rich, and they are both married to intelligent women.

3. Suburbanites tend to be conformists because they are similar in age, race, and politics, whereas city dwellers are less likely to conform due to their diversity in these respects.

4. Flying in an airplane is fast and noisy, whereas flying in a balloon is slow and quiet.

COPING WITH PROBLEMS IN WRITING THE SUPPORTED THESIS STATEMENT

Having begun to practice the most common form of the supported thesis statement, you may have met with some frustrating problems and wondered how to cope with them. Indeed, a good thesis statement is a challenge to write for a number of reasons, but with effort and practice, you should be able to master the problems.

First, *writing a supported thesis statement requires you to think through the main points of your composition, points that are summed up in the thesis*. It should be easy to sum up the main points once you have actually written the composition and know what it contains. If you have not written the composition but are simply practicing the thesis statement to learn its form and to think through the structure it represents, then you are on less familiar ground. In that case, you need to imagine what the composition might contain, what its main points would be. Hopefully, you will know something about the subject from your general experience and reading, and you will give it further thought as you write about it. However, *your practice thesis* will *necessarily* be *tentative or experimental*. You might think of it the way scientists view a *scientific hypothesis*, that is, as an *experimental conclusion to be tested and proved either right or wrong*. Your instructor may ask you and your classmates to share some of your practice thesis statements in class to see how well they hold up when examined and discussed, to see how well they are written, and to pool suggestions from the group for possible improvement. Such workshop sessions can be very helpful, but they are sometimes frustrating as well. You might keep in mind that learning to write a supported thesis statement is a complex matter. It is a process that takes time, effort, and patience. It should prove well worth your energy, however, because it will teach you to think and to organize your thoughts.

Another challenge is to *write the thesis statement* so the *supporting points*, though related, *are not repeated or overlapping*, two faults you can recognize in the following examples.

I avoid fast foods because they tend to be too salty, too high in calories, and too fattening.

It makes sense to buy a compact car because the purchase price is reasonable, the operating cost is low, and it saves on gas.

In the *first example* the problem is **repetition**, in this case saying the same thing in different words. What appear to be three supports are really only two, the second idea stated twice in differently worded versions. In the *second example* the problem is that the *second* and *third supports overlap*. *One support is a specific* and *the other* is a *general category in which the specific is contained*, the cost of gas being a part of the general cost of operating a car. One way to avoid this flaw is to decide in advance of writing your thesis whether your supports should consist of *general categories or specifics*. (Besides the cost of gas, other specifics within the general category of operating expense might include lubrication, oil change, tires, and other such expenses.) Whether you organize your supports by categories or by specifics may depend a good deal on how full or rich the subject is or how much you know about it. If you have a lot to say about the cost of gas, for example, and about one or two other related specifics, you might make each of them a main support of your thesis. However, remember that you must develop each support with a full paragraph or more in the discussion part of your composition. Think about it. Could you write a well-developed paragraph on the cost of gas? If not, you need a broader topic, that is, a category with enough specifics to build a good discussion paragraph.

Like the topic sentence studied earlier in this book, the ***thesis statement needs*** to be *clear* and *definite*, ***not vague*** and ***ambiguous***. Consider the following example:

Smoking should be banned in public places because it affects personal enjoyment and creates a safety hazard.

Exactly what is meant in the two supports is ***not clear***. First, the word *affects* by itself is vague. The probable intent is that smoking has an *adverse* effect on someone or something that the words *personal enjoyment* do not make clear. Whose enjoyment of what needs to be spelled out. In addition, the words *safety hazard* are ambiguous. Do they refer to secondhand smoke, fire, or something else? Be careful not to fall into the trap of thinking that you can explain later in the composition whatever the thesis does not make clear. Your readers cannot wait until the second page to understand what they are reading on the first page. You need to ***make yourself as clear as possible as you go along***. The thesis statement must be especially clear. The preceding statement might be improved in a number of ways. Here is one possibility:

Smoking should be banned in public places because it violates the rights of nonsmokers to breathe smoke-free and it creates a potential fire hazard.

You may discover that *the demands of the thesis statement sometimes pull you in opposite directions at the same time*. On the one hand, you should make the thesis as *concise* as you can. On the other, *you may find that to make it clear and definite rather* *than vague and ambiguous requires **additional words***, as in the preceding example. The improved version added 10 words to the original statement. However, it is improved because it is clearer and more definite, not because it is longer. ***Succinctness** is **still one of your objectives** in writing a supported thesis statement*. Say as much as you can, as clearly as you can, in as few words as possible. If these objectives try your patience by pulling you in two different directions at once, it may help to think of the thesis as a complex puzzle that needs to be solved very carefully.

Finally, as you work with the thesis statement, you may need to cope with ***mechanical problems*** such as sentence structure, grammar, or punctuation. Among its other requirements, *the thesis should be a **good sentence***. For example, the ***sentence structure should be parallel***. In the *following example*, the *structure* is ***not parallel***.

Jogging is a popular sport because it is good exercise and also for the scenery.

The first support in this thesis is a ***clause**, it is good exercise*, whereas the second support is a ***phrase*** (and not a very clear one), *for the scenery*. This difference in the structure of the two supports makes the sentence bumpy and unbalanced rather than smooth and even. To make the two supports line up better, ***both must be*** of the ***same construction***; that is, ***corresponding words, phrases, or clauses*** are needed in both. (See Chapter 15 for a fuller discussion of parallelism.) The preceding thesis could be corrected in several ways. One of them is the following:

Jogging is a popular sport because it provides good exercise for the body and a stimulating variety of scenery for the mind.

For further guidance with other mechanical requirements of the thesis statement or any good sentence, refer to Appendix B, "Correction Symbols," in the back of this book. In addition, you may find Chapter 4, "Practicing the Topic Sentence," useful, for almost all of what is presented there also applies to the thesis statement.

EXERCISE E15.   IDENTIFY FAULTINESS IN THESIS STATEMENTS

Each of the following thesis statements is faulty in some way. The defect may be that the supports of the thesis are (1) *repetitious* (saying the same thing in different words); (2) *overlapping* (one support is a general category and another is a specific within that category); (3) *vague* or *ambiguous* instead of clear and definite; or (4) *not parallel* (not of the same grammatical construction).

Write the letter "R" in the space next to the thesis statement if you think the supports are *repetitious*. Write the letter "O" if you think the supports are *overlapping*. Write the letters "V/A" if you think the supports are *vague* or *ambiguous*. Write the letters "NP" if you think the supports are *not parallel*.

You may wish to discuss and/or correct the statements once you have determined their faults.

_____ 1. I should lose weight to look better, to improve my health, and to lower my blood pressure.

_____ 2. My neighbors annoy me because their children play loud music and the barking of their dogs.

_____ 3. Many young people do not vote because they feel they have no representation in the government and because they feel no one in the government speaks for them.

_____ 4. The play is a big hit because of the cast, the music, and the star of the show.

_____ 5. Some students fail in college because they are lazy and unmotivated.

_____ 6. The volcano erupts to frighten people and when the goddess Pele is angry.

_____ 7. That exercise device increases endurance, conditions major muscle groups, and tones the thighs and hips.

_____ 8. Gum chewing should be prohibited in the classroom because it is a distraction and potential detriment to the environment.

_____ 9. Rap music does not appeal to some people because they think it lacks variety, is too repetitious, and too monotonous.

_____ 10. He likes to ride his motorcycle, renting movies, and to hang out at home with friends.

_____ 11. The candidate says he should be elected because he believes in patriotism and family values.

_____ 12. The hurricane made life miserable for the victims in three important ways: It destroyed their homes, it devastated their food supply, and it cut off their electricity.

_____ 13. His writing style is unimaginative, dull, and tedious.

_____ 14. She takes an ocean cruise in order to relax, to meet people, and for the pleasure of the food.

_____ 15. He faulted the University of Lipsync for its lack of academic standards, its mediocrity in teaching and scholarship, and its low admission requirements.

To pose a little greater challenge to you, the remaining five thesis statements have been written so they are faulty in more than one way. Each statement contains at least two defects, possibly even three. Use the system of letters ("R," "O," "V/A," or "NP") to identify the problems you find in the following:

_____ 16. Most fireplaces are wasteful, rob houses of heat, and pollute the air.

_____ 17. Singapore has become an economic power because of its manufacturing capabilities, its cheap and abundant labor force, and having people with a highly disciplined work ethic.

_____ 18. His conduct during the debate was childish, sophomoric, and acting immaturely.

_____ 19. I'll spend the summer at my cousin's farm to learn to feed the chickens, to milk the cows, to ride horses, and animal husbandry.

_____ 20. Anyone can see that John is a gentleman because of his politeness to everyone, his always correct manners, and how gracious he is in every situation.

EXERCISE E16. DEVELOP THESIS STATEMENTS IN RESPONSE TO QUESTIONS OR PROBLEMS

You will frequently need to formulate your thesis statements in response to questions or problems given by your instructors. The answers or solutions may not come to you easily in the form of good, clear, well-supported thesis statements. You may need to think and struggle over them. However, with effort you should cope very well.

The following questions or statements are designed to give you practice in developing thesis statements in response to questions or problems you might encounter in some of your college classes. Try to respond to them by writing thesis statements that are divided into two or three parts or supports. Generally you will want to use the most common form of the supported thesis statement, stating the subject first and then presenting the supports, but you may try out any of the forms you think appropriate. Study the following example, and then proceed to the exercises.

Example

QUESTION: What well-known person do you admire?

ANSWER: I admire Barbara Jordan for her outspoken political independence and her forceful, dignified presence.

1. Who should be the next president of the United States? Why?

2. Should children who have AIDS be permitted to attend public schools? Why or why not?

3. What are the primary benefits of a college or university education?

4. Is it good for parents to sacrifice for their children, or should parents look after their own interests first?

5. How do you account for the rise of sports figures as superstars?

6. Present arguments for or against single parenting as a choice or a necessity.

7. With which objectives of the women's movement do you agree or disagree?

8. What is the essence of soul food?

9. Is fidelity important or necessary in marriage?

10. Compare two presidents of the United States.

11. Give arguments for or against a woman's right to choose abortion.

12. Give arguments for or against divorce when there are young children involved.

13. Navajo weaving (rugs, blankets) is highly prized for many reasons. What are some of them?

14. What famous person, living or dead, do you admire and why?

15. What are the advantages or disadvantages of living in a small town, a city, or the country?

16. Which professional sport is most popular or well attended and why?

17. What does it mean to be poor?

18. What is your idea of an ideal job?

19. What importance do you place on the wilderness and wildlife?

20. If you could travel anywhere in the world, where would you most like to go and why?

21. What arguments can you present for or against marriage, for or against living with a person rather than being married to him or her?

22. Is the space program or the exploration of space important? Why or why not?

23. Is religious training important in the rearing of a child? Why or why not?

24. What do you know or think about the People's Republic of China, Chinese culture, or the Chinese people?

25. Do you think homosexuals are sick or healthy people? Except for their sexual preferences, are they like or different from heterosexuals?

26. Should every college student be required to study a foreign language? Why or why not?

27. Do you believe or have any faith in astrology? Why or why not?

28. Should euthanasia be legalized? Why or why not?

29. What place has television in your life? Do you prefer watching it to reading a good book or conversing with people?

30. What is your view of the relocation of Japanese Americans during World War II?

31. Do you honor your mother and father? Why or why not?

32. Is there more or less racism in America now than there was ten years ago?

33. What job, profession, or career do you think holds the most prestige? Why?

34. What is your most difficult subject in college? Why?

35. Explain the popularity of a certain form of music, such as country and western, rock, rap, or blues.

36. What is the finest sports car on the market today? Explain.

37. Do you have trouble trying to understand or make up your mind about a national or international situation, problem, or conflict? If so, about which situation or problem are you confused, and what is the nature of your confusion?

38. Are rodeos cruel to animals? Why or why not?

39. Which of your talents do you value the most and why?

40. Compare Martin Luther King, Jr., to Malcolm X.

41. Which Hispanic American do you most admire and why?

42. Do you think the current president of the United States is doing a good job? Why or why not?

43. What are your greatest fears or hopes about the future?

44. If you cold live in some age other than your own, which would it be and why?

45. Women do most of the cooking at home, but most of the world's great chefs are men. True or false? Why or why not?

46. Do you think the Equal Rights Amendment is a dead issue? Why or why not?

47. Which bills do you most dislike or resent having to pay? Why?

48. What is your prized material possession and why do you value it?

49. Do you believe in any form of censorship? Why or why not?

50. What drugs do you approve or disapprove of and why?

⌐

S U M M A R Y

The main idea of your thesis statement should be divided into two or three parts or supports. In the most common form of the supported thesis statement, you first state the main idea or subject and then proceed to state the parts or supports of it. The supports are often introduced by such words as *because*, *as*, or *due to* or by a punctuation mark, the colon (:). Sometimes the order of the thesis statement is reversed, the supports preceding the main idea for reasons of style or for emphasis. Another form of the thesis statement announces a comparison or contrast of two or more subjects.

You will find that all forms of the supported thesis statement require effort and practice to be mastered because they demand careful thinking and organizing. The effort and practice should prove worthwhile, however, because the skill you acquire will aid you greatly in all your college courses.

CHAPTER 12   ⟀

Evolve a Plan

When you first consider a subject and think about writing a composition about it, you may not be sure exactly what direction you will want to take with it. If you are unfamiliar with the subject, you will feel especially hesitant. You will need to do some research, study and think about it, possibly discuss it with people who know the topic well. If you are already familiar with the subject, it will probably still require some thought and imagination, some mulling over, before a plan for your composition begins to evolve in your mind and on paper. You may need to plunge into a rough draft without a plan and muddle about for a time, writing this way and that, until a light begins to dawn and something worthwhile starts to take shape. Then you might be ready to sketch out your first tentative thesis statement.

While you are in the rough draft stage, it might be well to think of your thesis, like every other aspect of your composition, as experimental. You may change your mind, try out different ideas, shift things around, even start over with a whole new approach. You may write several rough drafts before you are satisfied. However, once your direction is clear and your ideas and their development are firm, you should be ready to write your final draft. Your thesis statement will then become a fixed plan, an exact indication of the way the discussion is to be organized.

150

FOLLOW YOUR PLAN . . . EXACTLY!

If you are in command of the thesis statement, you should have no trouble organizing the discussion. However, an inexperienced writer sometimes fails to see there is a direct connection between the thesis and the discussion. He or she may write a beautiful thesis but then follow it with a discussion that is totally unrelated to it. Be sure you do not make this mistake! You need to understand that the thesis statement announces the plan of the discussion. Do not plan one thing and then do another. If you want to do another, plan another, but once you decide what it is, follow your plan!

The thesis statement gives an exact plan, and the discussion must *follow* it *exactly*. The thesis is divided into two to three parts or supports. These parts are restated in the discussion, becoming the topic sentences that begin the discussion paragraphs. The *order* of the thesis must also be maintained in the discussion. That is, the first part of the thesis becomes the first topic of the discussion. The second part is discussed next, and if there is a third part, it follows. The *wording* of the thesis is also approximated in the topic sentences of the discussion. The key words are the same, or for variety, synonyms or phrases meaning the same thing are used. The thesis statement sets up the basic structure of the discussion, and the discussion must not violate the thesis plan.

Examine Figure 12 – 1, which gives an overview of a whole composition based on a thesis statement that has three parts (*age*, *race*, and *politics*). The composition in this case is five paragraphs long, beginning with an introductory paragraph (the thesis statement may or may not constitute the entire introduction) and ending with a concluding paragraph. Notice that the topic sentences of the three discussion paragraphs (only the topic sentences are given, not the entire paragraphs) duplicate the arrangement of the thesis statement. The order is the same, and the wording, with some slight variation, is close to that of the thesis. In other words, the discussion follows the thesis plan. The two are an unmistakable match.

THE PLAN IS THE SAME, REGARDLESS OF LENGTH

If the composition were longer, each part of the thesis might be discussed in more than a single paragraph, but the principle of order and wording would remain the same. Suppose each part of the thesis in the preceding illustration were to be discussed in two paragraphs instead of one. Then it would be necessary to break each part into two subparts. For instance, consider the first topic sentence, "Suburbanites are alike in age." This topic might be divided into two parts (and two topic sentences) as follows: "Suburban adults are alike in age." "Suburban children are also similar in age." The first of these sentences might open up the discussion of age, and the second could continue it in a second paragraph. After that, the discussion would take up the

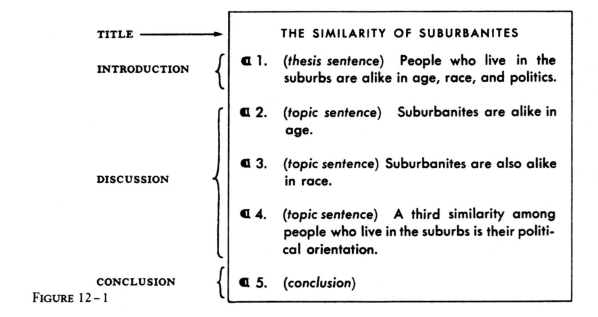

TITLE

INTRODUCTION

DISCUSSION

CONCLUSION

FIGURE 12–1

THE SIMILARITY OF SUBURBANITES

❡ 1. (*thesis sentence*) People who live in the suburbs are alike in age, race, and politics.

❡ 2. (*topic sentence*) Suburbanites are alike in age.

❡ 3. (*topic sentence*) Suburbanites are also alike in race.

❡ 4. (*topic sentence*) A third similarity among people who live in the suburbs is their political orientation.

❡ 5. (*conclusion*)

next topic given in the thesis. This, too, might be divided into two parts, and so with the third part of the thesis.

Notice the word *also* in the second of the two topic sentences, and be reminded of the need for transitional words to provide continuity (see Chapter 5) within the paragraph and between paragraphs. A well-organized discussion does not lose its reader along the way. It does everything possible to guide the reader. You need to signal your reader (see p. 133) when you are continuing in the same direction or changing direction in your discussion. Point the way so your reader can follow you.

WEIGHT OR LENGTH OF EACH PART DEPENDS ON THE THESIS

Ordinarily equal weight or length of discussion is given to each part of the thesis statement. In the illustration on the subject of suburbanites, for example, the three parts of the thesis (age, race, and politics) would be discussed at the same length — a paragraph of approximately the same length for each or two or three paragraphs for each. Nothing in the thesis suggests that one part is to be given more emphasis than another, and thus the discussion must treat each of the three equally.

It is also possible for the discussion to emphasize one part of the thesis more than another *if* that is what the thesis statement indicates the discussion will do. Remember, thesis and discussion must match! Suppose the thesis in the illustration on suburbanites were changed, for example, as follows:

People who live in the suburbs are alike in age, race, and especially in politics.

Now the thesis draws special attention to the last of its three parts, and therefore that part must be discussed more fully than the other two. The thesis might be changed in still another (and perhaps more current) way as follows:

People who live in the suburbs are more alike in age and politics than they are in race.

Now the thesis suggests greater similarity in the first two parts than it does in the third, and the discussion must follow accordingly. The most important point to remember about the relationship between the thesis statement and the discussion is that they must match. One (the thesis) announces the other (the discussion).

EXERCISE E17.   WRITE TOPIC SENTENCES THAT MIGHT BEGIN DISCUSSION PARAGRAPHS

The exercises that follow are designed to give you practice in organizing a discussion. Select a number of the following thesis statements, and for each one write the topic sentences that might begin each paragraph of the discussion. Notice that some of the thesis statements are divided into two parts and some contain three parts. Write your topic sentences accordingly. Take care that your topic sentences match the order and approximate the wording of the thesis statement. The key words should be the same or, for variety, synonyms or phrases meaning the same thing may be used. Remember to use transitional words where needed. Use the following example to guide you.

Example

(THESIS) People who live in the suburbs are alike in age, race, and politics.

(TOPIC SENTENCES) Suburbanites are alike in age.
Suburbanites are also alike in race.
A third similarity among people who live in the suburbs is their political orientation.

1. Cultivating a vegetable garden has three important benefits: It requires needed exercise, it produces fresh and nourishing food, and it saves money.

2. Jogging is good for both the body and the mind.

3. Children can be a headache when they are noisy, demanding, and destructive.

4. The Guessa is a fine automobile because the body is well designed, the motor is powerful, and the car is economical to operate.

5. The word *discrimination* has a positive as well as a negative meaning.

6. Poetry can be classified into three types: narrative, dramatic, and lyric.

7. Wilderness is needed in Alaska to preserve the polar bear and the caribou.

8. A good composition is well organized, well developed, and imaginative.

9. Three of my favorite comics are "Fred Basset," "For Better or for Worse," and "Doonesbury."

10. The excitement of the auction was due to the quality of the merchandise, the talent of the auctioneer, and the competitiveness of the bidders.

11. The female praying mantis is a remarkable creature that has five eyes, turns from green to brown as leaves do, and eats her spouse after mating with him.

12. Navajo rugs from the Two Gray Hills area are very finely woven and very expensive.

13. Television performs three important services: It entertains, it instructs, and it induces sleep.

14. Women are still struggling for rights and opportunities equal to those enjoyed by men.

15. Three of the most intelligent mammals of the ocean are also the most abused: the whale, the porpoise, and the dolphin.

DEVELOPMENT WITHIN THE PARAGRAPH MUST STAY ON COURSE

Keep in mind that while the thesis statement plots the course of the discussion, and the topic sentence of each paragraph holds that direction, the development within the paragraphs must also stay on course! It is not enough for the structure to be trim and in perfect order. The development of the discussion paragraphs must give that frame support and stiffening. Remember that each paragraph must contain no more than one central idea and must have unity. (See pp. 22–26.) Stick to the subject! Do not be distracted by interesting but unrelated ideas. Just as the topic sentences must follow the thesis plan, so the development of the discussion paragraphs must follow the topic sentences.

SUMMARY

Organizing the discussion is a matter of following the thesis statement, which announces the plan of the discussion. The parts or supports of the thesis statement determine the content, the order, and the approximate wording of the topic sentences that begin the paragraphs of the discussion. The topic sentences, in turn, indicate the organization of the paragraphs.

CHAPTER 13

DEVELOPING

THE

DISCUSSION

IS ANYBODY LISTENING?

Think about the meaning of the word *discussion*. When the word is applied to speaking rather than writing, it means two people or a group of people talking about or exchanging ideas about a given subject. In writing, of course, only one person does the "talking," but it is important to keep in mind that another person, your reader, is "listening." Your reader, furthermore, is an *active*, not a passive listener. In her mind she is constantly putting questions to your discussion. She asks such questions as "What do you mean by that?" and "What is your proof?" Your reader also has ideas of her own. She has been around, lived life, and been exposed to the kinds of issues or ideas you are likely to discuss. She may know quite a bit about your topic. She waits to see in your discussion how much you know and have thought about. If you disappoint her, she calls to you from the margin of your paper, "Develop!"

THINK ABOUT YOUR READER

Prepare your discussion with your reader in mind. Think about your reader as you write. Imagine you are speaking to a live person who is also a friendly stranger. He wants to know what you mean, but he doesn't know you well enough to guess your meaning. You have to spell it out for him. *Say* what you mean. Your reader is also not easily convinced. He hangs back. He has doubts. He thinks of counterarguments. He

156

waits to be impressed. He wants you to succeed, but he wants you to work at it, to make your discussion compelling, convincing, complete. Nothing is as frustrating to your reader as a promising discussion that doesn't deliver, goes nowhere, or dabbles where it ought to dig into a subject. Nothing is as pleasing to your reader as a discussion that fulfills its promises and realizes its potentialities. You can make your reader your adversary or your ally, depending on how well you develop your discussion.

WHAT DOES IT MEAN TO DEVELOP?

The word *develop* means to explain more clearly or fully, to enlarge on, to elaborate on, to bring out the possibilities of a topic, or to make it better known. In photography, the word means to make a picture visible. It is easy to apply this meaning to writing. An undeveloped discussion is like exposed but undeveloped film. Both have potential, but the possibilities of both lurk in the murk. Only through the process of development do they both gradually become clearer and clearer until they are finally sharp and vivid.

STUDY EXAMPLES

Following are examples of undeveloped discussion paragraphs and their improved, more fully developed versions. Notice that although the first paragraph in each set of two is shorter than the second, insufficient *length* is not its only or even its most important problem. Making a paragraph longer may or may not make it better, as a long paragraph may be as unclear or as unconvincing as a short one, if not more so.

The following three sets of paragraphs illustrate three different problems and their solutions. In the first paragraph that follows (A^1), the discussion does not satisfy the reader's need to know exactly what the writer means. The picture is murky rather than clear. As you read the paragraph, think about what is missing or what needs to be developed to satisfy the reader's question: *What do you mean by that?*

A^1 Another reason some people collect early California paintings is to satisfy their nostalgia for California as it once was or as they remember it. So much has changed that it is difficult to imagine the state as it was before it became so heavily developed and populated. However, early California paintings clarify this vision of the past and satisfy the longing of some people to return to it.

A^2 Another reason some people collect early California paintings is to satisfy their nostalgia for California as it once was or as they remember it. For example, they may want to visualize Yosemite when it was inhabited by Indians before it became the white man's park. They may want to see Spanish missions such as Santa Barbara or San Juan Bautista as they once were or other early settlements such as Fort Ross when it was occupied by Russian fur traders. San Francisco Bay with the old sailing ships in it or the Golden Gate before the bridge was built may hold a fascination. People may want to see San Jose when it was a sleepy little town or Berkeley when it was rolling hills and only a few farms. So much has changed that it is difficult to imagine the state as it was before it became so heavily developed and populated. However, early California paintings clarify this vision of the past and satisfy the longing of some people to return to it.

The second paragraph is clearer than the first in satisfying the reader's need to know exactly what the writer means. The examples of what some early California paintings depict help the reader understand the exact nature of the collector's nostalgia and specifically what he or she looks for and enjoys in these paintings. The subject is not so vague as it is in the first paragraph, becoming sharper and more vivid through example.

In the next paragraph the problem is not only being clear but being convincing. The first paragraph that follows makes claims but does not support them with evidence. As you read the paragraph, think about what is needed to satisfy the question: *What is your proof?*

B¹ Life — or death — looks truly absurd at times. A person may live his life very reasonably, taking few chances, yet he may be killed by an impulsive madman. On the other hand, a person may live quite dangerously, taking great risks, fighting in a war, perhaps, or simply overexposing himself to hazard or possible accident, yet he may die under the most innocuous circumstances. Life is not reasonable or rational. Living or dying often means confronting the absurd.

B² Life — or death — looks truly absurd at times. A person may live his life very reasonably, taking few chances, yet he may be killed by an impulsive madman. To illustrate, recently eight people were minding their own business, working in a Miami machine shop, when a disgruntled customer walked in and, without warning, blasted them into oblivion with a shotgun. The victims were ordinary people doing their daily work, and there was no way they could have anticipated the disaster or protected themselves. According to police, the killer "just went nuts." On the other hand, a person may live quite dangerously, taking great risks, fighting in a war, perhaps, or simply overexposing himself to hazard or possible accident, yet he may die under the most innocuous circumstances. The classic example is Albert Camus, the French writer who had been active in the Resistance movement during World War II. He was working in the theater when he was killed in an automobile accident after he decided at the last moment not to take the train but to return to Paris in a friend's car instead. In his pocket was found his unused railway ticket. Just as senseless and ironic was the death of Calvin Simmons, formerly the young conductor of the Oakland Symphony Orchestra. Resting from a strenuous schedule, he took a canoe out on a quiet pond in upstate New York. Although he was an experienced canoeist and had been to that pond many times before, his canoe overturned and he drowned. A young woman camping along the pond had got out her camera to record the peaceful twilight scene of the man in his canoe; instead, she witnessed his demise. With a brilliant career already established, an international reputation on the way, Simmons must have had many close calls as he traveled the world by plane, train, and car to keep up his frantic pace. Yet he died at 32 in a quiet pond in the wilderness. Thus life is not reasonable or rational. Living or dying often means confronting the absurd.

The second paragraph, unlike the first, presents evidence to support its claims. Because it supports and proves what it claims, it is more convincing and believable than the first. Keep in mind that it is not very meaningful to fill a discussion with unsubstantiated statements. You need to prove them with evidence, example, and further explanation to make them meaningful and convincing.

In the first paragraph that follows, evidence is needed not only to support the topic but to permit the reader to *participate* in the writer's experience. As you may see, the writer has left the heart out of the paragraph, for there is little indication of what has *caused* the intense reaction described at the end of the paragraph. Therefore, the experience is difficult for the reader to feel and understand.

C¹ One of my most frightening experiences occurred one summer on a two-lane highway in the Sierra mountains when I was driving back from Pinecrest Lake to the Bay Area. My friend Shirley and I had met Jim, a friend of hers, and two other young men at the lake, and we all enjoyed the lake together, as well as the discovery that the cars Jim and I drove were almost identical. When it was time to go home, we all decided that our twin convertible Fords should not be separated, so we followed each other down the mountains at a rather rapid pace, Shirley riding in Jim's car ahead of mine, one of the other men riding with me. With tops down, radios blaring, we spun turns as if we were immortal, laughing and making signs to each other from car to car. There was a sharp bend in the road where I lost sight of Jim's car. Then suddenly, going much too fast to stop, I discovered his car stopped in the road ahead of me. The next thing I knew I had got around Jim's car and was ahead of it, stopped and shaking while the others marveled at my maneuver that may have saved our lives.

C² One of my most frightening experiences occurred one summer on a two-lane highway in the Sierra mountains when I was driving back from Pinecrest Lake to the Bay Area. My friend Shirley and I had met Jim, a friend of hers, and two other young men at the lake, and we all enjoyed the lake together as well as the discovery that the cars Jim and I drove were almost identical. When it was time to go home, we all decided that our twin convertible Fords should not be separated, so we followed each other down the mountains at a rather rapid pace, Shirley riding in Jim's car ahead of mine, one of the other men riding with me. With tops down, radios blaring, we spun turns as if we were immortal, laughing and making signs to each other from car to car. There was a sharp bend in the road where I lost sight of Jim's car. Then suddenly, going much too fast to stop, I discovered his car stopped in the road ahead of me. The three in the car ahead turned in horror at what was about to happen, but then I spotted a trail winding up an embankment and around a tree just in back and to the right of them. It looked like an impossible route, for the bank could easily flip my convertible over, or I might just as easily run into the tree, but I had to try. Up we went, my companion turning green as he hung on, my concentration divided into too many parts: alternating gas and brake; turning the wheel; returning, while dirt kicked up and flew all over us; the tree scratching my car, our faces and arms. Then we skidded past the tree and miraculously bounded our way back down to the highway again, ahead of the car we had been following. I stopped my car, but I could not stop shaking while Shirley and Jim told about the traffic tieup that had blocked them. My passenger was speechless, but the others marveled at my maneuver that may have saved our lives.

The second paragraph, unlike the first, explains the *cause* of the reaction with which the paragraph ends, supplying the details needed to permit the reader to participate in the experience the writer has had, to follow the action and feel the terror of the near catastrophe. After reading the paragraph, the reader can say, "I see what you mean."

In developing your discussion paragraphs, keep in mind the reader's questions:

1. What do you mean by that?
2. What is your proof?

To these questions, add another:

3. How can I participate?

Make your meaning clear to your reader through explanation and example, using synonyms when needed. Support and prove your statements with convincing evidence. In addition, permit your reader to participate in your experiences, to feel and understand them, by explaining the causes, not just the results, of your reactions.

Do Not Simply Make the Discussion Longer

As mentioned earlier, developing a discussion is not simply a matter of making it longer. In fact, you make your discussion deadly dull by laboring it — that is, by overworking it with seemingly endless development. You should also avoid wordiness and repetition. As you develop your discussion, check to see you are really advancing it and making it more meaningful, not simply making it drag on and on. When you have made your point, stop!

Know Your Subject

A weak or poorly developed discussion is vague, too general, and/or not illustrated. It views its subject from too great a distance, with uncertainty, seeing it as a dim lump or an indefinite blur. It may be the writer does not know enough about the subject to write about it at all, much less with the particularity that is called for in a good discussion. Be sure you *know your subject*! A good writer always writes from experience, or acquires the experience that is necessary for good writing. If you have trouble developing your discussion, perhaps you need to consult materials at the library or go elsewhere to learn what you need to know before you can write about it.

EXERCISE E18. REVISE AND DEVELOP UNDERNOURISHED PARAGRAPHS

The exercises that follow are undernourished paragraphs that need revision and development. As you consider them, think about the reader's questions: (1) What do you mean by that? (2) What is your proof? (3) How can I participate? These questions should help guide you to the necessary corrections or developments. You may decide the following paragraphs need revision in one or more of these ways:

1. The exact meaning may be unclear. The paragraph may call for examples to clarify meaning and explanation and the use of synonyms to clarify certain words or terms.

2. The paragraph may be unconvincing or lack proof. It may call for evidence to support its claims. Explanation and example may be needed to make statements meaningful and believable.

3. The discussion, by presenting only the result and not the cause of something, may make it difficult or impossible for readers to participate in, feel, or understand the subject. The paragraph may call for detailing the action or event that produced the reaction given in the discussion. Such a paragraph will call for you to make up or invent a story in which readers can participate so they can feel and understand what is said in the paragraph.

4. The paragraph may simply be too brief and call for further development in one or more of the ways previously suggested.

The subjects of all the paragraphs that follow are relatively simple, so no specialized knowledge is required to develop them. Consequently, you must use your imagination as well as your reasoning ability to invent the development needed. Select a number of the following exercises and repair and develop them as you think necessary.

The dots (•) in the exercises indicate the points at which revision or development is appropriate, though you may be selective and not wish to develop every point. There is no need to change existing sentences. Just supply what is missing or needed.

1. Sometimes I feel sure my dog is my best friend. We are perfect companions. She understands me, and I understand her.• We get along well together, and we like a lot of the same things.• When I feel unloved by people, I am grateful for my dog, my friend who never deserts me.

2. *Star Wars* is one of the best movies I have ever seen. The action is exciting, and the special effects are fabulous.• The characters are good, too.• I liked the robots especially.• *Star Wars* lives up to its billing. It is a fantastic space odyssey nobody should miss.

3. English is my hardest class this semester, which doesn't surprise me. I've never been good in English, not even in high school, where it was a lot easier than it is in college.• I have trouble especially with compositions.• I just can't write. My instructor says I could be good if I tried, but I'm not interested, I guess.

4. Marijuana should be legalized because it is a benevolent drug. It makes people feel good.• It does not make them nasty the way alcohol does.• It does not have the bad aftereffects, either.• It is hard to understand why some people oppose the legalization of marijuana.

5. Teenagers are crazy about most video games, though they like some better than others.• These favorites are fascinating for reasons many older people do not understand.• Parents worry and wonder about the powerful grip of video games on their kids.

6. Barbara is a very blunt person. She is not afraid to speak her mind.• Sometimes she is so frank that I wonder how she keeps her friends.• Barbara calls her behavior being honest. I call it Barbara Blunt.

7. If disco dancing is on the way out, one may speculate about what the next rage will be. It might be something fast or slow.● It might be something complicated or very simple.● No doubt people will keep dancing!

8. My boss is difficult to get along with. She takes her job too seriously, and she treats the workers under her very badly.● Several of them have quit in the last few months because of her.● I'd like to quit and be done with her, too, but I can't afford to.

9. He was a loner, which was surprising because he had a lot of charm. When he told me what had happened to him, however, I understood his caution with people. He had been badly hurt as a teenager.● It was difficult for him to forget a hurt like that.

10. The trouble with many young people today is that they are lazy. They don't want to work.● They want money, but they don't want to earn it.● They want an easy life.● Young people used to have to work for a living. Now they play and get paid for it.

11. The divorce was a relief because the marriage had been a tragedy. They were not a perfect match to begin with.● They were very different kinds of people.● He was also unfaithful to her.● Then she became a nag.● He grew insulting.● The children became nervous and neurotic.● The divorce made all concerned feel reborn.

12. Disney World attracts people of all ages, not just children. There is much to see at Disney World and many activities that can be enjoyed by everyone.● It is no wonder the place is popular.

13. Housework is a dubious challenge to every homemaker. It is an accomplishment to be proud of when he or she manages to keep an orderly and smoothly running home, but the everyday task of doing it is hardly romantic.● The job requires fortitude as much as finesse.

14. Mildred is worn and weary. She has worked hard all her life, often doing incredibly difficult and draining labor.● She deserves a rest. Mildred has more than earned her retirement benefits.

15. A sports car is a must for anyone who wants top performance in an automobile. A sports car is superior to a standard or compact car in every way.● No other type of car performs as well as a sports car.

S U M M A R Y

It is important to think about your reader as well as your subject as you develop your discussion. To make your discussion clear and convincing, keep in mind the reader's questions, "What do you mean by that?" and "What is your proof?" To permit your reader to follow and feel experiences you relate, remember a third question, "How can I participate?" and supply the details needed of actions or events, not simply your reactions to them, so that the reader can understand them. Be careful to clarify general statements and to support them with specific explanation and example. Know your subject, and develop your discussion of it so that it fulfills its promises and realizes its potentialities.

CHAPTER 14

INTRODUCING,

CONCLUDING,

AND

TITLING

THE

SHORT

COMPOSITION

Introductory and concluding paragraphs are special, and different from discussion paragraphs. First, they are relatively short. The introduction may consist simply of one sentence, the thesis, although stated by itself without some preparation, the thesis may strike readers somewhat like a plunge into cold water. The composition may conclude even more abruptly with the final sentence of the last discussion paragraph, but the suddenness of such an ending can be unsettling. Instead of causing readers to reflect on the composition as a whole, such an ending may prompt them to see if the ink is dry or to search for a missing page. These extremes are not the desired goals of either the introduction or the conclusion, but brevity is. Three to five sentences, approximately, should suffice for each in a short composition.

A second way introductory and concluding paragraphs differ from discussion paragraphs is in their tendency to make general rather than specific statements or to typify rather than specify with a teaser or anecdote leading to the thesis sentence. The introduction approaches the subject of the composition and declares what it *will be*, but the subject *is not* discussed at that point except in the most general terms. The conclusion performs a similar function, only in reverse. Standing back from the subject, the conclusion indicates what it *has been*, and although the conclusion may make a final comment on the subject, it contains no further specific discussion of it. Such specific or concrete discussion is the task of the discussion paragraphs.

Finally, as already suggested, introductory and concluding paragraphs differ from discussion paragraphs in purpose or function. The purpose of the introduction is to prepare readers for the subject, to engage their interest in it, to explain it if necessary, and then to lead to the discussion of it. The purpose of the conclusion is to bring the discussion to a close, to summarize it briefly if necessary, to give its point in a culminating statement if possible, and to leave readers reflective and satisfied.

How Is the Introduction Organized?

Organize your introduction as follows:

1. Write an opening sentence or two to attract readers' attention and to focus their interest on the thesis or subject matter of the composition.
2. If necessary, write a sentence or two, either before the thesis or after it, to give background on the subject, to set the limits of the discussion, or to clarify the meaning of the key words to be used.
3. Write your thesis sentence.

How Is the Conclusion Organized?

Organize your conclusion as follows:

1. Make a general statement (a sentence or two) about the subject that will signal for readers a shift in focus from discussion to conclusion.
2. Write a sentence or two that summarizes or touches on the main points of the discussion.
3. If possible, end with a culminating sentence or one that gives special emphasis to the discussion.

CONSIDER SOME INTRODUCTORY TECHNIQUES

Keeping in mind that the main objective of an introduction is to be clear and concise, and that the most vital pat of the introduction is the thesis statement, you may find it helpful to consider some common techniques for writing introductions. These methods may help you get started and give your introductions greater smoothness, variety, and interest. Of course, you must remember that your subject matter or approach to it determines which of these techniques is not valuable or appropriate. Be sure your introductory statements are always *to the point of your thesis*, in keeping with both the content and mood of your subject. Be selective in your use of them. Among these techniques are the following:

A. Dramatize or present part of an anecdote. A vigorous way to begin your introduction is to present a brief dramatic scene or part of an interesting or humorous story, as in the introductions on pages 190, 203, and 208. In the opening two to three sentences of your introduction, it is impossible to tell a complete story, but you can present a representative part of it if you plan it carefully. The part might consist of a momentary glimpse of someone or something you will discuss later in your composition but wish to characterize beforehand, or it might be a highlight or preview of an incident you will present in a more complete form in your discussion.

B. Begin with a quotation. You may find a statement in such sources as plays, novels, short stories, poems, songs, newspapers, and magazines (sometimes even in textbooks) that you think captures or sums up an idea better than you can. The statement, properly acknowledged and set within quotation marks, may get your composition off to a good start. Be careful that the quotation is not too long, however. If it seems to be, consider using only part of it. A long quotation tends to drag down a composition, especially in an introduction, which should be as lively as possible. Moreover, your readers want to hear from *you* early in your introduction. Hence you should follow the quotation with your own words, making your use of it obvious. For examples of introductions using quotations, turn to pages 198 and 205.

C. Surprise with an unexpected point of view. One way to grab readers' attention is to begin your introduction with a point of view they do not expect or to contradict what you think they assume as true or right. Such an approach may catch your readers off guard and make them sit up and take notice. Be sure you startle your readers with cause, however, and know what you are doing, because you are obliged to make your unusual point of view meaningful, not just surprising. For examples of such introductions, turn to page 192.

D. Begin with a question. A rhetorical question is one to which no answer is expected or to which only one answer may be made—in this case, the answer presented in the thesis statement. The rhetorical question is a device to attract reader participation, that is, to engage readers in thinking actively about the question asked before they are led to the writer's conclusion as stated in the thesis statement. It is a somewhat worn technique that should be used with discretion. So if you decide to begin your introduction with a question, make it a good one. You will find an example of this device in the introduction on page 210.

E. Build background.   Sometimes the most forceful way to lead to the thesis sentence is to present background information in a series of statements that steadily build toward and strengthen the thesis. This method is particularly effective because it involves readers in the subject right from the beginning and continues to develop their interest until the climactic presentation of the thesis at the end of the introductory paragraph. This is perhaps one of the more difficult techniques because it calls for considerable knowledge of or experience with the subject, as well as sensitivity and skill in building the paragraph with increasing intensity. It is quite a rewarding challenge, however. For an example, see pages 192 and 194.

F. Combine these techniques or simplify them.   These introductory techniques are sometimes combined and can also be simplified. For instance, an anecdote can include a quotation (to be distinguished from dialogue, also set within quotation marks), or a rhetorical question may precede a surprise point of view. A dramatic scene can be simplified (not without losing some luster, however) by summing it up in a sentence rather than showing it acted out. Background information can also be shortened. As you practice writing introductions, experiment to see what works best for you.

Make the Conclusion Short and Simple
✑

You are essentially finished by the time you reach your conclusion, but if your discussion has been successful, it has gathered a momentum that needs to be slowed down before it is stopped. Your readers, who have been propelled along by your discussion, need a chance to shift gears, take a backward glance, and then come to a rest. This process is not complicated and should not be dragged out. Make your conclusion short and simple.

Study the conclusions in the model composition in Chapter 16 and notice how they are constructed. First, a general statement about the subject is made, to signal readers to shift their perspective from the specifics of the preceding discussion to the subject or discussion as a whole. This statement is usually followed by a sentence that touches on the main points of the discussion (which are taken from the thesis) or summarizes them. Finally, there may be a closing statement for special emphasis. The composition should not end abruptly or fade away. The end should come naturally, the main purpose completed, the final statement made.

GIVE THE COMPOSITION A TITLE

All formal compositions written in college are expected to have a title. You might think of this task as the fun part of composition writing. It's what you do near the end of your hard work on the composition, when you are ready to relax and reread your work (before you dash off to deliver it?). You may have been mulling over the possibilities for your title as you wrote, edited, and rewrote, but you shouldn't really focus on the task until the end, for it is the last step. (Never make the mistake of composing your title first and then trying to force your composition to fit it!)

What brief group of words can you come up with that will capture the essence of what you have been trying to present in your composition, and how can you motivate your reader to leap into your words with an intense desire to learn from you? Don't be too cute, too clever, too precious, but be creative and to the point. Here are some tips on composing a title:

1. **Don't go on and on unless you have some very special effect in mind.** An overly long title can drag down your composition, bring on yawns or resentment, making your reader feel a sense of forced and tedious labor, which is hardly the positive attitude you want to evoke with this, your first impression. Launch your composition with vigorous brevity.

2. **Be clear, not mysterious.** Don't write in code known only to you and maybe God. "Hold the Mustard!" may be meaningful to you, but it well may leave your reader without a clue. If you want to tease your reader into thought and into your composition, take care that your hints are clear enough to make sense. If necessary, make your title flat-footed and clear. Note that some of the titles in the composition exercises in Chapter 16 fall into the "simply clear" category, for example, "My Father" or "My Job as a Waitress." Neither of these is a potential prizewinner, but they have two important virtues: simplicity and clarity. Most readers, if they must choose, will pick clarity over cleverness.

3. **Provoke interest, if possible, while indicating what the composition is about.** The main point of a title is to identify the subject of the composition, but if you can at the same time fascinate or intrigue your reader, you'll give yourself an added advantage. "This looks like a live one! Shall I give myself a treat and read this one first, or save it to lift my spirits later?" These might be the reactions of your reader to an imaginative title. Remember, your reader is only human, and yours is just one in a set of papers to be read (next to several other sets?), and good first impressions matter.

4. **Don't forget a title!** Forcing your reader to plunge into your composition without the benefit of a title is a little like expecting two people to be comfortable conversing at length without knowing each other's names. It can be done, but it's awkward and rude.

5. Remember the mechanics of writing a title. As stated earlier in Chapter 9, a title is often a fragment (but not always) rather than a complete sentence. In addition, you should observe certain rules or customs regarding capitalization. For instance, prepositions and articles are not capitalized unless they are the first or last words of the title. Some people prefer to capitalize prepositions of five or six or more letters also. Examples of titles that might appear in student compositions are the following:

Ban the Handgun!

The Rustic Imagery of Robert Frost

Code Words for Racism

Looking at a Painting by Picasso

Who Is Not a Texan?

There are three other considerations regarding titles. First, a title is a unit separate from the composition; therefore, the first sentence of the composition cannot refer to the title or subject with a pronoun. The first sentence must be complete within itself, which usually calls for a noun. For instance, if your title is "An Examination of the Word *Tolerance*," your composition should not begin, "This has always bothered me." You need to start out fresh: "The word *tolerance* has always bothered me."

Second, your title should reflect your specific approach to a subject, not the subject in general. Suppose you are assigned to write on violence in America, but within that general subject you must select some specific aspect and give your perceptions of it. Your title should not be "Violence in America" but rather, for instance, "The Deadly Game of Car Jacking" or "Muggers Menace the Opera House." Be sure your title reflects your specific approach to the subject.

Finally, as noted in Chapter 9, remember where to place your title. It belongs in the upper part of your first page and should be centered there.*

ABOUT EXERCISES

There are no exercises as such in this chapter, although you are free to practice the structure and techniques suggested here. You should realize, however, that while the organization remains about the same in the introductions and conclusions you are likely to write, the techniques that govern content will vary considerably and will be determined by your *subject* and your *approach* to it. Therefore, think about and practice these beginnings and endings in relation to the composition as a whole. As

---

*When writers refer to the work of someone else, they place the title of that work in quotation marks. However, do not use quotes around your own title.

you practice the short composition in Chapter 16, you may want to turn back to this chapter from time to time for guidance.

SUMMARY

Introductory and concluding paragraphs differ from discussion paragraphs in their brevity, in their need to typify or generalize, and in their purpose. Organize them carefully to serve their purpose. There are a number of introductory techniques you can use, depending on subject and approach, and they must always be to the point of the thesis. Conclusions also vary but keep them short and simple. In addition, be sure to give your composition an effective title.

CHAPTER 15   ⟍

WRITING

MORE

SOPHISTICATED

SENTENCES

This chapter is different from the rest of the book. Until this point you have been asked to think primarily about *structure*, about organizing and developing the paragraph and the short composition. In this chapter you should turn your thoughts to *style*, to the effective use of language, particularly to the best ways to express yourself within sentences.

This chapter is probably best put off until you have worked with the preceding parts of the book. Turn to this chapter after you have written some of the more difficult paragraphs or as you begin to polish the content of your short compositions in their first or second drafts (you may write more drafts, depending on your need and motivation). As you look over your early drafts, you may notice some awkwardness in the way you have expressed yourself. For example, some of your sentences may lack clarity or variety, may be wordy or not as powerful as you might like them to be. What can you do about these problems? How can you become more skilled, more subtle, more sophisticated in your use of language, especially in your command of the sentence?

As you review and revise the early drafts of your paragraphs and compositions, consider the five aspects of the sentence discussed in this chapter that may make your writing more effective.

STRONG AND WEAK SENTENCE POSITIONS

STRONG	WEAK	STRONG
Beginning	Middle	Ending

FIGURE 15-1

Figure 15-1 represents a declarative sentence (one that makes a statement rather than asks a question) divided into three basic positions. The beginning and end positions are the strongest, that is, the weightiest or most emphatic. The most important ideas in a sentence should be placed in these positions. The middle position is the weakest; ideas of less or subordinate importance should be placed in this position. It is important to keep these positions in mind as you think about what you want to express. When you write your sentences, be sure to place your main or most important ideas in strong positions and your lesser ideas in the weak position.

Study the following pairs of sentences. The first sentence in each pair makes poor use of sentence positions whereas the second sentence makes good use of them, placing the most important parts of the sentence in the strongest positions.

1. a. On October 20,1991, in one of the most disastrous wildfires in U.S. history, 25 people were killed and over 2,000 homes destroyed in the Oakland hills near San Francisco.
    b. Twenty-five people were killed and over 2,000 homes destroyed in the Oakland hills near San Francisco on October 20, 1991, in one of the most disastrous wildfires in U.S. history.
2. a. Queen Elizabeth II spoke to an audience of 500 on the 40th anniversary of her accession to the throne, saying that 1992 had been a "horrible year" at a lunch given by the Lord Mayor of London.
    b. On the 40th anniversary of her accession to the throne, Queen Elizabeth II spoke to an audience of 500 at a lunch given by the Lord Mayor of London, saying that 1992 had been a "horrible year."

One of the best ways to judge the construction of a sentence is to read it aloud. Try doing that with the preceding sentences. What do you discover? What makes the second sentence of each pair better than the first? Do you find that the main ideas in the second sentences—in 1b the number of people killed, houses destroyed, relative national importance of the fire; in 2b the occasion contrasted with the quote—appear in the strong positions? When that main point is sandwiched into the weaker middle position, as in the first sentences, the point fails to stand out, becomes muddled or lost. Instead date and place appear stressed in 1a, and audience size and host are emphasized in 2a. As you study and revise the final drafts of your writing, read aloud some of your key or more important sentences to make sure you are positioning their contents for maximum clarity and impact.

EXERCISE E19. REVISE SENTENCES TO UTILIZE STRONG AND WEAK POSITIONS

Study the following sentences that have been written with purposeful disregard for the importance of strong and weak sentence positions. Decide what is important in each sentence and revise and rearrange it so that what is important takes a strong position in the sentence, what is less important is subordinated into the weak position. Remember that reading the sentence aloud may help you decide how to revise it.

1. They had a falling-out shortly before he died, so he didn't leave her a penny, although Erica had expected to inherit money from her uncle.

2. A person can be prochoice without being proabortion, in my opinion.

3. His family and friends were surprised when Dominique won a medal for track, because he was a gifted swimmer.

4. We all know the animals do not participate for the fun of it, regardless of how anyone may feel about whether or not rodeos are cruel.

5. My doctor has said that I can eat anything I want except foods containing MSG while my possible allergy is being tested this month.

6. A problem that is important to our nation, the economy, is one that politicians have only recently given much attention to.

7. An important feminist issue, sexual harassment, is finally coming to public consciousness.

8. The death sentence for a double murderer, who testified he would have voted for death if he were a juror, was upheld by the state supreme court.

9. He was becoming bored with college, and he decided to change his major after talking his problems over with his counselor.

10. After they had parked their rented car, trunk filled with all their possessions, along the French Riviera, they took only some change with them to buy ice cream at the beach, so they were horrified to discover the trunk open and everything—clothes, money, passports—stolen, when they returned to the car.

ACTIVE AND PASSIVE VOICE

Voice is a verb form that shows the relationship of the subject to the action of the verb. In the *active* voice the subject does the acting (she helps me) whereas in the *passive* voice the subject is acted upon (she is helped). Voice affects the construction of a sentence. Verbs in the *active* voice place the *doer* of the action in the *subject position* of the sentence; verbs in the *passive* voice place the *receiver* of the action in the *subject position*. Study the following:

	Subject	Predicate
ACTIVE Voice	Captain Kirk	landed the Star Ship *Enterprise* on Vulcan.
PASSIVE Voice	The Star Ship *Enterprise*	was landed on Vulcan by Captain Kirk.

Notice that the two preceding sentences are alternative ways of expressing essentially the same idea. Is one way better than the other? What do you think? Many experts caution developing writers to avoid the passive voice, criticizing it as indirect, awkward, wordy, and weak. However, they usually acknowledge there are situations that call for it. For example, the passive voice is useful when the doer of the action is unknown or unimportant, or when the writer wants to avoid revealing who the doer is. (Note that the doer of the action, "by . . . ," is often omitted, as in the example sentences that follow.) In addition, there are some cases in which a sentence constructed with the passive voice gives special emphasis to the receiver or object of the action by placing it where it may be unexpected, in the strong subject position. Examine the following sentences:

Subject (what the sentence is about)	Predicate (what is said about the subject)
Her topless picture	was published in all the tabloids.
Harvard, the oldest American college,	was founded in 1636.
That secret	was just revealed to me.

Who published the picture, founded the college, or told the secret is unknown, unimportant, concealed, or not the focus of the sentence. In each of the preceding instances, the doer of the action is superseded by the receiver or object of the action. In other words, ***what matters*** is ***what*** was ***done, not who did*** it. These examples illustrate appropriate uses of the passive voice.

Although there are circumstances that call for the passive voice, *most of what you write is probably best cast in the active voice.* By and large, the writing world is a *who did what* kind of place, and that message is expressed with the active voice. Your reader expects that message, wants you to be direct with it, to come to the point, to be forceful and concise, to be in command. The active voice may even be a sign (an illusion?) that you are a writer in control of your universe. At least when you use the active voice your sentences put the doer of the action front and center, in charge of the action.

Study the following pairs of sentences. The *first sentence* of each pair uses the *passive voice*, for the most part, whereas the *second sentence* employs the *active voice*. (The relevant parts of the sentences have been italicized for easy comparison.)

1. a. The students in the workshop displayed the projects that **had been made by them** during the semester.
   b. The students in the workshop displayed the projects that **they had made** during the semester.
2. a. **We were awakened** before dawn **by the manager** of our beachfront motel as **our door was rattled** and "Tidal wave! Get to higher ground!" **was shouted by him**.
   b. **The manager** of our beachfront motel **woke us** before dawn as **he rattled our door** and **shouted**, "Tidal wave! Get to higher ground!"
3. a. Miguel had planned to propose to Maria, but then he saw **José being kissed by her**.
   b. Miguel had planned to propose to Maria, but then he saw **her kissing José**.

What are the most noticeable differences between the first and second sentences of each of the preceding pairs? First, you can see that the passive voice in the first sentences requires more words, thus making the first sentences longer than the second. Notice that the passive voice in these particular sentences makes them indirect and awkward as well. Finally, by reading them aloud, you can easily recognize that the passive voice makes the first sentences less forceful than the second. Thus, in these sentences the active voice proves to be more concise, direct, smoother, and more forceful than the passive voice.

EXERCISE E20.   REWRITE SENTENCES, CHANGING VERBS TO ACTIVE VOICE

The following sentences are written with verbs in the passive voice. Rewrite and revise them by changing the verbs to active voice.

1. When the boss saw the mess that John had made, he was fired by her.
2. Excellent Vietnamese food is served by that restaurant.

3. Shortly after Bill was married by Ann, his money began to be spent by her, and countless affairs were had by him.

4. Low interest rates on savings accounts are not loved by retired people.

5. The instructor said that a quiz might be given by him at any time.

EXERCISE E21. RECONVERT WELL-KNOWN EXPRESSIONS TO ORIGINAL ACTIVE VOICE

The following are well-known expressions originated in the active voice. Here they are presented in the passive voice. For fun as well as enlightenment, reconvert them to their original wording in the active voice.

1. Four score and seven years ago a new nation was brought forth on this continent by our fathers . . .
2. A silver lining is had by every cloud.
3. The world is made to go around by love.
4. Company is loved by misery.
5. Seashells are sold by her by the seashore.
6. The broth is spoiled by too many cooks.
7. Waste is made by haste.
8. The worm is caught by the early bird.
9. Labor is made light by many hands.
10. The man is not made by clothes.
11. Nine are saved by a stitch in time.
12. A peck of pickled peppers were picked by Peter Piper.
13. Right is made by might.
14. Jack is made a dull boy by all work and no play.
15. The best is known by mother.

CONCISENESS AND WORDINESS

Being concise is the opposite of being wordy, a topic touched on earlier (see Problem D in Chapter 4) that bedevils many writers. Words are the medium with which the writer works, just as paint is basic to the painter. As with paint, so with the word, writers are tempted to lay it on a little thick, to spill it around, maybe even pour it right out of the can. Discipline and restraint tend to come with effort, after a painful process of trial and error and the frustration that may lead to tearing pages of deathless prose into heartfelt shreds.

The love of words makes some writers wallow in them. Some writers are indiscriminate in their wordiness, calling on all or most words in excess. Other writers may be driven to use only certain words over and over again. Occasionally writers seem to experience what amounts to momentary attacks by one or two words they repeat to the point of piercing pain.

It isn't always the love of words that makes writers overindulge in them. Some writers exercise a kind of false modesty with too many words, others hide behind words, some even decorate with words, as if they are off to some special place in their Sunday best. Another cause of wordiness is the inexact use of language, a poorly chosen noun, for example, and the attempt to correct it with a multitude of adjectives to make the poorly chosen word do a better job of conveying the desired meaning.

Before considering wordiness in further detail, think for a moment about what the words *concise* or *succinct* mean. They do not mean simply writing less or using fewer words. If they did, then the best writing would be none at all—zip. However, a good sentence is not necessarily a short one. Rather, it is one that packs its own weight. Think of a caravan, a string of vehicles or pack animals, journeying across rough terrain (communication is rarely easy) to a distant goal. The trip must be carefully planned. There can be no empty vehicles, no animals carrying nothing or so overloaded that they stagger under their burden. So with a well-constructed sentence: There is nothing extra, no empty words, nothing wasted. Well packed, a concise sentence carries just what it needs.

Now consider some of the causes and/or forms of wordiness as well as possible corrections.

FALSE MODESTY

Some writers, often inexperienced ones, may use extra words to avoid sounding too opinionated or arrogant when expressing an opinion or position on a given, perhaps debatable, topic. To illustrate:

Of course, I'm no authority, but in my humble opinion, **capital punishment is wrong**, at least from my ethical point of view.

Only the italicized words in the preceding statement are working words carrying content. The remaining words are excess baggage. They make the reader work harder (with unnecessary reading) to make the writer feel better.

POSSIBLE CORRECTION:

The intent to avoid a know-it-all or arrogant attitude is an honorable one, since that attitude is unpleasant, unrealistic, and quite likely to alienate a reader. However, the cure should not be worse than the disease. Instead of being wordy, adopt a concise, straightforward "this-is-how-I-see-it" presentation. Neither apologize for your views nor try to play God. Simply state your position and calmly offer reason and evidence to support it.

HIDING BEHIND WORDS

Writers who are unsure of themselves or their views may try to hide behind words, using indirect language and vague expressions, including verbs in the passive voice, that make it difficult for the reader to tell not only *what* the view is but *whose* view it is. These evasive statements usually require excessive words. For example:

Opinions on this matter differ according to the background of each person, and it is difficult to say who is right when even the experts disagree, and therefore a middle ground may be the choice of many, since no final conclusion can be reached. . . .

A form of gobbledygook (see Appendix B, "Correction Symbols") this evasive language is a wordy smoke screen that is most likely to turn up during times of duress such as exams or special deadlines. Pity the poor reader who is committed to read such language, struggling ever onward, praying for relief!

POSSIBLE CORRECTION:

Probably the best way to avoid such writing is to allow more time for study and thought, to make better preparation. Know your subject and have something real to say about it.

DECORATING WITH WORDS

A person who is not accustomed to writing formal compositions may think they call for dressed up language. Indeed, some care with language needs to be taken. Heavy dependence on slang or the most colloquial language is inappropriate except in special cases, for example, an essay on slang where it might be fitting to write, "Hey, man, what's happening?" Otherwise, the language of a composition is somewhat formal, elevated above the level of the most casual conversation. However, it is not fancy like putting on a top hat and tails or a party dress. Compare the two statements that follow:

My longtime male associate was excessively unpunctual at his place of employment, and therefore a management decision resulted in his termination.
My boyfriend was late to work so often that his boss fired him.

The first of the two preceding statements puts on airs in phrasing and word choice. Note that this kind of pretentiousness requires more words than the second sentence does. The second statement is a colloquial translation of the first but is not so informal that it is inappropriate in a composition, though some critics might prefer *employer* in place of *boss* or other slightly more formal substitutes for words used. The degree of formality, or the level of language appropriate for formal compositions, is not exact or easy to measure. Practice and experience tend to build, over time, a sense of what is needed.

Another mistake some writers, both experienced and inexperienced, make is to try to impress readers with the biggest or most multisyllabic words they know. Granting that multisyllabic words often serve a real purpose in communicating complex or highly technical ideas, these words can also be used in a pretentious or showy manner. The error in this case, as with dressed up language, is that the words call attention to themselves rather than serving their purpose to communicate. Hence they are distracting as well as annoying. Readers are not fools. They usually know when they are being subjected to affectation. They may even find it amusing, as in the multisyllabic version of the time-honored drinking song:

Indicate the way to my residence
I'm fatigued and desire to retire . . .

Some decorative wordiness may result when developing writers are experimenting with language or perhaps trying to evolve their own writing style. It may be useful for such people to study the styles of various contemporary writers and also to compare current taste with that of earlier periods. For instance, Victorians favored a much more flowery style than is in use today. Compare the two sentences that follow, the first published in 1904, the second a contemporary statement.

The right use of the breathing apparatus, in connection with the exercise of the voice, ought, therefore, to be the first subject to which the attention of the student of Elocution is called.

A speech student must first learn to breathe correctly.

How many differences in style or sentence structure can you find in the two preceding statements that convey essentially the same message?

POSSIBLE CORRECTION:

Remember, your aim with words is to communicate, to express, not impress. The best language does not call attention to itself but rather to the content, the ideas it is designed to present. The language need not be drab or dull. In fact, it should be alive and exciting. However, it should not dress up or show off in order to inspire. The current trend in writing style is somewhat like the going look in auto design:

understatement, function, performance. The great whitewall tires and massive chrome of the past are gone. As you develop your own unique writing style, be sure you are also in touch with the standard language of your time so you can communicate effectively with others.

TOO MANY MODIFIERS

Modifiers, words that adjust, change, or qualify other words, are vital to writers, making possible the fine tuning of language. However, modifiers can be overused and abused, in which case they contribute to wordiness.

The italicized words that follow are examples of modifiers: adjectives (modifying nouns and pronouns) and adverbs (modifying verbs, adjectives, and other adverbs).

adjectives: *red* house, *old* man, *bad* movie

adverbs: walked *slowly*, *very* cheerful, *too quickly*

When modifiers are overused or used as crutches to try to cope with poorly chosen words, they overload a sentence and drag it down. For example, examine the following sentence that contains too many modifiers (italicized for easy identification):

Her *gnarled* and *crooked* fingers moved *very slowly* over the *time-stained* keys of the *dark old* piano, making a *faint* sound that *gradually* filled the *dimly lighted* room with *dense* and *heavy* gloom.

The preceding sentence has too much frosting, not enough cake. It labors for effect, and the effect is almost comical with excess.

Consider another sentence that attempts to compensate for poorly chosen words with an excessive use of modifiers (italicized for easy identification):

My father was *really very* mad at me for breaking my promise and *completely* lost his temper, but I felt *absolutely* terrible when he scolded me *so much* in front of my friends.

Writers need to beware of the temptation of modifiers such as *really, very, completely, absolutely, so, so much, most, great, clearly, quite, extremely, greatly, many,* and other so-called intensives that tend to be overused. They may be symptomatic of sickly sentences in need of more exact as well as more concise expression. A good dose of *Roget's Thesaurus* may be the medicine needed to help with better word choice. The preceding example might be improved with more exact wording such as the following (note the italicized words):

My father was *furious* with me for breaking my promise and *flew into a rage*, but I felt *humiliated* when he *reprimanded* me in front of my friends.

POSSIBLE CORRECTION:

Most people are familiar with the cliché "One picture is worth a thousand words." Another saying might be coined from that expression: A well-chosen word is worth innumerable modifiers. You cannot do without modifiers entirely, but if you find yourself writing sentences with too many, check to see if you might be overdoing a good thing. Try to choose your words carefully so they express your meaning as exactly as possible. Thus you will not need to struggle with too many modifiers.

GENERAL WORDINESS

Wordiness comes in many forms, and critics who have been exposed to it for any length of time tend to have their pet peeves. One general category of wordiness is often called *deadwood*, which means useless phrasing of any kind. Included in this category is the unnecessary repetition of ideas or expressions, a pet peeve among critics. Consider these examples:

In my opinion, I think . . .
In this modern world of today . . .
To repeat again . . .

As you go over your second or third drafts, check introductory parts of sentences to see if you find deadwood that needs pruning. Don't be surprised if you discover your entire introductory paragraph needs editing or revising because that is the place in composition writing where the maximum wheel spinning is likely to occur. Sometimes an introductory paragraph is where you find out, with much effort, what it is you want to write about. It may take you many useless words before you find that critical focus. But the words will not have been entirely useless if they helped you develop your thesis. However, they are not words you want to share with others necessarily. Once you know your direction, cut, cut, cut, and rewrite.

Another form of wordiness might be termed "taking the long way" to express a point. Instead of concise, direct wording, the writer uses roundabout and often awkward ways to express an idea:

It is the recommendation of the chairman that . . .
It is the determination of the board that . . .

These ponderous expressions, sometimes sounding like decrees from on high, tend to work their way into formal business communications, but they are not the concise language called for in college compositions. Instead, write:

The chairman recommends that . . .
The board has determined that . . .

POSSIBLE CORRECTION:

Cut any word you can do without. Keep only what you need, what is essential to clarity and completeness. When you submit your composition, remember that your name is on it; your reader knows your composition contains your views, thus "in my opinion" may be entirely unnecessary or can be reduced to a bare minimum. Be concise.

EXERCISE E22. IDENTIFY FIVE FORMS OF WORDINESS

Each of the following sentences contains one of the five forms of wordiness discussed earlier. Place an "A" in the space next to a sentence you think contains *false modesty*; write a "B" for *hiding behind words*; write a "C" for *decorating with words*; write a "D" for *too many modifiers*; write an "E" for *general wordiness*. You may also want to revise and rewrite the sentences.

_____ 1. His new car is really very well designed and extremely powerful.

_____ 2. In my opinion, I believe that women should receive the same pay as men for comparable work.

_____ 3. Having lost parental aegis, I experienced the inevitable exigencies associated with seeking gainful employment.

_____ 4. It was a very dark and extremely stormy night, and the prevailing wind blew quite fiercely.

_____ 5. It is my tentative understanding that aerosol is harmful to the earth's atmosphere, but then my research is limited as I am only just beginning my graduate studies in meteorology.

_____ 6. He declined the invitation as necessity called upon him to peruse his textbooks assiduously prior to his undertaking final examinations.

_____ 7. That period of history is not well known, and since many people did not read and write at the time, what has been recorded depended originally on word of mouth, which is not entirely reliable, and so there are various versions of events, many of them in conflict.

_____ 8. The crisp, yellow, ranch style house stood sedately behind a bright green, well-manicured lawn, and when the automatic door of the two-car garage lifted to reveal a large, practical station wagon, two sweet children skipped happily from their protective abode, tugging eagerly on their adoring mother's reliable hands, and the doting threesome piled merrily into the ample car and drove away.

_____ 9. I think it may rain, perhaps, if I'm not mistaken, but of course I'm not a weather person.

_____ 10. I must repeat again that, in my opinion, I think this matter merits our immediate attention.

VARIETY

It is the dead of night in the old house, and from downstairs comes the sound of the kitchen faucet, the steady drip, drip, drip, drip, drip. You imagine your hand tightening the faucet. How easy it would be. Just a simple turn. But you are warm in your bed. Drip, drip, drip, drip, drip. You will try not to listen, you think, as you pull a pillow over your head.

Sentences that are too regular, too uniform, all of the same length, approximately, and the same construction, may have the effect on your reader of a steadily dripping faucet. They might even drive your reader down the stairs in desperation to replace the washer, at the very least.

VARY SENTENCE LENGTH

Of course, the length of the sentence is related to its content. Complex ideas often require longer sentences to explain and clarify, though some complicated thoughts can be reduced to shorter sentences than might at first be apparent. However, a mixture of longer and shorter sentences is more likely to keep a reader attentive and involved than an extended series of long or a seemingly endless succession of short sentences.

Think for a moment about sentence rhythms. Long sentences (with notable exceptions, some of them by Gilbert and Sullivan) tend to have a meandering, smooth, legato style and pace. Short sentences are more often staccato, sharp and choppy. Sentence length alone, regardless of content, has an effect on a reader that you need to keep in mind as you write. If you write too many long sentences, your reader may start to drift off, no matter how intriguing the content. If you write nothing but short and choppy sentences, your reader could become agitated enough to get up and dance away from your composition! Therefore, to keep your reader tuned, use a variety of sentence rhythms.

VARY SENTENCE CONSTRUCTION

Consider this brief paragraph containing sentences of approximately the same length and construction:

My brother is very lazy. He doesn't make his bed. He doesn't pick up his clothes. He doesn't brush his teeth. He doesn't do his chores. He doesn't take out the garbage. He doesn't feed the dog. He doesn't mow the lawn. He doesn't wash the car. He doesn't do much of anything.

The preceding paragraph contains nothing but short sentences, each, except for the topic sentence, having exactly the same construction, each beginning in the same way with the same word. The cumulative effect is something like a dentist's drill.

You already know that the preceding example might be improved by varying the length of the sentences. Now consider how the paragraph might be made more interesting by varying the sentence construction.

1. Vary the beginning of the sentence.
    "He doesn't" becomes painful with repetition. Instead of repeating "he," use variations for this beginning such as "my brother," "the lazy boy," "the loafer," "the do-nothing." Substitutes for "doesn't" could be "won't" or "will not," "refuses to," or other such words.

2. Use transitions.
    The jerky singsong of the preceding example might be broken up with transitional expressions that would also make the paragraph flow better. Placed at the beginning or end of some of the sentences, these expressions might include *moreover, usually, besides, either,* and others. (See Chapter 5 for a list of transitional expressions.)

3. Combine sentences.
    The preceding example is constructed entirely of short, choppy sentences. Some of them might be combined. For example,

SHORT SENTENCES: He doesn't make his bed. He doesn't pick up his clothes.

COMBINED: He doesn't make his bed or pick up his clothes.

4. Vary sentence types.
    All the sentences in the example given earlier are of the same grammatical type: *simple* sentences with one independent clause. The other grammatical types that might be used are *compound* sentences, having two or more independent clauses; *complex* sentences, consisting of one independent and one or more dependent clauses; or *compound–complex* sentences, having two or more independent clauses and one or more dependent clauses. These variations are illustrated in the following sentences:

SIMPLE: He doesn't mow the lawn.

COMPOUND: He doesn't mow the lawn, and he doesn't wash the car.

COMPLEX: He doesn't mow the lawn when our parents ask him.

COMPOUND–COMPLEX: He doesn't mow the lawn, and he doesn't wash the car, even when our parents ask him.

If you need further or fuller explanation of these various sentence types, turn to an English handbook or workbook that includes an indepth examination of grammar. In addition, study the application of a mixture of these types in the following revision of the earlier example:

My brother is very lazy. He doesn't make his bed, though our mother reminds him to repeatedly. He doesn't pick up his clothes when she asks him, either. My lazy brother doesn't even brush his teeth regularly. Besides, he often neglects his chores. He doesn't take out the garbage when he's supposed to, though our father rants and raves about it, and he frequently forgets to feed the dog. This lazybones also fails to mow the lawn or wash the car, as a rule, though these are two of his assigned duties. In fact, my brother doesn't do much of anything.

PARALLELISM

Shortly after a horse is born, it begins to cope with parallelism, that is, with trying to bring its legs into alignment so it can stand and walk. At first its legs appear to go every which way, and the foal staggers about and falls, but before long the legs begin to line up, and miraculously, the newborn can function.

Just as lining up its legs helps a young horse to hang together in one piece, so parallelism in writing, which puts like units of thought in the same grammatical form, contributes to effectiveness and coherence. Parallel structure is important in sentences containing a pair or series of units that are equal in importance. Study the sentences that follow (the nonparallel parts are italicized for easy identification).

NONPARALLEL: It is better to have loved and lost than never **having** loved at all.

PARALLEL: It is better to have loved and lost than never to have loved at all.

NONPARALLEL: Having a persuasive manner, being well versed in criminal law, and **because she possesses** astute methods of interrogation, Mary should become a defense lawyer.

PARALLEL: Having a persuasive manner, being well versed in criminal law, and possessing astute methods of interrogation, Mary should become a defense lawyer.

NONPARALLEL: His father taught him about growing corn, bringing in the harvest, and **to respect** all farm animals.

PARALLEL: His father taught him about growing corn, bringing in the harvest, and respecting all farm animals.

NONPARALLEL: I take the class to earn credit and **for mind expansion**.

PARALLEL: I take the class to earn credit and to expand my mind.

NONPARALLEL: . . . that government of the people, by the people, **benefiting each person** shall not perish from the earth.

PARALLEL: . . . that government of the people, by the people, for the people, shall not perish from the earth.

Think through sentences that pair units of thought or present them in a series. The wording you use in the beginning of such a sentence sets the pattern for what follows. Of course, you may decide to reword a sentence totally, favoring wording that comes to you as you write the middle or end of a sentence. Then you need to restate the beginning to match the middle and end. In any case, all units must match. Parallelism means agreement in wording, however it comes about.

Notice that the preceding parallel sentences are better packaged, to use a term from the advertising field, than the nonparallel sentences. Parallelism helps to bind the words together in one sentence, to point up the ideas, sometimes to make them memorable, as in the last example.

Parallelism works its effect within paragraphs as well as within sentences. Return for a moment to the first version of the paragraph about the lazy brother in the preceding section on variety. Perhaps the only virtue of that paragraph in its early version is the parallelism that binds the paragraph together and keeps it moving in one direction. Of course, that virtue is overdone and carried to a fault so the paragraph calls out desperately for variety within the sameness. But note the similarity in the length and construction of the sentences from the perspective of parallelism as well as from the need for variety and change. These two perspectives call forth an important lesson in writing if not in life in general: Balance one need against another. Consider one lesson in terms of another. Parallelism without variety, for instance, leads right back to the pain of the dentist's drill.*

EXERCISE E23. IDENTIFY PARALLEL OR NONPARALLEL SENTENCES

Some of the sentences that follow are parallel. Some are not. Place a "P" in the space next to a sentence you think is parallel. Write an "N" in the space next to a sentence you think is nonparallel. You may also wish to correct or improve the nonparallel sentences.

*See Appendix B, "Correction Symbols," for a brief additional discussion of parallelism.

    1. He came, he saw, he conquered.

    2. I enjoy sawing wood for the exercise and to meditate.

    3. To swim and walking are my favorite morning activities.

    4. I like Japanese food for its lovely appearance, its delectable flavor, and being nourishing, as well.

    5. He chased the cat down the stairs, out the door, and around the block.

    6. I know nothing about shooting a rifle, casting a fishing line, or to build a fire without matches.

    7. It is better to have run the race and lost than never having run.

    8. She may look mean, but she has a big heart.

    9. She was overwhelmed by the splendor of the ballroom, the beauty of the prince, and fearing that all this would soon disappear.

    10. He runs to keep in shape and for pleasure.

S U M M A R Y

As you review and edit the final drafts of your compositions, be sure to think about the writing techniques that can make your sentences forceful and effective. First, remember the concept of strong and weak sentence positions so your placement of major ideas within sentences gives them maximum impact. Second, consider the uses of active and passive voice, especially the benefits of the active voice in making sentences smooth, concise, and forceful. Third, bear in mind the need for conciseness and the risks of wordiness, particularly the trap of using too many modifiers to compensate for inexact language.

Finally, think about variety and parallelism in your sentences. Keep in mind the usefulness of varying sentence length and construction to ensure that your reader remains interested and involved in your composition. Consider parallelism in your sentences when you present ideas in pairs or in a series, and let the common form in the sentences underscore the content they share, compare, or contrast.

These techniques, together with practice and experience, should help you write more skillful and sophisticated sentences.

CHAPTER 16

PRACTICING

THE

SHORT

COMPOSITION

The main purpose of the model compositions that follow is to guide the structure, or organization, of your own compositions. However, the following examples may be helpful in other ways as well. They may irritate or soothe you with their subject matter. They may stimulate you to think. They may suggest ways in which you can develop as well as structure your own ideas. If the models are successful, you should do quite well without them before long.

EXERCISE 31. WRITE A PORTRAIT OF A RELATIVE

Write a composition in which you present a verbal picture of one of your relatives. (You might repeat this exercise using a friend or a fictional character as the subject.) Your portrait might concentrate on aspects of your relative's personality or on his or her physical appearance, or on both. Because this composition, your first, is not expected to be very long or complex, you will need to be selective, limiting yourself to only the most outstanding aspects of your relative.

Make your composition about as long as the following example, which has four paragraphs. The first paragraph is a brief introduction that terminates with the thesis statement. Divide your thesis into *two* parts or supports. Discuss the first part in paragraph 2 of your composition; discuss the second part in paragraph 3. The final paragraph is a brief conclusion.

Be careful to use verb tenses that are appropriate to your subject. If your relative is living, use present tenses. If your relative is deceased, as in the following example, past tenses are called for.

Example

MY FATHER

"I hate the bloody stuff," my father used to say, tossing down straight shots of whiskey. "Ah . . ." Once he had conquered the agony of getting it down, he glowed with the pleasure of it. His response to life was a little like his reaction to whiskey, which he hated and loved. (THESIS STATEMENT) My father had a mercurial Irish personality, and his facial features could be just as changeable.

My father was Irish in the extreme and abrupt changeability of his moods. In the middle of intense anger, he could break himself up laughing. Once when I had driven a 7-inch spike, on which I had planned to hang my saddle, completely through the side of our garage, through the wall, the outside stucco and all, with the point of the nail glaring at my father from the outside, he flew into one of his rages. ". . . ! . . . !" he screamed, "don't you know you should hammer a nail into the studs, not into the siding? And why in hell did you use such a big nail?" I stood there, sheepishly, taking my what for from my father, when suddenly he burst into laughter, covering his mouth with his hands as he always did with a big laugh. He finally said, "How in hell did you do it?" True, I was only nine years old at the time, and I had worked very hard banging at that big nail before I got it through the wall. Though what I had done had made him mad, my father could also appreciate my effort.

Besides being quick in altering his moods, my father could also make dramatic changes in his facial expression. He had very thick and very long eyebrows that, together with his dark eyes, probably said as much or more than any other part of his bony face and body. When he was mad, his eyebrows whipped about and then lowered, so his eyes almost disappeared except for the fire that I could see or feel was in them. That was the look that sent dogs under chairs and children running for cover. Even adults backed off, giving my father the widest possible berth. When he was joyous or sentimental in song (he could not sing; he knew it, but he tried anyway), his eyebrows would lift into an arch above his nose. At the top of the arch, they pointed heavenward, like a steeple, and under the steeple, his eyes glowed multicolored, like the windows of a fine old church.

These memories of my father go back many years, but time has sharpened rather than dimmed the aspects of his personality and face that I remember. If he were alive today, I'm sure my father would look at this portrait and say, "I'm damned if that isn't me!"

Suggested topics: father; mother; brother; sister; uncle; aunt; grandfather or grandmother; cousin; husband; wife; son; daughter; in-law. (Remember to limit your portrait to only a few or the most outstanding aspects of your relative's personality and/or physical features.)

EXERCISE 32. EXPLAIN WHAT YOU ADMIRE ABOUT A FRIEND

Write a composition in which you explain two or three of the qualities you admire in a close friend. Although this is somewhat like Exercise 31, its focus is different. Here you are asked not only to describe your friend, but to make clear that you are praising him or her for the characteristics you describe. This process is called a *eulogy*, which is a tribute to someone's virtues or achievements.

Present the qualities or characteristics of your friend in a thesis divided into *two* or *three* parts or supports. Each of the parts of the thesis should be developed into a paragraph of the discussion. In addition, write a brief introduction and conclusion. Use the following example as a guide.

Example

MY FRIEND ANNE

She doesn't go out of her way for most people: she almost never gives a party, she rarely invites people to dinner, she seldom calls anyone on the phone. Most people tend to bore her. Is she an unhappy, maladjusted recluse? Quite the contrary; people are attracted to her because she is so well adjusted. (THESIS STATEMENT) I admire my friend Anne Perry because she is self-assured and discriminating.

Unlike some people I know, Anne has confidence in herself. She is not plagued with insecurity and self-doubt. Some people carry little monsters in their heads that tell them, "You're no good. Don't try to dress well; you have no taste. Don't go to that elegant restaurant, the waiter will snub you. Don't try to meet that important person; you're not interesting. Stay in your hole and hang your head." Not so with Anne. A happy little troll lives in her head, and it says, "Hi, sweetie, glad you're here. What can I offer you? Make yourself at home!" Anne is not so self-assured that she is arrogant, but she likes herself. As a result, it is a pleasure to be with her. She relaxes people because she does not lean on them neurotically for support. Her faith in herself is contagious. Her self-possession inspires others to be like her, and her appreciation of life spills over to her friends.

Being confident probably helps Anne to be discriminating. She sees no reason to settle for second best, and she hardly ever does. Why spend an evening with boring people just to be with people? Why not spend an interesting evening at home alone? Why go to a bad play or sit in a bad seat to see a good one? Instead, wait for a good play and save money, if need be, to sit in a good seat. These are the choices Anne makes. She prefers old friends to strangers or mere acquaintances, and she will do just about anything for her friends — short of making dinner for them, which she does rarely because she wants to do it well or not at all. As infrequent as her invitations are, they are highly prized because she is a gourmet cook. Few people I know are as discriminating as Anne is, and I admire her for her insight and her taste. She knows that life is precious, and because she is selective, she makes the most of it.

Anne is aware that some people call her a snob, but those who know her well respect her for her confident and discriminating personality. As a result, the few who are chosen are honored to be her friends.

Suggested topics: virtues such as being thoughtful or considerate, fun or funny, wise or witty, clever, creative, conscientious, honest, a good listener, talented or entertaining, helpful, loyal, a good critic, supportive, patient, understanding, a hard worker, a good sport, fair; achievements such as being a good athlete, student, salesperson, teacher, painter or sculptor, driver, musician, writer, cook, model, dresser, housekeeper, parent, gardener, dancer.

EXERCISE 33. DISCUSS SOMETHING YOU DISLIKE

Write a composition in which you present two or three reasons why you dislike something *or* in which you present two or three things you dislike, as in the example that follows. If you choose to do the latter, be sure the things you write about are closely related; for instance, two sounds or noises, as in the example. This exercise contrasts with the preceding one; however, you may or may not write about a person here. Your objective is to focus on something, an object or experience, that irritates, offends, embarrasses, or angers you. Think about what is generally true for you rather than a single event you have experienced. Note the list of suggested topics following the example.

Divide your thesis into *two* or *three* parts or supports. Develop each part into a paragraph of discussion in which you explain and illustrate your meaning in some detail. Also write a brief introduction and conclusion. Use the following example as a guide.

Example

TWO HATEFUL NOISEMAKERS

The world is becoming a painfully noisy place. Lately even my relatively peaceful neighborhood has turned to bedlam with the sounds of construction. Houses being built require the work of bulldozers and other heavy equipment, huge trucks to haul dirt downhill, others to struggle slowly uphill with concrete. Some trucks spend much of the day in reverse, it seems, repeating a high, piercing, electronic signal. These and other harsh sounds that have lessened the quality of life in the vicinity make me think about the noisemakers I like least in all the world. (THESIS STATEMENT) Among them, two of the most hateful are the chain saw and the leaf blower.

The chain saw makes an ugly sound, partly because of what it does. When I hear one at work, I have a horrible fantasy of the parched earth being covered over with Astroturf as yet another tree is denuded and then cut down. "The damned thing blocks my view," I can hear a neighbor say to the man who will spike his way up the pine. The tree man whines away to the top, and great limbs fall, while another man below drags them off to the chipper where they are processed into little bits. The trunk is bare after a few hours and looks pathetic with its short stumps where the branches had been, and then the trunk is dropped, slab by slab. Throughout this transformation, the chain saw works in furious spurts, sometimes wailing to a high pitch, sometimes choking up, getting snagged, stopping abruptly. For a moment my ears almost ring with the quiet, but the relief is brief, the racket resumes, the saw snarling and splitting the poor pine into oblivion. I wait for the chain saw to go away eventually, but it never does. It simply moves around, sometimes off in the distance, sometimes nearer, always somewhere, like an insistent, buzzing insect I cannot wave away.

Cacophonous mate to the chain saw, the leaf blower may be even more offensive. Its sound almost unbearable, the leaf blower (illegal in some areas) goes into a high-pitched roar and stays there, without relief, until the job is done. A misbegotten cure where there was no disease, the leaf blower replaces the simple rake, and its only justification is that it saves a little time and effort, effort that used to keep gardeners trim and time that permitted them to stay in touch with nature and their own souls. Now gardeners come upon the scene like pneumatic tyrants, like enemies at war with the garden, and they huff and puff them into submission, using nonrenewable fossil fuel to do the work. The shrill blasts send the leaves flying into the street or into the yards of neighbors as gardeners work at a steady pace, their ears plugged or tuned to a favorite channel of their stereo headset radios. They appear to be unconnected to what they do and unaware of how they disturb the neighborhood with that jarring noise. Relief comes only when they leave, though they are never fully gone. The leaf blower, like the chain saw, is always somewhere in the area.

The chain saw and the leaf blower are conveniences that are not likely to disappear from the workaday world. However, if these two hateful sounds are not soon muffled, the day will come, as in the movie *Network*, when I will open my window and cry out to all the world, "I'm mad as hell, and I'm not going to take it anymore!"

Suggested topics: sounds such as barking dogs, honking horns, house or auto security alarms, dental drills, nails on a chalkboard, snoring, construction noises, airplanes flying too low or fast; odors such as strong cheese, sour milk, an outgoing tide, strong perfume, body odor; sights such as garbage or litter in the streets, dying flowers, billboards, ashtrays full of cigarettes, air pollution, too much makeup; experiences with other people such as guests arriving late or early, someone forgetting a date with you, someone standing too close, lecturing, or otherwise boring you; independent experiences such as forgetting someone's name or birthday, breaking a shoelace, getting junk mail, missing a bus, losing track of time.

EXERCISE 34. DISCUSS A GOOD OR BAD JOB

Think of the various part-time or full-time jobs you have held, and write about one you have either liked or disliked. Consider what has made the job a good one for you or a bad one, and present your case for or against the job in a thesis divided into *three* parts or supports. Each of the three parts of the thesis should be developed in a paragraph of discussion, making the composition, together with an introductory and concluding paragraph, a total of five paragraphs in length. Use the example that follows to guide you.

Example

MY JOB AS A WAITRESS

While working my way through college, I have held some dull and difficult jobs. I have spent a summer picking tomatoes in hot and seemingly endless fields. I have sold toys during the Christmas rush to screaming children and harassed parents in the crowded basement of a large department store. I have worked through the night sorting mail in a cold and dreary post office. However, none of these jobs was as bad as my work as a waitress in a combination restaurant and ice cream parlor. (THESIS STATEMENT) The work there was physically hard; the pay was poor; and most of all, the working conditions were deplorable.

First of all, the job made great demands on my energy and endurance. From 4:30 in the afternoon until 1 or 2 o'clock in the morning, I spent most of my time on my feet waiting on customers; walking from counter to kitchen to table; carrying trays heavy with plates of food and giant ice cream sundaes, sodas, and shakes. The restaurant was a popular hangout for teenagers, whose needs for another straw, another spoon, another glass of water kept me in almost constant motion. Families were also drawn to the place and overflowed the booths, their little ones spewing milk shakes down the seats, often followed by broken glass — targets for the broom and mop that I wielded in my ''spare'' time. In fact, in the rare moments when business slowed down, I was expected to mop the entire floor and to clean down walls as well as to polish the extensive fountain area. In addition to waiting tables, I was required to work in the kitchen some of the time and to make the ice cream orders for all of my customers. My hands and arms ached by the end of the night from scooping hard ice cream. When I went home, I had to soak my sore body in a tub for at least a half hour before I could sleep.

The physical hardship might not have been so hard to bear if the pay had not been so poor. I was paid the minimum wage, which was at that time $3.25 an hour, and on a good night, I made another three or four dollars in tips. Because of the low pay, I often worked overtime on weekends to increase my paycheck. I was naive and didn't at first realize that weekends attracted the "big spenders," who promised substantial tips that rarely materialized in return for extra attention and faster service. Although I catered to them and flew as fast as I could, when I cleared their tables I might find a dollar or sometimes nothing at all as tip for a table of four and a bill of $40 or more. Of course, in addition to longer hours, weekends meant heavier traffic in the restaurant, but as a rule I made little more money on weekends than I did on my regular shifts. My take-home pay was usually under $300 a week, including tips. I was promised a Christmas bonus of a two-pound box of candy, but I forfeited that reward by leaving the job the week before.

Even worse than the physical strain and the low pay, what upset me about the job were the working conditions. My boss was a slave driver and a dirty old man who liked to pinch pennies as well as various parts of my anatomy. On the cook's days off, he did the cooking himself but expected me to help him out in the kitchen in addition to my regular work. While I cleaned vegetables, prepared salads, and made desserts, I also had to listen to his obscene jokes and fight off his amorous advances. Rejecting him put him in an ugly mood, and then he would find special jobs for me, such as cleaning the ovens and scraping down the grills. He would demand that I work harder, and he would criticize me when I sat down for the brief rest breaks that were due me. During rush hours his wife sometimes worked as cashier, and her raised eyebrows and insinuating remarks about my relationship with her husband made me furious. Finally, when she came right out and accused me of trying to seduce him, I told her what I really thought of him as well as the job. There was a terrible scene, and it wasn't clear at that point whether I quit or was fired. It was enough to know I would never work there again.

I had worked at that job for seven months, barely able to endure the work load, the poor pay, and the degrading working conditions. When the moment of my liberation came, I was too enraged to worry about how I would continue to support myself and pay for my education, but that miserable job made me even more determined to do so.

Suggested topics: any part-time or full-time job such as clerk, cashier, salesperson, gardener, bank teller, waiter, bus boy/girl, dishwasher, custodian, cleaning person, gas station attendant, hospital worker, field hand, laundry worker, medical assistant, office worker, baby-sitter, handyperson.

EXERCISE 35. EXPLAIN A RULE BY WHICH YOU LIVE

Write a composition in which you discuss *one* of the rules by which you live. Explain why you believe in this rule or why and how it works for you. Your thesis statement should present your rule or belief with *three* divisions of the subject or supports for your position. Each of the three parts of the thesis should be developed in a paragraph of discussion, making the composition, together with an introductory and concluding paragraph, a total of five paragraphs long. Use the following example to guide you.

Example

LIVING IN THE PRESENT

About one of humanity's frailties Thomas Wolfe wrote, "He talks of the future and he wastes it as it comes." This observation is related to a principle by which I try (without always succeeding) to live. (THESIS STATEMENT) I believe in living in the present because it is futile to dwell on the past, to worry about the future, or to miss anything in the only reality I know.

It is futile to dwell on the past. What existed or happened in the past may have been beautiful or exciting and may now bring profound and precious memories; but the past is dead, and it is not healthy for living spirits to linger over a world inhabited by ghosts. The past may also be a place of horror, of regret, of spilled milk, of unfortunate deeds that cannot be undone, of sad words like "might have been." However, it is painful and pointless to fixate on a period that cannot be relieved or repaired. It is unproductive self-punishment. The past must be kept in its place, outlived and outgrown.

It is also useless to worry about the future. Why fly to heaven before it's time? What anxious visions haunt people who think too much about the future? They may envision the horrible mushroom cloud; the earth shriveling from radiation; the overpopulated, abused earth gone dead. They may imagine their own lives going awry, appointments missed; advancements given to someone else; their houses burned to the ground; their loves lost; everything in their lives, as in a nightmare, slipping away. There is no end to the disasters people can worry about when focusing anxiously on the future. There are events in the future, including their own deaths, over which they have little or no control, but which can ruin their lives if they worry about them. There are some disasters they may be able to prevent, but they must do that by living well in the present, not simply by worrying about the future.

The present moment, which is even now moving into the past, is the only reality I know, and I don't want to miss it. The wild cherry cough drop dissolving in my mouth is sweet and soothing. Even my sore throat and backache have meaning. The cool night air, the crackling noises of my furnace, my cat yawning and stretching — these are the tangible realities I can recognize. They exist in this moment, together with my own breathing, the warm lamp overhead, the jerking of my typewriter. Along with these are the realities of other people and of all life on this earth, which matter to me now, not at some past or future time.

Everyone needs a sense of history, I think, particularly a feeling for his or her own roots, but history needs to keep its distance to be appreciated. It is also vital to have some sense of direction, which means making plans for the future but not becoming preoccupied with them. What is most important, I believe, is living in the present, that is, being alive *now*.

Suggested topics: being friendly; being helpful; trusting people; turning the other cheek; expecting the best or worst in people; being honest; looking out for number one; winning, losing, playing the game; being competitive; being loyal or faithful; being aggressive; doing all things in moderation; living dangerously; taking chances; playing it safe; being selfish or unselfish; being rich or poor; getting exercise; being a vegetarian; eating healthful foods, dieting, or fasting; getting close to nature; being outgoing; being defensive; working hard; being independent; being loving; traveling in the fast lane.

EXERCISE 36. PRESENT TWO SIDES OF AN ISSUE

Write a composition in which you present the advantages and disadvantages of something or in which you argue both for and against something. Present the two sides in your thesis statement, and in your discussion devote two or three paragraphs to each side. Try to be objective and fair in discussing each side, giving about equal time or space to each. In your conclusion you may or may not show that you favor one side over the other.

Be careful in your thesis statement to present two sides of *one* issue. Don't be confused into thinking that your objective is to give first the advantages of one thing and then the disadvantages of something else. On the other hand, some topics suggest or imply others. For example, if you discuss the advantages and disadvantages of owning a home, you will naturally think of the subject in terms of its alternatives, such as renting a home or renting an apartment. Keep your focus, nonetheless, on home ownership. Don't shift it to the alternatives. Don't even discuss the alternatives, except as they clarify your arguments for and against owning a home.

Notice also that your thesis statement may give categories, as in the example that follows, rather than the specifics within those categories that can be dealt with later in the discussion. For instance, one of the advantages given in the following thesis is "general well-being." This category is later presented more specifically in terms of improved prosperity, savings in wear and tear and cleaning of clothes, improved personal hygiene, and a calmer disposition. You may use this scheme or you may employ specifics immediately in your thesis statement.

Example

The Advantages and Disadvantages of Being a Recovering Smoker

Reforming can be a risky business. Prime examples are recovering smokers who exhibit holier-than-thou smugness that alienates and antagonizes everyone around them, including people who have never smoked as well as those who still do. Research indicates that former smokers are wise to have stopped, but they do not automatically fall into paradise for having done so. There are not only advantages but also some disadvantages in giving up cigarettes. (THESIS STATEMENT) Among the advantages to recovering smokers are better prospects for good health and general well-being, but the disadvantages include some interpersonal as well as personal problems.

The prime advantage in giving up cigarettes is that it gives recovering smokers a better chance of having good health. For example, it comes as a pleasant surprise to former smokers that coughing is not the most natural way of coming to consciousness every morning. They may wake, as usual, with their feet on an icy floor, but they go about the morning, with a difference, ever so quietly, without hack, sneeze, or wheeze. They discover the joy of breathing deeply in the morning air, of tasting their food, of feeling energy they thought they had lost in the smoky passing of the years. Their dentists praise them for their bright new gums. Their doctors note the clearing of their lungs. Their blood pressure goes down. They have fewer colds. Indeed, there is no guarantee for long life, but they are healthier, and indications are that they may stay that way for a reasonable stretch of time, thanks in part, at least, to conquering their addiction to cigarettes.

Besides better health, recovering smokers enjoy an improved sense of general well-being. For one thing, they are a bit more prosperous for having given up an increasingly expensive habit, which formerly included not only cigarettes but also such equipment as cigarette holders, lighters, cases, and so forth. In addition, they no longer need to worry about burn holes in their clothing that required expensive "invisible" mending, and their clothes do not need to be cleaned as often, nor do they any longer grow rank and reek with smoke. Their personal hygiene has improved immeasurably, since neither their bodies nor their hair is contaminated by cigarettes. Finally, they are calmer and more contained persons who no longer need to wonder about their next cigarette break or feel the desperate agitation that comes from needing nicotine. They can enjoy a leisurely dinner without interruption and the theater without a mad dash to the lobby. These are now pleasures in themselves, not impediments to the next cigarette.

Not at first as apparent as the advantages, perhaps, the disadvantages of being a recovering smoker include some knotty interpersonal problems. Partly to reinforce the effort to break their smoking addiction, former smokers may adopt an attitude of new purity and clean up their immediate environment, ridding themselves of any positive associations with smoking. Ashtrays, some of them handsome pieces, have to go as well as the cigarette containers offered guests, and all cigarettes, lighters, and matches. After that, suppose the new nonsmokers give their first dinner party. Old friends arrive, and many of them still smoke. So much for purity, as the house disappears in clouds of smoke, and cigarette butts develop longer and longer ashes. "Where are all the ashtrays?" someone asks, and the hosts unhappily find a very small one for everyone to share. The hosts resent their guests smoking and want to ask them to do it outside, but haven't the courage to say so. However, very gradually, especially as more and more people stop smoking and the general attitude begins to change, some disgruntled smokers do learn to step outside, though it is hard to insist on that consideration when the weather is harsh. But there is always the clod who will light up at the dinner table, even while others are eating, and create a scene if asked to smoke elsewhere. Similarly, in planes, restaurants, and elsewhere, it can be difficult for smokers and nonsmokers to relate.

Another disadvantage of being a recovering smoker is that the new reform poses a number of personal problems. One of the worst is fat. Few people quit smoking without gaining weight. Besides the natural weight-gaining changes they experience in response to cigarette withdrawal, former smokers overcompensate for lost oral pleasures by munching. After all, meals no longer end when there is no cigarette with which to conclude them. Instead, they spill into each other. In the first few months, the most difficult period in the smoke-ending process, it is not unusual for former smokers to gain twenty pounds or more, tough to carry around and hard on their self-esteem. Recovering smokers also tend to become grouchy. The more mean and hateful they become, the less they like themselves, and only their best friends can tolerate them. Their outlook on the world grows worse, in addition, as their sense of smell returns. While smokers, they had been deprived of the things they liked to smell as well as those they didn't. Now, besides the smell of bread baking and other lovely cooking aromas, they can smell the exhaust from cars and buses, the stench of sewers, the leaden scent of heavy perfume, the pollution of the world. It is a grim life without cigarettes, at least at first. Personal problems may linger for months or years before recovering smokers finally adjust.

To stop smoking requires all kinds of grit and will power and is not nearly as romantic as smoking promised to be, when it was sold through song and sexy sales pitches. Smokers who want to recover from the addiction may need to weigh the advantages of quitting to health and general well-being against the personal and interpersonal disadvantages. However, they might enjoy life more fully, in this case, if they accepted the costs and quit.

Suggested topics: getting married; staying single; having a large (small) family; being a child in a large (small) family; being an only child; getting a divorce; being a child of divorced parents; owning a car; owning a compact car; making a career in the army or navy; going to college; working for a large (small) company; being self-employed; being an older student returning to college; being a working wife or mother; marrying someone of another race or religion; living in a big city; living in a small town; living in suburbia; living in the country; having a job that requires a lot of traveling; owning a home; renting an apartment; being a man; being a woman; being in love.

EXERCISE 37. DESCRIBE AN EVENT IN YOUR LIFE

Write a composition of four to five paragraphs in which you narrate an event in your life or tell a story about an experience you have had. Your thesis statement should indicate the nature, scope, and chronology of the event so that the reader can anticipate what is coming in the composition and how it will be presented. Use the example that follows to guide you.

Example

RIDING AN OUTRIGGER

At the precise moment when the big wave began to swell and roll shoreward, the beach boy sitting in the stern of the outrigger shouted to us, ''Now paddle! Wikiwiki!'' A tourist in Hawaii, I was sitting in the middle of the boat with other tourists as we all began to paddle furiously to catch the big wave. Catching it just right, we lifted our paddles up and felt it hurl us toward the beach. (THESIS SENTENCE) This moment was the greatest thrill of riding an outrigger canoe, an experience I found exciting from beginning to end.

The adventure began with amusing contrast. Against the beautifully tanned and muscular bodies of the beach boys, we pale or sunburned tourists, who ranged in age from six to sixty, appeared especially knobby-kneed and pot-bellied. The laughing faces of the beach boys exposed incredibly white and perfect teeth as they welcomed us to make our way awkwardly into the hollowed-out boat. We tourists sat like ducks in a line in the boat, each of us grasping a short-handled, fat paddle with two hands. The beach boys pushed the canoe out into the surf, jumped into it, and with the help of their inexperienced crew, conveyed the craft seaward.

The way out was fairly effortless for us tourists. The beach boys did most of the work while at the same time explaining to us the method and objective of the experience that was to come. Once we reached the desired point in the water, we waited. It was a delightful period in which we appreciated the balmy air of the semitropics, the magnificent view of the island paradise, and the blue-green water which, because it was shallow, revealed a myriad of coral formations beneath it. The luxury of relaxing in the sunkissed canoe was heightened by the expectancy we crew members felt as the beach boys awaited the right wave and prepared to give the signal for all of us to paddle. Then the wave came.

''Now paddle! Wikiwiki! Fast! Everybody go!'' Suddenly and furiously, we obeyed the command. All paddles slashed into the water. Again and again, faster and faster — dip, out, dip, out — our paddles moved. We knew the boat must be just slightly ahead of the big wave to catch the swell. ''Paddles up.'' Now the wave did the work. Swiftly, still more swiftly, our canoe raced toward the shore. The spray of the foam, the power of the wave, the speed of the craft, the soft breeze all combined into the excitement unique to riding an outrigger. The trip beachward was really some distance but seemed short and needed repeating. By the second and third time we had repeated the experience, we tourists were completely exhilarated by the skill as well as the romance of it.

There is the belief in Hawaii that anyone who visits the islands must return again someday. It must follow that anyone who once enjoys the sport of riding an outrigger canoe, as I did, cannot resist trying it again when he or she returns.

Suggested topics: visiting the Empire State Building; touring through a museum; skiing in the mountains or on the water; meeting a famous person; meeting a bear or a rattlesnake; flying somewhere in an airplane; visiting a strange city; seeing a bullfight; learning a new dance; learning a new custom in a foreign country; trying to speak a foreign language; going deep-sea fishing; learning to ride a horse; seeing a circus; attending a concert; experiencing your first day of college; running for office; campaigning for a political candidate; collecting funds for a charitable organization; earning your first paycheck; shopping for a new car; meeting the man or woman you plan to marry; traveling on a train; fighting a forest fire; having an automobile accident or seeing one; winning or losing a race; learning a lesson; achieving a goal. (Bear in mind that your composition is to be relatively short. You may not be able to tell everything about a camping trip in the mountains, for example, but you can describe an episode or some event that took place during it.)

EXERCISE 38. DESCRIBE A PLACE OR SCENE

Write a composition of six to eight paragraphs in which you describe a place or scene. Your thesis statement should indicate not only the nature and scope of your subject, but also that you intend to organize your composition geographically. Use the example that follows as a guide.

Example

THE GRANDEST STATE OF ALL

"I love you, California. You're the grandest state of all." These words from a sentimental old song sum up the feelings of most Californians about their home state. (THESIS SENTENCE) Other states make many claims about their beautiful mountains, deserts, lakes, cities, and people, but California, from the top to the bottom of the state, has all these attributes and many of them in greater abundance than any other state. In fact, California has just about everything.

Northern California offers the cool climate and scenic beauty that is claimed by Oregon and Washington. On the coast, near the Oregon line, is the Del Norte Coast Redwoods State Park with its fern-carpeted forest of rugged redwood trees. Tourists can drive or hike through the dense forest to the ocean where the giant redwoods, found only on the Pacific coast, grow almost to the shore. Also to be enjoyed from April to July are outstanding displays of rhododendrons and azaleas. Inland in the north are many other beautiful parks, including Mount Shasta. Besides an abundance of skiing terrain, this park contains white water in deep canyons, exquisite lakes, thick forests, and open valleys. Not far from Mount Shasta is Lassen Volcanic National Park with over 150 miles of trails leading to a remarkable variety of natural wonders: glacial lakes, permanent snowpacks, boiling hot springs, striking waterfalls, and lush meadows. California also owns the greater portion of the beautiful Lake Tahoe, the largest body of water on the continent at its elevation, a small part of which it shares with Nevada.

Traveling down the state toward San Francisco, tourists can experience natural wonders that equal or surpass most of those in all the northern states. They may choose the inland route through the Sierra, the largest single mountain range in the country, with peaks of 14,000 feet, and then across the fertile Sacramento Valley. The city of Sacramento, once a boom town with its roots in the gold rush of 1849, is now the state capital with a beautifully restored capitol building surrounded by a park, an oasis on hot valley days, with forty acres of plants and trees from all over the world. Instead of going inland, travelers may decide to journey down the virtually unspoiled coast that stretches almost four hundred miles from the southern border of Oregon to the San Francisco Bay. The oceanside highway offers magnificent views of the dramatic coast with its precipitous cliffs and rocky, windswept shore. The highway passes numerous beaches, many of them spacious and uncrowded, and interesting sites such as Mendocino, a nineteenth-century town of weathered wood houses, now an artists' mecca; Gualala, an old lumber port; and Fort Ross, once a Russian outpost. Finally, visitors come to one of the engineering wonders of the world — the Golden Gate Bridge, the northern entrance to San Francisco.

San Francisco, though not the largest city in the country, is probably the most cosmopolitan, with a unique blend of races, customs, and nationalities, including the largest Asian community outside the Orient centered in its colorful if overcrowded Chinatown. The city's many fine restaurants reflect its international character and offer the gourmet numerous choices, including Chinese, Japanese, Vietnamese, Korean, Indian, Italian, Spanish, Greek, and a variety of other menus. The city also offers cultural opportunities with its excellent museums, its civic center with one of the country's finest opera houses, symphony hall, theater, library, subterranean exhibit hall, and civic auditorium. The city's downtown and other areas are a delight to shoppers. Surrounded on three sides by water, San Francisco is a compact city of hills. From one of its hill-climbing cable cars or from the tops of its many excellent hotels, the view of the bay area with its great bridges, the neighboring cities in the distance, including Berkeley, headquarters of the world's largest university system, is an unforgettable vista.

Leaving San Francisco, travelers can journey inland again and enjoy some of the nation's greatest parks — Yosemite, King's Canyon, or Sequoia — for either summer or winter sports, including a hike up Mount Whitney, the highest peak in the continental United States. Visitors can also head south along the scenic coast highway or along the San Francisco Peninsula through an area called Silicon Valley for its large electronics industry, and then past another great university, Stanford, to the Santa Cruz region with its excellent beach parks. Before long they will come to the beautiful Monterey Peninsula. Characterized by white beaches, craggy rocks, pounding surf, and twisted cypresses, the peninsula contains an exceptionally scenic route known as 17 Mile Drive, permitting tourists to drive through thick woods, past elegant homes and clubs, and along a spectacular shoreline. Monterey, Carmel, and their neighbor to the south, Santa Barbara, all attractive because of their setting and intriguing shopping, are also interesting historically, vestiges of early settlements still evident, among them the Franciscan missions. Parallel to these early Spanish and Mexican mission sites are inland valleys that are among the richest agricultural areas in the country. From Salinas, famous for lettuce as well as John Steinbeck, through Merced, Fresno, and Bakersfield, the soil is as productive as any found in such midwestern states as Kansas, Iowa, or Minnesota. Citrus groves, which appear in the lower valleys, tell travelers that they are in Southern California and nearing Los Angeles.

Los Angeles, California's largest city, is a vast sprawl of intermingling communities held together by the most extensive freeway system in the world. The best way to get around the city is by car, and though the freeways are constantly crowded, the system works quite well when understood and carefully followed. Seeing the immense expanse the city has become, it is difficult to imagine the small Mexican community, founded in 1781, that it once was, though a tiny sample of that beginning remains on Olivera Street, closed to traffic and preserved as a Mexican street of over a century ago. Los Angeles expanded greatly during World War II and is now noted for its large aircraft and missile industry, for such places as Beverly Hills with its elegant Rodeo Drive, as well as for movie stars, and is one of the most populated cities in the country. In the summertime, much of this population can be seen along the many fine beaches that stretch between Los Angeles and San Diego. In fact, Southern California is a paradise for sunlovers, from its coast to its inland desert areas, including the famous Death Valley National Monument. Southern California offers just about everything that states such as Arizona, Colorado, and New Mexico boast of. It also competes with the pleasures of Florida.

California has just about everything, from cowboys to Indians and from urbia to suburbia. It has Texas oil. It has Minnesota lakes. It has Arizona deserts, Vermont snow, and Wyoming mountains. It has more people than New York. The sentimental old song was never truer of California than it is today. It is the grandest state of all.

Suggested topics: your block; your neighborhood; your hometown; your part of a state or your whole state; your school; a nearby park; the place where you work; a place where you used to live; a place you have visited many times; your house or yard; a scene from your window; your room; a building or place in your town you particularly like or dislike; a painting you enjoy. (Be sure you write about an area you really know, and limit your area; the model composition covers more ground than you may want to try to cope with.)

EXERCISE 39. DISCUSS YOUR EXPERIENCE WITH MECHANIZATION AND/OR DEPERSONALIZATION

Write a composition in which you discuss a negative or adverse experience you have had with mechanization and/or depersonalization. The word *mechanization* refers to operations or labor done by machine, making a task automatic, unspontaneous, routine, or monotonous. *Depersonalization* means the state or condition in which a person is deprived of his or her individual character or personality, that is, made impersonal.

The advantages of the machine age are numerous, and few people want to give up their multicycled washing machines to return to scrubbing boards, for example. However, so-called progress has brought about losses as well as gains. Many people who used to keep healthy through vigorous labor now have to compensate for the machines that have made life easy for them by taking exercise classes or jogging. In addition, mechanization can make life humdrum or monotonous, turning out products that are uniform or that lack individuality, and organizing or translating people into numbers, codes, or other systems that tend to deprive them of their uniqueness and personality. Thus, mechanization and depersonalization can be closely related.

Think about your experience with mechanization and/or depersonalization and decide on the influence of one or both on your life, your attitudes, or values. Present these influences in a thesis statement divided into *two* or *three* parts or supports. Develop each part into a paragraph of discussion in which you explain and illustrate your view. In addition, write a brief introduction and conclusion. Use the following example as a guide.

Example

HELLO. THIS IS A RECORDING. . . .

Faint memory returns of a time, light-years ago, or so it seems, when there were no dials on the telephone. To make a call, I first took the receiver off the hook and then waited for the dulcet tones of the telephone operator, "Number, please." That was a live voice, not a recording, and for an instant there was a real transaction, a dynamic relationship between us, and we spoke to each other. That page of my tattered memory book has almost disintegrated with the passage of time, and I have long since become so conditioned by mechanization and depersonalization that I am startled and disoriented by such things as live voices. (THESIS STATEMENT) Sometimes I am convinced that machines and the impersonal people who work for them are making me an automaton.

Mechanization may systematize and speed up the process of the working world, but it is also making me feel like a zombie. If I am injured and bleeding, for instance, do

I hurry to the nearest doctor? Of course not. Instead, I prepare myself to be processed at the emergency hospital, medical card in hand, slowly sinking while I am coded and properly entered into the computer system, which may, at last, permit me to receive aid. If I want to dispute a bill with a large department store, I gear myself for the experience as I pick up the telephone. There will be the first recording, and then the music, for it is clear that I must never be left alone with my thoughts while I await the accounts person. After ten minutes of soporific music, I am reduced to such a trancelike state that I must make notes to myself to remember why I placed the call. One time when I went to Europe for the summer, I paid a large credit system twice the normal amount, attaching a note of explanation. When I returned, however, I was in trouble, for the system could not read my note, could not be paid ahead of time, could not but fault me for being away when it was time to pay. Now when I travel abroad, picking my way through the glorious ruins of the Acropolis, admiring Paris from atop the Eiffel Tower, or being spirited by gondola through fascinating Venice, I know the moment when it comes, and I drop everything else so that I can sit down and write out my check to the Big System. Such is the hold the mechanized world has on me.

Strongly resembling the machines for which they work, the people who staff the mechanized world also have a deadening effect on my spirit. Most often we connect by telephone, for I have learned that it does not pay to appear in person if I want fast action. Clerks and other servicepersons always give the telephone top priority, letting other customers wait. I get the most attention when I am an anonymous voice. "Hello, this is . . ." I start to say, when I am interrupted by the other voice, with even, steel courtesy, totally devoid of human imperfection or identity. "Your account number, please?" it says, and then I quickly survey my statement for the correct series of numbers, and I note that one goes clear across the page. The time that I got in trouble with the Big System, the other voice grew rigid with authority. "That is against company policy," the other voice said, with a sober sense of righteousness, in complete support of the machine that couldn't read and couldn't make exceptions. "Is there someone else that I can speak to?" I asked. "Just a moment, please," it measured out, like toothpaste. The next voice, more velvety but just as rigid in supporting policy, said, "The computer is programmed to expect payment every month." At last I reached an officer with some authority, and a "lifetime exception" was made for me to clear my credit. "Do you mean that literally?" I asked. "Yes, this is the one exception we can ever make for you." "Ever in my life?" I suppressed my anguished giggles, but there was no humor in the affirmative reply. As I put down the telephone I felt as if I had been doomed to spend a lifetime on probation, with detached and heartless voices ready to seal my fate if I should ever slip again.

It is a long time since I used to take the receiver off the hook of an upright telephone and wait for the human warmth and lively interaction that could ensue. Now when my telephone rings, I cope automatically with the world of machines and impersonal people. "Hello," my message begins. "This is a recording. . . ."

Suggested topics: experiences you have had with machines and/or impersonal people and your reactions to either or both in the following situations: on the job or applying for a job; drawing unemployment benefits or medical or other insurance; at your college during registration or another procedure; at home when you are approached in person by a representative of a company or reached by telephone or when you try to approach or reach the same; when you try to make travel arrangements or obtain tickets to the theater, a concert, or a sports event; when you want to make a complaint about a product or dispute a bill; when you use the automatic teller at your bank.

EXERCISE 40. DISCUSS LOVE

Write a composition in which you discuss love. You may write about romantic love or some other kind of love, such as love of country or parental love. The important objective in this exercise is to find a fresh or unusual approach to the subject. You should not labor to say what has already been worn out about the subject. Ponder the subject (or perhaps your particular love object) for a while until you come up with a thesis that is fresh and meaningful. You may put a question to yourself about love, as in the following example, and then proceed to answer it.

Example

STACCATO OR LEGATO?

Among the more curious questions that can be asked about love is this: is it staccato or legato? That is, when one feels romantic love, does he or she feel it in breaks, with interruptions or changes, or does one feel it continuously, without interruption or change? (THESIS SENTENCE) Although the legato position about love is appealing, the staccato argument is probably more realistic.

Poetry and song seduce one into thinking love legato. "Love is not love which alters when it alteration finds," wrote Shakespeare in one of his famous sonnets. Love is "an ever-fixed mark that looks on tempests and is never shaken," he continued. And Elizabeth Barrett Browning wrote of her constancy to her husband Robert in such lines as this: "What I do and what I dream include thee." Some of the greatest arias of opera are gloriously legato about love. Tosca, Tristan and Isolde, and Madame Butterfly are only a few of the operatic lovers whose steadfast devotion is proved by their dying for it. "True Love" and "I Love You Truly" are two of the best-known popular songs that go on and on about how love goes on.

In reality, love is probably staccato. First, it is difficult to suppose that one can experience anything continuously. Sleep interrupts wakefulness, and sleep itself is interrupted by dreams and nightmares. The feeling one has for a lover during wakefulness may be blotted out or intensified by sleep. In either case, the feeling changes.

When a person is awake, attention cannot be fixed constantly on a single object. He must blink, if nothing else. More likely he will look to something else for variety or from necessity. His mind may turn to the stock market or he may become fascinated by the operation of a pile driver on the way to work. His focus for much of the day is on work. As he closes the door to the office, his thoughts may turn to love, but sitting at the desk, his eyes fix on the print and figures there. He may fall out of love and into work, or he may catch the faint perfume of his secretary.

Pain and pleasure, either one, can distract a lover from concentrating on love. Pain calls everything to itself. One can forget one's love for a period even over a stubbed toe. The pleasure of too much food or drink can be totally absorbing. The pleasure even of one's lover may pall periodically. Often the greatest distraction is oneself. At times the preoccupation with self, the worry over self, the development of self, the delight in self admit no other thought.

As lovely as legato is, one can neither live nor love continuously. At best, a lover can only echo the words of the poet Ernest Dowson, and say, "I have been faithful to thee, Cynara! in my fashion."

Suggested topics: the eternal triangle; monogamy; bigamy; polygamy; consecutive or sequential monogamy; long separation; dependence, independence, interdependence; marriage contracts; open marriages; sexual relations with or without love; the effect of the first (or other) child on love between husband and wife; teenage love; puppy love; infatuation distinguished from love; falling in or out of love; love for parents; love for children; love for sister or brother; love for one's people.

APPENDIXES

Appendix A

Appearance and Form of the Submitted Paper

To make a good first impression of your work, you should submit a paper that is neat and easy to read. Such a paper invites readers, in a pleasant manner, to begin their work. If the paper is a mess, it obviously is not very inviting. In fact, your instructor may return your paper without reading it if it is too difficult to read. Be considerate of your readers. Turn in a paper that not only reads well but looks good.

Directions for the form of the paper are as follows:

1. Write or type on every other line and on one side of the page only.
2. Leave generous margins for your instructor's comments or corrections.
3. Check with your instructor for the exact format or layout for your paper. All instructors want you to submit your manuscripts with *pages numbered* and in their *proper order*, so that they can be read beginning with page one, continuing to page two, and so on. Some instructors want your manuscript to *lie open* and *flat* (Figure A-1), with your name, the course, the assignment, and the date in

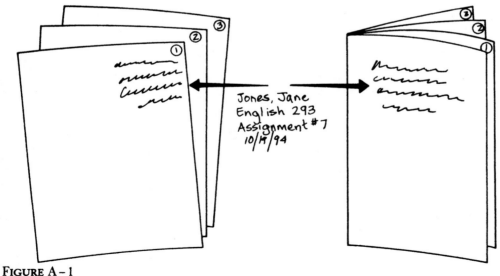

FIGURE A-1

FIGURE A-2

the upper right-hand corner. You may be asked to clip or attach the pages together in some way. Other instructors may ask you to *fold* your paper *lengthwise*, so that it looks like a little book (Figure A-2), with your name and other information on the front cover. Most instructors will ask you to make and *keep a copy of your paper.*

Be sure to ask about these technical requirements. They make a difference!

Appendix B

Correction Symbols

agr   **Agreement**

The verb must agree with the subject. If the subject is singular, the verb must be singular; if the subject is plural, the verb must be plural.

Neither John nor Mary are to be blamed for the accident. (Neither John nor Mary *is* to be blamed for the accident.)*

A pronoun must agree in number and in gender with its antecedent, that is, the noun to which the pronoun refers.

Each of the men must buy *their* (his) own uniforms. Neither Anne nor Joan brought *their* (her) lunch.

ambig   **Ambiguous**

The meaning is not clear because of the possibility of two or more interpretations of the idea.

San Francisco is farther from Los Angeles than Elko, Nevada. (Which city's distance from which city is being compared?)

ap   **Apostrophe Needed**

Her movements were as calculating as a cobra. (. . . as a cobra's. The idea refers to a *cobra's* movements.)

---

*All words, phrases, and sentences within parentheses are either the correction of the errors in the preceding sentence or observations leading to the correction of the preceding sentence.

awk   **Awkward or Confused Phrasing**

Muskrats work on the dikes before we get to them by burrowing through between two ponds and thus connect them when their contents are supposed to be kept separate. (Muskrats burrow tunnels through the dikes between the ponds. Through these openings the water flows from one pond to another.)

Bpr   **Broad Pronoun Reference**

A pronoun must have a specific noun antecedent. A pronoun's antecedent cannot be implied, nor can it refer to an entire preceding action or statement.

On the first floor we were shown where the fiction books were kept; <u>this</u> completed the tour. (The tour was completed when we were shown where the fiction books were kept.)

Ca   **Wrong Case Used**

The boy will give the book to <u>whomever</u> (whoever) comes into the room first. The secretary notified Maria and I (<u>me</u>) to come to the office.

Cap   **Capital Letter Needed**

Paul Guildford, a Jefferson <u>h</u>igh <u>s</u>chool graduate, won the Thomas Paine <u>c</u>itizen <u>a</u>ward. (Jefferson High School, Thomas Paine Citizen Award)

Coh   **Faulty Coherence**

The sentences in the paragraph are not arranged and tied together in such a way that the reader can easily and readily follow the train of thought of the development. The relationship of ideas between sentences is not clear. The reader loses the sense of focus and/or direction.

Cst   **Faulty Sentence Construction**

Sentence sense is confused, illogical, or obscure because of faulty construction of the sentence.

Privacy hindered my studying while in high school because living in a house where there are many children it is very hard to secure privacy. (A lack of privacy hindered my studying while I was in high school because I lived in a house where there were many children who distracted me.)

d   **Faulty Diction (Word) Selection**

Colloquialism, slang, jargon, obsolete and archaic words, and dialect should be avoided in formal types of writing.

He <u>calculated</u> that the <u>dude</u> could be <u>banked on</u>. (He determined that the man was reliable.)

Frequently, the only food they had was what the mother could <u>tote</u> (carry) home after work.

DM Dangling Modifier

Revise the sentence so that the modifier is coherently related to the word it is meant to modify.

<u>Running across campus</u>, the bell tower struck five. (While I was running across the campus, I heard the bell tower strike five.)

<u>If cold</u>, an overcoat should be worn. (Is the overcoat cold or is the weather cold?)

DR Divided Reference of the Pronoun

John told William that <u>he</u> had made the mistake. (Can you tell who made the mistake?)

fact Authenticity Questionable

Gold was discovered in California in 1860. (It was discovered in 1849.)

focus Lack of Focus or Lack of Sense of Direction

The reader is confused about what you are aiming at or exactly what point you are trying to make.

frag Fragment Rather than a Sentence

He came to the office Monday afternoon. Immediately <u>after he arrived from New York</u>. (After having arrived in New York Monday afternoon, he immediately came to the office.)

The winters are cold. <u>Although the autumns are pleasant</u>. (Although the autumns are pleasant, the winters are cold.)

F/Sub Faulty Subordination

In general, in sentences that contain a main clause and one or more subordinate clauses, the main focus—the central idea—must be placed in the main clause, not the subordinate clause.

I was looking in the store window <u>when the thief ran off with my briefcase</u>.

Probably the more important idea is the thief running off with your briefcase, not your looking in the store window.

The thief ran off with my briefcase as I was looking in the store window.

gob   **Unintelligibility of Concept**

In essence, this symbol indicates that the reader is unable to make sense out of what you are saying. You seem to be putting words together in such a way that they make no discernible sense. Some English handbooks identify this type of writing as *gobbledygook*.

As a child my grandmother perambulated hyperbolically to imbibe multitudinous prevarications.

gr   **Grammar Error**

This symbol identifies all grammar errors not specifically discussed under other headings.

He walked slow and careful. (He walked *slowly* and *carefully*.)

John should have spoke about this accident before. (John should have *spoken* about this accident before.)

He is the most tallest boy in the class. (He is the *tallest* boy in the class.)

Id   **Unidiomatic Phrasing**

This symbol indicates your use of an unidiomatic expression. He has agreed on the plans. (He has agreed *to* the plans.)

illeg   **Illegible Word**

It   **Italics**

Underline words to signify that they are to be italicized.

His favorite book is Thomas Hardy's Return of the Native; his favorite magazine is the London Literary Times.

logic   **Invalid Inference, Faulty Reasoning**

?   **Meaning Is Unclear**

n/a   **No Abbreviation**

Do not use abbreviations.

J. Smith went to Cal. in Berk., Cal., in Aug. '74 & took a course in chem. tech. w/Prof. Jones. (James Smith went to the University of California in Berkeley, California, in August 1974, and took a course in chemical technology with Professor Jones.)

n/ap   No Apostrophe Needed

John returned the book to it's (*its*) owner.

There are several kind's (*kinds*) of flowers in that garden.

n/cap   No Capital Letter Needed

Six High School students won Medals for Good Citizenship. (Six high school students won medals for good citizenship.)

n/pgr
or *n/¶*   No New Paragraph Needed

The material in this paragraph should be part of the development of the preceding paragraph. It is further support for the topic sentence of the preceding paragraph.

nwo
or ∧   Necessary Word or Words Omitted

The problem has and will be carefully studied. (The omission is *been*.)

O   Superfluous Punctuation

You have used unnecessary marks of punctuation.

The cat⌒sitting on the roof⌒is mine.

Well, just what kind of a girl do you think I am?⊘⊘

= ∫   Faulty Parallel Structure

Elements placed in a series must be of the same grammatical structure.

The duties of the vice president were to call the meeting to order, <u>collecting</u> the dues, and he <u>appointed</u> the chairmen of the various committees. (The duties of the vice president were to call the meeting to order, *collect* the dues, and to *appoint* the chairmen of the various committees.)

p   Punctuation Error

This symbol identifies all errors in punctuation (comma, semicolon, colon, period, dash, parentheses, quotation marks, question mark, and exclamation point) other than those errors listed as RTS (run-together sentences). Needless or superfluous punctuation is listed under *O*.

There are three colors in the flag; red, white, and blue. (There are three colors in the flag: red, white, and blue.)

pgr or *¶*　New Paragraph Needed

When you have finished developing one idea and shift to a new direction, you need also to start a new paragraph.

pgr D　Inadequate Paragraph Development

You have not given sufficient concrete and specific details to establish or prove the topic sentence or the central idea of the paragraph.

pgr O　Weak Paragraph Organization

The factors within the development of your paragraph are not well organized or structured. The material should be revised so the progression of your thought from the beginning to the end has a better sense of coherence and continuity.

pgr U　Lack of Paragraph Unity

You have material in the paragraph that is not to the point of the topic sentence or central idea and also distracts from it.

Red　Redundancies

Redundant terms, expressions, and ideas are to be avoided. Do not say the same thing twice. "Repeat <u>again</u>," "combined <u>together</u>," "<u>important</u> essentials," 2 A.M. <u>in the morning</u>" are examples of saying the same thing twice.

Rep　Repetitious

Avoid being repetitious. Do not say the same thing over again. (The preceding are repetitious statements.) Because you change the wording does not mean you have changed the content of the thought; you have merely trodden over the same ground in a different dress.

Good students turn their compositions in on time. They always have their work ready on the day it is due. They do not turn it in on the day after or the week after the instructor asks that it be submitted. They are never late.

The preceding statements convey the same idea four times.

R T S　Run-together Sentences

You have linked independent clauses within the sentence without the proper punctuation. Independent clauses must be joined with either a semicolon or with a comma, provided you are using a coordinating conjunction (*and, but, for,* or *nor*) when you use the comma. Examples of the error:

The story was not true however it was interesting. (The story was not true; however, it was interesting.)

The jaws of the scoop swung open, out tumbled the dirt and debris. (A comma has been used instead of the required semicolon.)

John collected over $30 but Tom collected only $20. (A comma must be placed before the *but.*)

ℐ C   Split Construction

Do not shift from the active voice to the passive voice in the same sentence.

We <u>flew</u> over Chicago at noon, and the Golden Gate <u>was seen</u> by sunset. (We flew over Chicago at noon and *saw* the Golden Gate by sunset.)

ℐ N   Shift in Number

Do not shift the number of nouns, particularly of persons.

Be sure to take your <u>passport</u>; the customs officials always look at <u>them</u> (*it*).

Every boy in the room took off <u>their hats</u> (*his* hat).

Sp   Spelling Error

Check the dictionary.

He was <u>disatisfied</u> with the grade that he had <u>recieved</u> from the <u>profesor</u>. (*dissatisfied, received, professor*)

S/p   Shift in Person

Don't shift from <u>I</u> to <u>you</u> to <u>one</u> to <u>he</u>, and so on.

I first will buy some seeds. Then <u>you</u> place them in some water. In a few days <u>a person</u> will begin to see them sprout. (After the seeds have been bought, they should be placed in some water. After a few days the seeds will begin to sprout.)

To the <u>student</u>, going to summer school is worse than having no vacation at all, for when <u>you</u> have no vacation, you do not think about all the things <u>a person</u> could do if <u>he</u> had one. (To the student, going to summer school is worse than having no vacation at all, for when he has no vacation, he does not think about all the things he could be doing if he had one.)

spec Specific

Be more specific and provide details; avoid the abstract.

In high school I studied Shakespeare and a Victorian novelist. (In high school I studied Shakespeare's play Hamlet and Charles Dickens's novel Oliver Twist.)

Because the weather was unpleasant outside, we didn't do much of anything. (As it was exceedingly hot and muggy outside, we sat inside sipping iced tea and occasionally playing a game of canasta.)

ST Shift in Tense

You must keep the same tense of the verb throughout the discussion of the subject.

For months I had admired Susan from afar, but I haven't the courage to ask her for a date. (Use either "had admired" and "hadn't the courage" or "have admired" and "haven't the courage," but be consistent.)

Sub Subordination of Ideas

Effective writing sets up relationships between ideas by subordinating secondary ideas to primary ideas. Subordinate the underlined sentence or sentences.

The Bethel River Project was approved by the governor in 1989. The plans were ready the following year. However, the actual construction did not begin until 1992. (Although plans for the Bethel River Project were ready in 1990, one year after the governor approved the project, actual construction did not begin until 1992.)

Subj Subjunctive Mood of the Verb Required

If I was (*were*) the chairperson, I would veto the measure.

It is necessary that each student keeps (*keep*) his or her own notes.

Trans Transitional Link Necessary

The change of thought or direction is too abrupt between the two sentences or paragraphs. You need to provide a link between the two so the reader can follow the progression of your thought. Build a bridge to serve as the transitional device.

Modern machinery often makes people its slaves. Last summer I worked for the Great Lakes Motor Company. (That modern machinery often makes people its slaves is a conclusion that I came to after having worked for the Great Lakes Motor Company last summer.)

trite   Clichés, Hackneyed Expressions, Overused Phrases, Trite Observations

"A budding genius," "at one fell swoop," "nipped in the bud," "seething mass of humanity," "launched into eternity," "good as gold," and so on.

Vague   Need More Specific Details

Your development is lacking in a sufficient number of concrete details to make the meaning of your generalization clear to the reader. The generalization may be a valid one, but the reader is not aware of what you mean by it. A generalization can always be made exact and clear if you follow it with one or more specific examples. It is always advisable to follow an abstract idea with a specific for purposes of clarification.

The food in the cafeteria is dull.

What does *dull* mean — there are no spices used, the food is unimaginatively prepared or served, there is little selection? The reader would know exactly what you meant by that generalization if you were to follow it with an explanation like this:

Day after day the only two courses offered on the menu are spaghetti and meatloaf.

wd   Wordiness

You are using too many words. Say the same thing in fewer words. Strike out all that is superfluous.

The boy had a temperature that would be regarded under all circumstances as a dangerously high one. (The boy had a dangerously high temperature.)

WR   Weak Reference of Pronoun

You need to establish more exactly the antecedent of the pronoun.

When the baby is through drinking the milk, it should be sterilized in boiling water. (Should the bottle or the baby be sterilized?)

WT   **Wrong Tense**

The wrong tense of the verb has been used.

In the drama the hero <u>was slain</u>. (In the drama the hero *is* slain.)

This scientific article, written two months ago, <u>said</u> (*says*) that the use of Drug X is dangerous.

WW   **Wrong Word**

You've used an inappropriate or wrong word.

The <u>principle</u> (*principal*) speaker was James Thorne.

He <u>excepted</u> (*accepted*) the money.

I do not believe that teachers should be allowed to administer <u>capital punishment</u> (*corporal punishment*) to students.

The darling girl is a child <u>progeny</u> (*prodigy*).

APPENDIX C

PARAGRAPH EVALUATION

	A	B	C	D	F
1. Is the topic sentence clearly stated?					
2. Is the paragraph well developed and organized?					
a. Does the paragraph contain one idea only?					
b. Is the topic adequately developed or supported?					
c. Is the paragraph unified and coherent?					
d. Does the paragraph have continuity or smooth transitions?					
3. Does the paragraph contain good sentence structure?					
4. Is the word choice effective?					
5. Is the paragraph free of errors in grammar, punctuation, and spelling?					
6. Is the treatment of the subject matter imaginative and thought provoking?					

Paragraph Grade _____

Additional Comments:

APPENDIX D

COMPOSITION EVALUATION

	A	B	C	D	F

1. Is the thesis statement clear and well supported?
2. Is the composition well organized and developed?
   a. Is the order or arrangement of the material in the composition as a whole correct, clear, and easy to follow?
   b. Does the discussion part of the composition keep a balance and support the purpose of the composition?
   c. Is there sufficient use of specific, concrete details to support any generalizations made in the composition?
   d. Is each of the paragraphs well organized and developed and is there continuity between them?
3. Is the word choice effective and does the composition avoid wordiness?
4. Is the composition free of errors in grammar, punctuation, spelling, sentence construction, and so forth?
5. Is the title appropriate and effective?
6. Does the composition as a whole reflect thought? Is it both logical and imaginative?

Composition Grade _____

Additional Comments:

APPENDIX E

300 WORDS MOST FREQUENTLY MISSPELLED

1. accelerate
   accidentally
   accommodate
   accompanied
   accumulate
   achievement
   acquainted
   across
   address
10. advice
    aggravate
    all right
    altogether
    always
    amateur
    among
    amount
    apparent
    appearance
20. appetite
    approaching
    appropriate
    approximately
    arctic
    argument
    around
    arrangement
    article
    athletic
30. awkward
    barbarous

before
beginning
believed
benefited
breathe
brilliant
bulletin
buried
40. business
    carrying
    cemetery
    changeable
    chosen
    clothes
    coming
    committee
    comparative
    competition
50. conceive
    conquer
    conscientious
    consider
    continually
    control
    convenience
    cooly
    copies
    corner
60. course
    courteous
    criticism

curiosity
dealt
decided
decision
definite
definition
dependent
70. description
    desirable
    despair
    desperate
    destroy
    develop
    different
    dining
    disappeared
    disappointed
80. disastrous
    discipline
    diseases
    dissatisfied
    dissipation
    divided
    division
    doesn't
    eighth
    efficiency
90. eliminated
    embarrassed
    emphasize
    environment

equipped
especially
exaggerated
excellent
excitement
exhausted
100. exhilaration
existence
experience
explanation
familiar
fascinating
finally
foreign
formally
formerly
110. forty
fourth
friend
gardener
generally
genius
government
grammar
grievance
guard
120. handle
height
hindrance
hurriedly
imagination
immediately
incidentally
independent
indispensable
intelligence
130. interesting
interfere
interpreted
interrupted
irresistible
its
itself

knowledge
laboratory
laid
140. led
leisure
lightning
livelihood
loneliness
lose
losing
maintenance
mathematics
meant
150. medicine
miniature
minute
mischievous
mysterious
naturally
necessary
nevertheless
nickel
niece
160. ninety
ninth
noisily
noticeable
nowadays
obstacle
occasion
occasionally
occurred
occurrence
170. off
omission
omitted
operate
opinion
optimistic
opportunity
original
outrageous
paid

180. parallel
paralyzed
parliament
particularly
partner
pastime
perform
perhaps
permissible
perseverance
190. persistent
persuade
phenomenon
physically
piece
pleasant
portrayed
possess
practically
preceding
200. preference
preferred
prejudice
preparations
principal
principles
privilege
probably
procedure
proceeded
210. professional
professor
prominent
propeller
psychology
pursue
quantity
quiet
quite
quitting
220. quizzes
realize
really

received
recognize
recommend
referred
relieve
religious
remembrance
230. repetition
resource
restaurant
rhythm
ridiculous
sacrifice
safety
satisfactorily
scarcely
schedule
240. secretary
seize
sense
separate
sergeant
severely
shining
similar
sincerely

sophomore
250. source
specimen
speech
stopped
strength
strenuously
stretched
studying
succeed
successful
260. superintendent
supersede
suppress
surely
surprise
synonym
temperament
their
there
together
270. too
toward
tragedy
transferring
tremendous

tries
truly
twelfth
undoubtedly
unnecessary
280. until
usually
valleys
valuable
varieties
vegetable
vengeance
view
vigorous
village
290. villain
weather
whether
whole
wholly
who's
whose
women
worrying
writing
300. written